Please return to,

Helen Garner.

THE FRUIT OF THE SPIRIT

M.T. Holman
34 The High Street
Ardingly
West St
RH17 6

GW00480905

This book is dedicated to my daughter Krissy in the hope that her life may be fruitful in the way this book describes.

THE FRUIT OF THE SPIRIT

The Thoughts and intents of the Christian heart

Colin J. Attridge

"THE DAWN" BOOK SUPPLY

First published 1998
Reprinted 2000
Reprinted 2003
Reprinted 2006

ISBN 1 874508 11 9

Published by "The Dawn" Book Supply
66 Carlton Road, Nottingham, NG3 2AP, England

Printed and bound in Great Britain

CONTENTS

PREFACE

Back in January 1989, I was asked to give a short talk on the subject of The Fruit of the Spirit. Getting some thoughts together for that event made me acutely aware of the importance of the subject and how little I knew about it. (This was going to take twenty talks not twenty minutes!) But more particularly, I became uncomfortably aware how much I lacked this fruit.

Making a private study of it seemed the best way to remedy my personal deficiency. Then it occurred to me that other believers might find the work helpful. In fact the subject is so vital that none of us can afford to ignore it. Where our characters are concerned the fruit of the Spirit may well encompass everything Christ will be looking for in you and me at his return. It really is *that* important.

Writing the chapters that follow has certainly helped me to understand more of what is required of a believer. I don't say that I now exhibit fully all the fine qualities of the fruit of the Spirit (family and friends would soon put me right if I did). What I do say is that I now have a clearer vision of what I'm aiming for.

Unless you know what you are aiming for, it's almost certain that you'll miss! We know we need to develop the sort of character Christ will approve when he comes. But if we're not clear about what should go into that character, if we're vague and general about it, then the chances are high we won't develop properly. We'll achieve a lop-sided development, over-emphasizing some things and missing others.

The fruit of the Spirit represents the whole, balanced, Spiritual personality. Unless we are aware of what it is, and know how to work towards it through the days of our probation, we may fail to produce it. This is why the subject of the fruit of the Spirit impressed me as being so vital.

And please bear in mind that if anything you read on these pages should sound as if it comes from some higher moral ground, this book was written for me before it was written for you.

The only man to have exhibited the fruit of the Spirit perfectly is the Lord Jesus Christ who learned it from his Father in heaven. May your own delight and meditation in the Father's Word help you to do the same.

C.J.A.

Acknowledgements

My grateful thanks are due to all those who helped shape the contents of this book by their helpful comments. The talks and tapes based on the original manuscript produced much useful feedback. For this reason the book differs from the tapes.

Thanks are specifically due to my daughter Krissy for typing the book from my, at times, unreadable manuscript. I'm very grateful to Lizzy Clay for her keen eye and good humour as a proof reader. And I absolutely must thank Jane Toms for her lovely interpretation of 'a tree by a river' for the front cover.

Note on Biblical Versions used

AV = Authorised Version of 1611 (King James Version)

NKJV = New King James Version of 1982

RAV = Revised Authorised Version of 1982

NEB = New English Bible of 1970

RV = Revised Version of 1885

RSV = Revised Standard Version of 1946-52

NIV = New International Version of 1978

INTRODUCTION

"But the fruit of the Spirit is

love,

joy,

peace,

longsuffering,

gentleness,

goodness,

faith,

meekness,

temperance:

...against such there is no law."

These are the aspects of the fruit described in Galatians 5:22,3 which are the subject of this book.

We'll be looking at each of these qualities in turn in the chapters that follow. There are also some scene-setting and rounding-up chapters to provide the bread on either side of this spiritual sandwich.

The opening chapter is devoted to showing the relevance to daily life of the fruit of the Spirit. Because if it has no practical bearing on your life, why should you bother with it? Somebody once wryly commented, "What's relevance got to do with anything?" But it's a serious question for Bible readers. In spiritual matters it's easy to lose sight of relevance and forget that what we read and study has to be useful for day to day living. We need to be able to use what we study to enhance our love of God, our enjoyment of His Word, our ability to live the Truth and handle everyday conflicts with the flesh, and to strengthen our grip on basic doctrines.

The gradual enhancement of these things (which is a lifetime's work) is summed up in the phrase 'spiritual development'. This is what the fruit of the Spirit is all about. The fruit is above all practical. And the impact it can have on our lives is the substance of the first chapter.

Then we shall look at how fruit is used as a symbol in the Scriptures. We'll also touch upon what is meant by that phrase *of the Spirit*. How are we to understand that the fruit is *of the Spirit*?

After which we'll get into what the book is really about, the nine aspects of the fruit. And in each case we'll look at **what the Bible has to say** about love, joy, peace, etc., rather than ruminate on what we think these things mean, or what they generally mean in everyday speech and writing. Which can be different!

Chapters five and six introduce a theme which continues throughout. In these chapters I offer the idea that there is only one fruit of the Spirit, which is *agape* (Paul's word for love in Galatians 5.22), and that the other eight items on Paul's menu are the characteristics that go together to make *agape*. The fruit is like an orange: love is the whole orange and the segments are joy, peace, and so on. This is, as I hope you'll agree, a Scripturally plausible idea. I'm certainly not the first to put it forward.

In order to help with the practical application of the fruit, I've added a section (chapters fifteen to nineteen) on the works of the flesh. This section describes how the fruit of the Spirit and the works of the flesh interact. The two are mutually exclusive, and to whatever degree you produce the fruit you eliminate the works. This section is intended to serve as a guide to which aspect of the fruit you may need to cultivate.

Note for non-Christadelphian readers

I'm a Christadelphian, but I realise that not everyone reading this book will be a Christadelphian. Although initially aimed at a Christadelphian readership, the book has no doctrinal corner to defend (it's about successful living), the message applies to everyone. There's one very minor problem, though, that I should mention. Like most groups of people, from those in chess clubs to scientific societies, we Christadelphians[1] have inevitably developed our own shorthand words and phrases which are constantly

---

[1] Should you want to know what we believe and why, I suggest you contact the Dawn Book Supply for a copy of the book *Thine is the Kingdom*.

in use and instantly intelligible among us. But this jargon leaves others in the dark. I have tried to eliminate as much as I can from these pages (with partial success!), but one phrase I have been careful to retain is **the Truth,** with a capital T.

The Truth is shorthand for a life which embraces all the fundamental principles and practices of Biblical Christianity. To speak of *living* the Truth is to speak of living according to Biblical Christianity. To be *in* the Truth is to have committed yourself to following the teachings of Scripture. I have kept the phrase in because it serves its purpose well and not least because it has the backing of the apostle John: "The elder unto the elect lady and her children whom I love in the truth..." (2 John:1). The phrase is used a number of times like this in John's letters 2 and 3.

CHAPTER ONE

"ONE THING IS NEEDFUL"

L IFE in the Truth ought to be the most satisfying and fulfilling way of life available to anyone living on this planet. That's a bold statement to start with. To substantiate it, let's begin by thinking for a moment of some of the things people generally agree go together to make a satisfying and fulfilling life. These are not in order of merit.

1. Sufficient food.
2. Sufficient clothing.
3. A place to live.
4. Sufficient money.
5. Good physical health.
6. Good emotional health (self worth, security).
7. Good mental health (lack of anxiety or neurosis).
8. Good relationships.
9. A sense of purpose (a belief that life is meaningful).
10. Enjoyment (that doesn't rob us of any of the above).

In most people's minds these ten items add up to a satisfying and fulfilling life. It's sad how few people actually achieve even half of them. They fail to balance it out in most cases. That's why I was careful to say for the last item: Enjoyment *that doesn't rob us of any of the above.* So often people go for an enjoyment, or the extreme of an enjoyment, that will cancel out one or more of the other vital factors for a successful life.

The man who enjoys living just for the moment is likely to wake up one morning feeling his life has no sense of purpose, which could in turn affect his emotional and mental health with the onset of depression. The woman who goes for the enjoyment of an extra-marital affair drives a steam-roller through the relationships department of her life. The man who enjoys gambling may not have sufficient money to pay for necessities. And in many other smaller and bigger ways people mess things up for themselves and fail to live satisfying lives.

But to achieve all ten of those items (or a good percentage of them), the remarkable truth is that you don't have to strive for them all. You don't in fact have to *strive* for any of them. **You have to concentrate on one thing only.** All you need to focus your attention on is your spiritual life.

Read, discover, believe and, most importantly, be permanently filled with the following spiritual truths: that you can cast *all* your cares upon God because He cares for you (1 Pet.5:7); that if you spend your time looking for righteousness and the way to the Kingdom of God you don't have to worry about having sufficient food and clothing, these things will come (Matt.6:33); that God knows all the things you have need of, whatever they are, before you even ask Him about them (Matt.6:8) because He keeps a very close watch over you (Matt.10:30,31); that *all* things work together for good in the lives of those who pay attention to their spiritual life (Rom.8:28).

Once these truths take root you're well on your way to attaining everything you need for a satisfying and fulfilling life. Because those very needs are fulfilled as a by-product of the spiritual life. As is sometimes said of happiness: you don't achieve it by directly striving for it, it generally comes as a by-product of doing other things. The *pursuit* of happiness puts happiness forever in the future. Be like the wise old tomcat who realizes that when he stops chasing his tail it follows him around anyway. Don't chase after all the things you think will bring happiness; simply focus on your spiritual life and those things will take care of themselves— and the happiness will follow.

"One thing is needful," said Jesus.
"This one thing I do," said Paul.

In Luke 10:38-42 Jesus said to Martha that she was *"careful and troubled about many things"* she reckoned

2

were of great importance. She was busy in the kitchen getting food ready for Christ and his disciples who'd just descended on the house. But her sister Mary was eager first of all to know about spiritual things. Rather than disappear into the kitchen, Mary grasped the opportunity to listen to the Truth from the lips of Jesus. Preparing food could wait —this was an unmissable experience! She chose the one thing that was needful, and Jesus told her so.

I'm not saying that everyday chores should be ignored. That you should let your house turn into a dump, and give up feeding the children, just so that you can spend your whole time soaking up spiritual truths. I'm sure that wasn't the extreme lesson Jesus was trying to teach Martha.

The lesson is surely that we can trust God that the mundane things will fall into place if we put spiritual matters first. Martha felt that if she didn't get on with preparing the food then nothing would get done. "I haven't got time to sit around talking!" She thought it was vital that the meal was organised immediately. No it wasn't! They wouldn't starve. Somehow they would all have eaten. A little late maybe, but so what! Martha might starve, however, of needful spiritual food if she continued to busy herself with chores at the expense of her spirituality.

How could anyone pass up a unique opportunity to hear the wisdom of the Master himself in order to slice bread or cook meat! Imagine having Jesus himself in your front room talking about the meaning of life, and you go off and get busy in the kitchen! If you could let such an opportunity as that slip, what would it say about your general enthusiasm for spiritual things? What did it say about Martha's? She had a wrong attitude. She was never going to find fulfilment in life by relegating her spirituality to second place behind the daily grind. So many people say they are too busy for God. So many people are unhappy! And often they keep busy to avoid facing the fact that they are unhappy. To break free, just one thing is needful. The Marthas (and their male equivalents) need to pay attention to their spiritual life.

Always it can be said, whatever the situation, *"one thing is needful"*– trust in God. Lesser matters will fall into place. And remember, **everything else is a lesser matter.**

In Philippians 3:13,14 Paul said, "This one thing I do ... I press toward the mark for the prize of the high calling of God in Christ Jesus." Spiritual health was Paul's primary aim in life. Not, of course, that he never did anything else. He travelled, he wrote letters, he even found time to make tents, and did a lot of other things besides. But everything else he did was secondary to the over-ruling passion of his life. The one thing that he did above all else was give attention to his spiritual life.

Therefore we say that life in the Truth, the spiritual life, *ought* to be the most satisfying and fulfilling life for any man or woman. God, who created us and continually sustains us, teaches us by His Word how best to live the life He has given us.

Red and green lights

The Bible is the Book of how to do it—for life. Because like most things there's a right way and a wrong way to do it, a safe way and a dangerous way.

When you're driving a car you keep to the instruction book called the Highway Code (well, hopefully you do!). If you have any sense you don't drive regardless of it, saying to yourself: "Why should I stop at red lights?—I'm going to ignore them. I don't *have* to stop! Nobody tells me what to do."

BANG! You stop. You have hit another car.

The Bible has a lot of 'red lights' in it. They are all those *Thou shalt nots* and *don't do this and thats*. They are there for our safety and protection. But they make a lot of people dislike God's Word. "It's so full of restrictions."

How come so very few people take the same attitude to the Highway Code? You don't hear people saying, "I can't take it, it's so full of don'ts: Don't cross red lights, don't pull out without looking, don't park on crossings." We *know* these don'ts are there for our own safety and the safety of others. And so it is with all the don'ts in the Bible. You can go through a whole lot of Bible red lights, ignoring them cavalier fashion. You'll probably be 'lucky' for a while and get away with it. You'll have a few near misses and might even think it quite exciting. But as sure as 'eggs is eggs' your 'luck' will run out one day, and, *BANG!*—you're in serious trouble.

Bible don'ts are the red lights put there for our safety. But there are a whole lot of green lights in the Bible, too. In fact all the aspects of the fruit of the Spirit are green lights. It tells us so, right there in Galatians 5:23 where the fruit is detailed that these are things "*against which there is no law.*" There's no law against peace, joy, faith, and all the others. All green lights. Do these. It's safe for you to go this way.

The One who authored the instruction book knows. The One who created us knows the best way for us to go. He tells us in His Word how best to live the lives He has given us. And we can prove that to ourselves by learning and living what His Word has to teach us. We're not left to muddle through this life in frustration and ignorance, living *"lives of quiet desperation,"* to quote the words of Henry Thoreau, which he said, *"the mass of men lead."* Life is meant to be a whole lot better than that!

You can have all that is necessary for a satisfying life when you follow the way of the Spirit.

So what's the catch?

But there's a catch—or at least what seems to be a catch. It's more of a rider really. We had to emphasize that word *ought* when we said earlier that life in the Truth *ought* to be the most satisfying way of life. Because often, in conversation with fellow believers, one gets the distinct impression that they don't feel too overjoyed about *their* life in the Truth much of the time. Sometimes they say bluntly that life is giving them too many hard knocks. So what has gone wrong? And why do so many believers seem to live well below their spiritual potential?

The two main reasons I've come across (to be honest, *experienced*!) are **the problem of trials**, and **the problem of vagueness about spiritual development.**

Trials

Trials are the "catch" or rider I mentioned earlier. While it's true that God says He will do many things to help those who seriously pursue the spiritual path through life, the rider is that He will also test everyone who travels that path. "For whom the Lord loveth he chasteneth, and scourgeth every son whom he receiveth. If ye endure chastening, God dealeth with you as with sons; for what son is he whom the father chasteneth not?" (Heb.12:6,7).

We don't take too well to chastening, do we? We didn't like it when our parents inflicted it on us "for your own good" when we were children, and quite naturally we react against it when our Heavenly Father inflicts it when we become His children. We doubted that it was really all for our own good when our parents did it; we suspected that it was sometimes done for *their* good! If they dealt sharply with us, they had a quieter life, because we were put in our place. The writer of the letter to the Hebrews makes this very point: "For they [our parents] for a few days chastened us after their own pleasure; but he [God] for our profit, that we might be partakers of his holiness."

6

We will be tested with problems and difficulties. And these tests will always hit us in one or more of those ten items we mentioned earlier that go to make a satisfying life. What's more, the test will probably hit us where it hurts the most. For the indications are that God tests believers through the very things they prize the most: sufficient money perhaps, or health, or self-esteem. There's a case in the New Testament (Luke 18:18-23) where this principle comes to light. A man described as a rich young ruler went to Christ and asked what he should do to inherit eternal life.

What do you lack?

This ruler was already keeping the commandments, or so he claimed, yet he felt he lacked something. Or perhaps, which is likely, he wanted to know what new thing Jesus was teaching that he should do over and above what the Law of Moses already required of him. Wasn't that Law enough? Was Jesus saying he needed more than that? The young man said he already kept all the commandments of the Law. So what did he lack? As expected, Jesus went instantly to the heart of the matter. "Yet lackest thou one thing: sell all that thou hast, and distribute unto the poor, and thou shalt have treasure in heaven: and come, follow me. And when he heard this, he was very sorrowful: for he was very rich" (Luke 18:22,23).

The man was already on the spiritual path. He was observing the law, and we assume he made a genuine enquiry of Jesus, but there was an area of his life in which he was vulnerable. He lacked *one thing which was needful*: a truly full commitment to the spiritual path.

He had not yet faced an unpleasant truth about himself, that his wealth was more important than his spirituality. All the while he had everything he needed, he felt secure in his religion. But if his religion made demands that might be fatal to his wealth, he would rather side with his wealth. He believed that to lose his money was more than he could cope with. It wasn't of course, and Jesus would not have suggested he part with it if it were completely out of the question. We don't know how the story ended. The last we see of the man is his droopy-shouldered departure from Jesus. I like to think that God later re-tested him in this area of his wealth, and proved to him that he could cope: that he found treasure in heaven when he got his priorities straightened out—and was not exactly destitute as a result, as he feared.

Don't misunderstand me. We don't all have to give everything we have to the poor in order to follow the spiritual path. The point being made is that we are better off doing without whatever blocks our progress along the path. The man's attachment to his wealth was the problem, not the wealth itself. Your problem may not be wealth, even if you have it. You may need testing in an entirely different area.

God certainly tests believers, and this is one reason why many believers are less than content with life in the Truth. So often, I'm sure, we fail to learn the lesson that comes to us. So often we don't see the problem on our path as a test from God, but think of it instead as just one of life's hard knocks that we have to suffer and that drags us down. So we don't rise above it. We don't learn anything about ourselves—except, perhaps, that we're pretty useless at trying to live the Truth, which is not what God is attempting to show us! Consequently there is no spiritual development, no fruit of the Spirit; there is only complaint and dissatisfaction.

Being rightly exercised

The key verses on this subject of our trials are Hebrews 12:11-13:

> "Now no chastening for the present seemeth to be joyous, but grievous: nevertheless afterward it yieldeth the peaceable fruit of righteousness unto them which are exercised thereby. Wherefore lift up the hands which hang down, and the feeble knees; and make straight paths for your feet, lest that which is lame be turned out of the way; but let it rather be healed."

8

All the turmoil and mental agitation of our trials, whatever they are, could give way to the peaceable (peaceful) fruit of righteousness, if only we would *allow* that to happen. If, instead of feeling sorry for ourselves and dispirited about life's set-backs (with our hands hanging dejectedly and our knees too feeble to move us ahead), we would only lift up those hands in prayer, and lift those knees (a figurative way of describing getting going along the spiritual path), then we would be healed, and not lame.

Our present problems can seem like a rough and difficult road that we are stuck on. Spiritually, our knees are feeble and we're in danger of going lame as we tramp along this unfriendly terrain. That's how life seems sometimes, and we might even say, or feel like saying. "I can't go on." The way looks too hard.

But the answer is in our own hands (and feet). It is for us (and nobody else!) to "make straight the path of [our] feet." We have to take responsibility for our own spiritual progress. (It's not up to God to drag us along and *make* us develop spiritually.) The verses in Hebrews tell us we can do this by being rightly exercised by our problems. And how apt to say that our lameness and feebleness will be cured by exercise.

The spiritual muscle is like any other muscle in the body in the important sense that if we hardly use it, it becomes feeble and useless, and needs exercise to get it back into shape. People off their feet in hospital for long periods need to get the strength back in their legs before they can walk confidently. Unused muscles need exercise, or they may eventually atrophy and become totally useless.

The problems God puts our way are to strengthen our spiritual muscle, not weaken it. God will pick out the areas in our lives that need attention and send something to build us up in those areas. If we let the problems exercise us correctly, the outcome will be good. Undoubtedly.

The trouble is that we have a tendency to go lame when we hit rough patches. We don't allow ourselves to be exercised by them. We so easily let the hard times shake our faith instead of firming it up. But that's never God's intention for us when he tests and chastens us. His intention is that we should develop and grow spiritually. That we should in fact develop the fruit of the Spirit. And one of the aspects of the fruit is mentioned right there in those verses from Hebrews 12.

If we are exercised rightly by the chastening of the Lord "it yieldeth the peaceable [peaceful] fruit of righteousness." Righteousness means being right with God—which brings peace.

So the outcome of accepting the difficulties we face in life in the right spirit (spirit equals *attitude* here) is peace. Which makes perfect sense, doesn't it? If we see the hand of God in our problems, they cease, in reality, to be problems. They become exercises for learning, for strengthening our spiritual muscle. The Lord's chastening leads us, in fact, to develop the fruit of the Spirit.

Only peace is mentioned in those verses from Hebrews, but other aspects of the fruit will also be developed.

Though hold on just a moment...!

...Just think of the benefits of peace alone! So many people lack *true* peace in their lives in this age of anxiety. Having just that one aspect of the fruit will bring with it many of those things which most people agree are necessary for a fulfilled and satisfying life. Peace alone brings good emotional and mental health, which often leads to better physical health, which in turn makes us better able to enjoy life, to earn our living, and have other necessary things.

One thing is needful. Get the spiritual side of life right, and no matter what comes your way, good or 'bad', you'll see that it has God in it, and so it can't really be bad. You'll be able to handle it. It may not go away, but you'll be able to handle it. You'll be rightly exercised by it. And you'll discover you have all you need for a satisfying life. Keep in mind that the Bible says "all things work together **for** good" in the life of a believer, not that all things **are** good.

Man in a wheelchair

The other day I was walking home from the office and saw a young man in a wheelchair ahead of me on the path. He was moving slowly because of the incline and I soon caught up. As I passed by I saw how hard he was working with his arms to keep the wheelchair going. I wondered if I should help.

A short way ahead I turned and looked back to see how he was doing. The path was getting steeper and he was hardly moving forward at all. The wheelchair was going more from side to side than forwards. The young man was obviously struggling. I couldn't just walk off and leave him puffing his heart out! So I walked back and said, "Can I give you a push up this steep bit?"

To my amazement he looked up, smiled, and between breaths said, "No thanks. This is good exercise."

Good exercise! I could hardly believe it. He was having a really tough time moving that chair up that slope. It looked like torture. But to him it was just "good exercise". He was actually enjoying himself!

What a good way that is to be about life. In fact, it's the only way for a true believer to be about life. Not to moan and complain when things are hard, but to smile and see them as good exercise. Does that sound impossible to you? Well, it isn't. The Apostle Paul wrote in one of his letters about "glorying in tribulations" (Rom.5:3). That means being happy even when things are hard. Paul could be happy when life was difficult (as it certainly was sometimes) because he trusted that God was always with him. As he saw it, he didn't really have anything to worry about. All believers need to have that same truth engraved on their hearts. Whatever happens, God will look after us and see us through. For us there are no events over which God does not have control, and nothing that is truly bad can happen to us. The 'bad' is merely "good exercise".

The other reason

We said there were two reasons why believers often live below their spiritual capabilities. One is that we don't learn from our problems, and we let them sap our spiritual and physical energy. The other is that **we go through life with only a vague notion of what spiritual development is**.

As a consequence we don't commit ourselves strongly enough to it. We blithely mark time in the Truth, thinking that just being *in* the Truth is all that matters. But it's not *having* the Truth that counts, it's what you do with it when you've got it! The transfer from being "in Adam" to being "in Christ" is only a *transfer,* it's not a transformation! The transformation of our character happens slowly afterwards, as we continue to apply our minds to spiritual things in a purposeful way– or it doesn't happen because we don't. Therefore we stagnate spiritually– and find life in the Truth rather less than fulfilling.

This transformation of our character is the development of the fruit of the Spirit. It's as simple as that. And once we know that, we know what we're aiming for. Spiritual development ceases to be vague. It is the process of bringing the nine aspects of the fruit of the Spirit into our character.

And as we involve ourselves in this process, we learn one of life's greatest lessons. A God-given law of life comes into operation. We learn, as the fruit of the Spirit develops, that we can more easily handle the tests God puts our way. We lose those old feelings of stagnation, of being spiritually becalmed, that we may have had before.

We lose any dissatisfaction with life in the Truth that being vague about our spiritual direction generates. We arrive at the wonderful conclusion that life in the Truth *is* the most satisfying and fulfilling way of life available to anyone living on this planet.

Hopefully, your journey through this book will help reinforce that conclusion for you. Or help you towards it.

One final point: Prosperity Theology

There is one final point I must make about spiritual living before closing this chapter. It is true that God looks after us when we focus on the one thing that is needful. But there is a school of thought that goes a lot further, and claims that the spiritual life will bring all sorts of superabundance into our lives—*NOW!*

This is known as Prosperity Theology. The claim is that if we can get ourselves rightly attuned to God's will for us, He will shower us with blessings, make us *super* rich, *super* healthy, *super* attractive, *super* confident.

The idea that following God will turn you into superman or superwoman is very appealing. But it has more to do with the American Dream than the promises of God. It's the message of many of the television evangelists of America and Canada– the sort of people who are now starting up television channels over here. And they seem to be getting a following in certain sections of the church.

It's as if the religion of the Bible had fallen into the hands of a clever advertising agency who'd seen a better way to market Christianity. Which probably isn't too wide of the mark. The message is: if you want to do well for yourself, be the sort of person you always dreamed of being, then Christianity is your answer. GOD WANTS YOU RICH is the sort of banner it marches under.

Like all the best untruths, like all the most appealing lies, there is an element of truth in it. Undoubtedly, our quality of life is greatly improved by the addition of a spiritual dimension, but we should not be looking for superstar status.

The satisfying and fulfilling life the Scriptures promise us now is not in that direction. True satisfaction and fulfilment are rarely found that way. That's why when I listed the ten things that go to make up the truly good life, I said **sufficient** food and money, **good** health and relationships etc., not SUPER-ABUNDANT! and EXCELLENT!

On being normal

Producing the fruit of the Spirit– the all-round Christian character– will not make us *super*-people with everything we ever dreamed of, but it will make us **NORMAL PEOPLE**. "Ah," I hear you say politely, a little unimpressed. "What's so good about being normal?" What encouragement is there for me to gain the fruit of the Spirit if all it does for me is make me normal? Who wants to be just plain *normal*? Doesn't everyone want to be special?

I happen to have a passion for normality. I think the normal should be pursued with great fervour. In fact I'd like us all to be *excessively* normal. This is because I believe, on the basis of what the Bible says, that *normal* is an awful lot more than most people experience. The majority of people undoubtedly operate below what God intended as normal for us.

One of the Proverbs says: "Give me neither poverty nor riches; feed me with food convenient for me: lest I be full and deny thee, and say, Who is the Lord? or lest I be poor, and steal, and take the name of my God in vain" (Prov.30:8,9). This applies to more things in life than money and food. This is the norm. This is what the fruit of the Spirit is geared to. Not lack, not superabundance, but sufficiency. And we can be certain that what God sees as sufficient will not be penny-pinching.

God, I'm sure, would love to shower us with unlimited blessings. He knows how to give good gifts to His children. And He gives us as much as He safely can without creating problems for us, without giving us things that will mis-shape our characters. As Jesus said: "What man is there among you who, if his son asks for bread will give him a stone? Or if he asks for a fish, will he give him a serpent?" (Matt.7:9,10 RAV). So why should we expect any less from our loving Father? The true version of normal is well above the subsistence levels in most areas of life—well above what passes for normal!

So I am all for being normal. Not so over-blessed in my wealth, possessions, wit, charm and abilities (no problems here, so far), that I forget my God; not so under-blessed that I carp and whinge at life's bad breaks, forgetting and cursing God in the process.

The fruit of the Spirit will not turn us into *super* people, the envy of the neighbours and toast of the town, but it will turn us into normal people in the sight of God.

So why be less than normal? Normal is, in fact, rather special. To be normal is to be extremely successful. It might even include material success– abundance in some aspects of life– but that isn't the purpose of travelling the spiritual path. It may come as a by-product of pursuing the real satisfaction and fulfilment that the **one thing that is needful** brings. Then again, material success may even come as a trial.

I know it's an old cliché that wealth doesn't bring happiness, but that makes it no less true. The casualties of success are legion. The 'successful' have everything— including an aching void that says, "Is this *all* there is?" And unless they have something other than, and *better* than, wealth and success, they are doomed to enjoy neither.

Far better to make the finest qualities of character your goal in the first place. Go for what is normal, not what appears to be super normal. This book is not about becoming a superstar through Prosperity Theology. It's a book for those who aspire to achieve normality with God. Such unusually wise people will one day "shine as the stars for ever and ever" (Dan.12:3).

CHAPTER TWO

"LIKE A TREE PLANTED BY THE RIVERS OF WATER"

A TREE that bears fruit is worthwhile. It gives something useful. It gives us something to eat which is healthy and refreshing. Such a tree is also vital for producing more trees after its own kind. Fruitless trees would be the end of 'tree-kind' as we know it.

Fruit-laden trees are a feast for the eyes as well as the stomach. How amazing an orange grove looks in full fruit!—and what about the pastel whites and pinks that precede a bumper crop of apples! Fruit looks good, it tastes good, and it does you good.

All these points were established back in Genesis chapters 1 and 2, when "the Lord God planted a garden eastward in Eden" for the first man and woman and "Out of the ground made the Lord God to grow every tree that is pleasant to the sight, and good for food..." (Gen.2:9).

On the other hand, a fruit tree that bears no fruit is worthless. Especially if you depend on it for your food or livelihood. You might as well dig it up and plant something useful in its place. There's no point having it. You don't have to be an expert gardener to know this is all sound horticultural commonsense. Good husbandry dictates that, having first done what you could for the unfruitful tree— tended it, given it more time—if it still produced little or no fruit, you would have to do the sensible thing and remove it. Get yourself a healthy tree. In fact Jesus told a parable along these very lines.

The parable of the fig tree in the vineyard

"A certain man had a fig tree planted in his vineyard; and he came and sought fruit thereon, and

16

found none. Then he said unto the dresser of his vineyard, Behold, these three years I come seeking fruit on this fig tree, and find none: cut it down; why cumbereth it the ground? And he answering said unto him, Lord, let it alone this year also, till I shall dig about it, and dung it: And if it bear fruit, well; and if not, then after that thou shalt cut it down" (Luke 13:6-9).

It's a parable about Israel. There's little doubt about that. The fig tree is used as a symbol for the nation of Israel (Matt.21:19; 24:32; Joel 1:7; Jer.24; Psalm 80:8-17 and others). Jesus, as the dresser of the vineyard (as all the prophets God sent to tend Israel before him had been), had for three years of his ministry attempted to make some spiritual impact on the nation. He met with very little success. There was still no fruit to speak of. On each of those years the Lord God, the owner of the vineyard of Israel, had looked in to see what success His dresser was having, and he was disappointed each time. Israel might as well be "cut down" in the opinion of Heaven.

But Jesus must have said in effect, *"No. Let me make one last special effort. I may yet be able to coax some fruit from it in what time I have left."*

The fruit of the parable obviously represents the spiritual fruit Christ was hoping to encourage from Israel.

Fruit, naturally speaking, is the visible evidence and expression of a tree's good health. The tree that comes to fruit has done what it was meant to do. It has done what it was designed by God to do. It has perfectly fulfilled its function. From which we can tell how best to understand spiritual fruit. Spiritual fruit is the visible evidence and expression of a believer's good spiritual health. Likewise, the believer who comes to spiritual fruit has done what he or she was meant to do—what he or she was designed by God to do.

The parable of the vine-dresser tells us Christ was looking for a change of heart from the nation of Israel. He was trying to convert them from the works of the flesh to the fruit of the Spirit. He was working hard to turn the people away from their dead, legalistic slavery to the Law of Moses, which had made the Law a burden to them, towards a healthy understanding of the love that was actually expressed *through* the Law, and which would make it a joy for them to observe. This new enlightenment would also help prepare the people for the transfer that was soon coming from Law to grace—from the Old Covenant through Moses to the New Covenant in Christ.

It's almost certain that many of the people Jesus wanted to change in this way had experienced the baptism of John three years previously. And what was it that John told them on that occasion?—"Bring forth therefore fruits meet for repentance"—*spiritual* fruit. John also added, significantly, "And now also the axe is laid unto the root of the trees: therefore every tree which bringeth not forth good fruit is hewn down, and cast into the fire" (Matt.3:10).

John's warning

The parable of Jesus is an unmistakable echo of what John had said. *"Fruits meet for repentance"* had so far not been forthcoming, and the axeman's hand had been stayed long enough. *"Cut it down,"* said the owner of the vineyard. But Jesus' compassion for his people, and his plea on their behalf, moved the Father to wait a little longer.

Admittedly, it's difficult to fit the parable precisely to the events that occurred historically, because the "cutting down" of Israel cannot truly be said to have happened until AD70, when Rome finally lost patience with her and scattered her across the globe. That's **forty years later** rather than the extra one year's reprieve that the dresser of the vineyard had petitioned for. But that's not really a problem. We should see it rather as an example of the mercy of God. We are told that "The effectual fervent prayer of a righteous man availeth much" (Jas.5:16). Bearing in mind *who* the righteous man was in this case, it's no small wonder that Israel's reprieve lasted forty years! How earnestly Jesus must have prayed for his people!

From the natural to the personal

What we're chiefly concerned about with regard to the parable of the vine-dresser is that it shows us that the Scriptures employ the cultivation of fruit to portray spiritual development. Failure to produce fruit as lack of spiritual development. In the parable it was applied nationally: the nation of Israel was the tree. But, as other Scripture shows, the symbol can also apply to individuals.

John the Baptist likened the individuals approaching him for baptism to trees which might be cut down if unfruitful. Your spiritual development and mine is our "fruit" in Scriptural terms. And John made it abundantly clear that there simply have to be *"fruits meet for repentance"* ("in keeping with repentance" NIV), or we trees will be good for nothing but to be cut down. In other words, following baptism there has to be spiritual development, a visible expression of our growing spiritual health. Our characters must be transformed into characters which Christ will approve.

But this won't happen overnight! Which is one of the important things that likening our spiritual development to the production of fruit tells us. Fruit grows and ripens gradually. The vine-dresser in the parable could hardly have said, "Let's just wait another couple of days and see what happens." Nothing would have happened. Quite reasonably, he had to wait for the vine to go through its cycle of production. The fruit would be ready, or not, in due season.

But to be sure of fruit *some day* we must be active now. It's not next year, or even next month when we must make a start. The time to be developing our fruit is always *now*.

19

We'll be doing it all our lives until Christ comes. Then there will be what he calls the harvest in many parables: the gathering in of the fruit.

Spiritual fruit is the same as physical fruit in that it doesn't appear suddenly a few days before the harvest. Barren trees don't suddenly explode with fruit a day or two before the apple-pickers start rolling up their sleeves or cranking up their machinery. This is one of the important reasons why the parallel is made between the appearance of fruit on trees and our spiritual development. It can't be done instantly. The tree can't put it off until a few days before the harvest, and neither can we. That's the message.

We said at the start of this chapter that for a tree to produce good fruit it must be healthy. So, in our turn, in order to produce spiritual fruit we have to be spiritually healthy. In nature, for a tree to be healthy three factors come into play: good soil, sufficient sunlight, and, most important of all, *water*. Water is the crucial element that can often make up for poor soil and even sparse sunlight. As this world is a spiritual desert, and a place of near spiritual darkness until the Light of the World returns (John 9:5), our only hope is good water! Without a good water supply a tree is doomed. Which brings us to Psalm 1.

The spiritual man or woman: a tree by a river

In Psalm 1 a picture of the perfect tree (meaning the true spiritual man or woman) is provided for us. Here the godly person is described in these terms:

> "And he shall be like a tree planted by the rivers of water, that bringeth forth his fruit in his season; his leaf also shall not wither; and whatsoever he doeth shall prosper" (Ps.1:3).

Jeremiah paints a similar picture:

> "For he shall be as a tree planted by the waters, and that spreadeth out her roots by the river, and shall not see when heat cometh, but her leaf shall

be green; and shall not be careful in the year of drought, neither shall cease from yielding fruit" (Jeremiah 17:8).

The chief reason these trees are healthy, we are told, is because they are planted by a good water supply. They spread their roots along the river-bank, so even in a time of drought they can find the hidden sustenance beneath the river-bed. Now, if we take a look at the preceding verse in Psalm 1 and in Jeremiah 17, we learn exactly what makes the tree, the man or woman of God, healthy and fruitful.

Delight and meditation

In the Psalm we are told it's because "his delight is in the law of the Lord; and in his law doth he meditate day and night." **That's why he's like the fruitful tree.** And in Jeremiah we're told, "Blessed is the man that trusteth in the Lord, and whose hope the Lord is. For he shall be as a tree...."**That's what makes him a fruitful tree.**

- DELIGHT in the law of the Lord
- MEDITATION day and night in His law
- TRUST in the Lord
- HOPE in the Lord

These four items are what makes the man of God like a fruitful tree. These four correspond to a good water supply nourishing the tree. **So it follows that our development of spiritual fruit depends on these very things.**

The development of the fruit of the Spirit will only occur if we are planted by the good, health-giving waters of delight and meditation. Meaning, of course, that we must get our roots down firmly into the water of life that is in God's life-giving Word. *Delight* in it and *meditate* upon it, in order to suck up *trust* and *hope* from its depths to sustain us through this twentieth century spiritual drought.

The sort of meditation mentioned in Psalm 1 doesn't involve emptying our minds, as in Eastern meditation where

21

the idea is to achieve a calm inner state by stilling the 'chattering monkey', as the Easterns call the perpetual dialogue we have going with ourselves inside our heads.

There is some benefit to be had from that sort of mind-clearing relaxation, but it's not what the Scriptures mean. The Hebrew idea couldn't be more different. The word actually means *mutter*! The Psalmist is telling us to fill our minds, not empty them! To fill them, of course, with the Word of God. Where spiritual development is concerned there is no substitute for a good acquaintance with the Word. There is no other way to cultivate "fruits meet for repentance." No other way to develop the sort of characters Christ will approve.

But spiritual fruit will never result from a casual acquaintance with the Word. As the Psalm says, it comes from meditating upon it day and night: that is, filling our lives with it, delighting in it. That doesn't mean, of course, that we have to be actively reading every spare moment, almost permanently holding an open Bible! That much study is impractical, and would very likely make us *mad*—to borrow Festus' word to Paul on the subject of too much study (Acts 26:24). But the *quality* of our study, when we do it, needs to be sufficiently good to give us something to chew over most of the time so that it has constant influence on our lives. That sort of quality only comes when we truly take delight in reading the Word and take time to think over properly what we read.

The fruit of the Spirit grows from delighting and meditating in the Word of God. This is why the fruit is said by Paul to be **"of the spirit".** It comes from the spirit Word. But that's the topic of the next chapter.

CHAPTER THREE

"OF THE SPIRIT"

NOBODY but God can make a fruit. No fruit-farmer or vine-dresser in the world can actually make an apple or a grape. All he can do is create the most favourable conditions for growth, and let the natural laws established by God bring about the fruit.

So in a very real sense all **natural** fruit is of the Spirit, because God has brought it into existence, not man. Every item of produce that emerges from the ground and appears on your meal table is directly attributable to the hand of God. Hence the very excellent custom of giving thanks before eating.

But our subject is not fruit that grows on trees and vines. It's more important than the mere food on our tables. "Is not the life more than meat?" (Matt.6:25).

According to the Apostle Paul, writing by the Spirit of God, *"the fruit of the Spirit is love, joy, peace, longsuffering, gentleness, goodness, faith, meekness, temperance."*

This fruit is extra special. It brings together all the qualities of character which are produced in the heart of a believer by the Spirit. And in a sense, in the same way that no man can make an apple or a grape, so no man can manufacture these qualities for himself. As Paul says, they are *"of the Spirit"*.

Simply *deciding* to make these qualities ours won't change us in any appreciable way. As if to say, "Name a virtue and it's yours!" We can't turn the aspects of the fruit into something like a list of New Year resolutions, and expect to have them. If we do that, they'll go the way of most New Year resolutions. Probably sooner! Just deciding to have these things, by an effort of will, won't generate them. Fruit has to go through a process of growth. You can no more demand spiritual fruit of yourself than you can demand apples of a tree. This fruit is of the Spirit, not of our own wills.

Not the real thing

I also believe that the good works of the unchristian of the world fail to please God because they are *not* the fruit of the Spirit. Dare I say that the love, joy, peace, longsuffering, gentleness etc. which the world exhibits is only a synthetic fruit. Laudable as it is—and sometimes in appearance and effect it puts true believers to shame—it is not the genuine article, but mimics the real fruit of the Spirit.

This may seem like a harsh thing to say, bearing in mind all the energy and sincerity that undoubtedly goes into the good works of the world, but if all the qualities of the fruit are in a person, and he or she has not obtained them through delighting and meditating in the Word according to a sound understanding of the gospel, what else can we call this fruit but imitation? Though it's hard to accept that the well-intentioned and sincere good characters we often encounter are viewed by God as mere imitations of what He really expects, I find it hard to escape this view.

But the fact that the only character acceptable to God is one which exhibits the fruit of the Spirit does help us understand why so many very good people are actually unacceptable to God. **What they have only appears to be what God wants.** You may be the greatest philanthropist on earth, but still be a long way short of what God wants from you.

Not a gift of the Spirit

One thing we must get clear in our minds is that the fruit is **of the Spirit**, and *not* a gift of the Spirit. The qualities that make up the fruit are not conferred by the Holy Spirit. Believers have never had the fruit of the Spirit bestowed upon them as they once had the Spirit gifts. If that were to

24

happen it would make a nonsense of believers' probations, the whole point of which is to instill these qualities into their characters.

To have one's character suddenly and miraculously changed by the Holy Spirit (presumably at baptism, or shortly after) would make all the warnings and exhortations of the New Testament about failure a complete waste of Bible space.

With supernaturally changed characters we would never need to be told what to do and what not to do; it would come naturally. No-one would ever leave the Truth. The very notion of God's re-programming us for righteousness not only flies in the face of Christian experience (meaning it doesn't happen), but it's contrary to the way God has historically dealt with us. God wants our free-will response. And love, the first (and probably the whole) of the fruit of the Spirit, is impossible to programme into someone.

Try programming your computer to say "I love you" and you'll quickly realize that the response is less than satisfying! Do you really think it means it? That certainly isn't love.

The fruit of the Spirit was never a gift of the Spirit to alter us regardless of our own efforts and intentions. Even those powers that *were* gifts of the Spirit never *made* the first century believers righteous. They still had problems and failed.

The fruit is of the Spirit because...

So, if it isn't a gift of the Holy Spirit, how is the fruit to be understood as being of the Spirit? **It is of the Spirit because it results from the influence of the Spirit Word.**

"Of the Spirit"

Perhaps it will be helpful to look at some parallel phrases from the New Testament.

> "Fruit of the Spirit" (Gal.5:22)
> "mind of the Spirit" (Rom.8:27)
> "spiritually minded" (Rom.8:6)
> [minding] the things of the Spirit" (Rom.8:5)
> "mind of Christ" (1 Cor.2:16, Phil.2:5)
> "Spirit of Christ" (Rom.8:9)
> "Spirit of life in Christ Jesus" (Rom.8:2)
> "Walk in the Spirit" (Gal.5:16)

All these phrases amount to the same thing. They all refer to a mind which is dominated by spiritual thinking, a mind influenced by the Spirit Word, as opposed to fleshly thinking. None of these phrases refers to the direct influence of the Holy Spirit on the mind. *Walking in the Spirit* is taking the spiritual path through life, not the fleshly path dominated by self. *The mind of the Spirit* is the mind influenced and directed by the Spirit Word.

Spirit in all these cases is used as the opposite to flesh. God's Spirit way is contrasted with our natural inclinations. Most of the phrases above come from Romans 8, and if you look at that chapter you'll see that this spirit-and-flesh antagonism is the theme of the chapter. The same is true of Galatians 5 where the fruit of the Spirit is set against the works of the flesh.

If we attempt to make the word *Spirit* in Romans 8 mean the direct influence of the Holy Spirit, then we have the very nonsense we mentioned earlier. We have a situation where the Holy Spirit makes people righteous. For in verse 13, Paul writes: "For if ye live after the flesh, ye shall die: but if ye through the Spirit do mortify the deeds of the body, ye shall live." The Holy Spirit did not *make* believers righteous by mortifying the flesh (deeds of the body); the believers themselves were asked to do that through the Spirit—that is, through acquiring a spiritual mind. They would accomplish it through their delight and meditation in the Spirit word, not through any gift of the Holy Spirit.

The mind of Christ

A phrase of particular interest among those quoted above is *"the mind of Christ."* Without doubt Christ exhibited the fruit of the Spirit to perfection. **To have the mind of Christ is to have the fruit in all its aspects.** It hardly seems necessary to prove it, but here is the proof anyway: all these refer to Christ:

"... love one another as I have **LOVED** you" (John 15:12)

"... that my **JOY** might remain in you..." (John 15:11)

"... my **PEACE** I give unto you..." (John 14:27)

"... Jesus Christ might shew forth all **LONGSUFFERING**." (1 Tim.1:16)

"... the Lord [Jesus] is gracious [Gk. *chrestos*, **KIND** = gentleness**] (1 Pet. 2.3)

"Can there any **GOOD** thing come out of Nazareth?... Come and see" (John 1:46)

"... Christ Jesus who was **FAITHFUL** to him that appointed him" (Heb.3:2)

"...by the **MEEKNESS** and gentleness of Christ" (2 Cor.10:1)

"Every man that striveth for the mastery is **TEMPERATE** in all things" (1 Cor.9:25) [includes Christ]

Of course, as I believe *agape*/LOVE is the *whole* fruit, encompassing all the aspects of Galatians 5:22,23, it's really only necessary for me to point out the verses which attribute *agape* to Christ in order to demonstrate he had the fruit in full. But the verses listed above do make an interesting collection. They do confirm that the *mind of Christ* is what we get when we produce the fruit of the Spirit. All the qualities of the fruit are found in the perfect character of Christ. When the production of the fruit of the Spirit is our goal in life, we are really seeking to make the character of Christ our own.

God is love

Taking this a step further, it has to be remembered that *God is love.* God is *agape,* in fact, as the word is in 1 John 4.16. God is the great originator and epitome of this love. And Jesus the Son is spiritually the image of the Father (Heb.1:3). The mind of Christ is a true reflection of the mind of the Father.

The mind of the Father is expressed in His Word. Jesus found it there, delighted in it and meditated day and night upon it, to the full exclusion of the mind of the flesh. He achieved a likemindedness with God unequalled in man before or since. He could always think or say, "as the scripture hath said," or "how readest thou?" or "have ye not read this scripture ...?" He was so in tune with his Father's thinking that he could say that he and his Father were *one*.

Our aim, too, is to get ourselves in tune with the thinking of the Father. And we will achieve success in this enterprise to whatever degree we apply ourselves to the Spirit Word. The Scriptures are the only place in this world where the mind of God, and subsequently of Christ, is shown.

Delight and meditation in the Word will slowly, almost imperceptibly, produce the fruit of the Spirit for us, where no amount of will-power can. Fruit is not summoned into existence; it will grow in its own good time. We cannot force it. But we *can* create the most favourable conditions for growth (like the successful farmer), and let the natural laws established by God bring about the fruit.

This is not the operation of the Holy Spirit working directly upon us, but the bringing together, over a sustained period, of the mind of God and a receptive heart. These are the only favourable conditions for the production of the fruit of the Spirit.

CHAPTER FOUR

BEING AND DOING

THE development of love has to be one of the prime concerns of all who seriously want to follow Christ. Yet how many of us are clear enough in our own minds about what Christian love really is, and make the development of it a conscious goal in our lives?

It's very easy to be vague about Christian love, to exercise it in an indeterminate manner, and to acquire the notion that it's nothing more than "doing good." Obviously "doing good" comes into it, but it's nowhere near the whole story. In fact "doing good" is more of a by-product of Christian love, the result of it rather than the object of it.

This is why Paul could say that "love is the fulfilling of the law" (Rom.13:10). Adultery, murder, theft, false witnessing, covetousness, and all other such wrongs, simply don't happen when people have love (which is a paraphrase of Rom.13:9). Doing good occurs instead. Doing good happens when we give attention to who we **are** rather than what we **do**.

Love is about being

One of the most important things to learn about love is that **it has more to do with being than doing.** It concerns what we *are* rather more that what we *do*. The fruit of the Spirit , which I believe is love, is something which grows and ripens in our character and personality, bringing about a gradual inner transformation. It is not developed by our deeds; it is developed by the Spirit through our delight and meditation in the Spirit Word.

How easy it is for us to get things back-to-front and imagine that it's by all our doing that we will eventually evolve the right sort of Christ-like characters for ourselves. It's not so. The simple truth is that the transformation of our characters *from within* must come first, and then the deeds will take care of themselves. Getting it the wrong way round and putting deeds first will produce the sort of imitation fruit of the Spirit that the world produces with all its good deeds. God does not approve it because it's phoney fruit.

The Apostle Paul teaches us in his famous chapter on love (1 Cor.13) that we can do all manner of wondrous things in the service of God and our fellow man, but these will count for nothing if we don't first have love– that is, if we don't put ourselves internally right first. Love is more about being than doing! The error of getting it back-to-front manifests itself in at least three different but similar types of unfulfillment.

1. The joyless worker

Why is it that some believers find themselves overburdened by trying to live the Truth? Life in the Truth is the most satisfying and fulfilling way of life available to anyone living on this planet, as we said at the outset of this book. Yet some people work flat out at "doing" the Truth with very little satisfaction, as their weariness will betray, (barring the dubious satisfaction of grumbling about all those who aren't so overloaded!). A law of diminishing returns sets in. Too much time and effort spent in doing and not enough attention given to being (to what we are *inside*) can make life go spiritually flat, like old *Coca Cola*. The joy of doing will eventually wear thin if the joy of being hasn't preceded it.

2. Non-starters

Then again, there are some believers who have the opposite but equally unsatisfying problem. Theirs is not the problem of being unfulfilled by a demanding work schedule; theirs is the problem of being defeated even before they start. They have a fixation on the doing, and there seems to be such an unclimbable mountain of things for them to do that they give up at square one.

It's all too much, they think. They can never hope to do it all– or as much as person B, C and D are doing– so why bother? They have seen *doing* as the most important thing in Christian life and they have backed away from it, feeling inadequate to do as much as they feel they ought to do, or as much as they see others doing. If only they would concentrate on being and not doing, the problem would go away.

3. The becalmed

The third type of unfulfilled believer is closely related to the last. He or she would certainly find it hard to say, hand on heart, that their life in the Truth is the most satisfying and fulfilling way of life. I'm talking about those who are the spiritually becalmed.

When you're on a sailing boat which is becalmed, you're stuck out in mid-sea with no wind in your sails. And if you don't have a motor, you have a problem. You're not going anywhere. You just drift with the tide. The situation could get life-threatening.

Believers can become spiritually becalmed. In this state all their years in the Truth seem to have produced very little by way of spiritual progress. They had such grand aspirations when they started out on the spiritual journey, but they have grossly underachieved.

Probably most believers feel a bit like that from time to time (and rightly so, because self-satisfaction in the spiritual life is the fast lane to stagnation), but the believers I have in mind are the chronically dissatisfied. They're stuck. They can't get started any more, and they don't see any way of *getting* themselves started. Here again, the problem is usually too much attention to external achievement and too little on internal development.

It's the mistake of believing that only when they *do well* will they *be well*. So they give up trying, because every time they try, they get all fired up and busy in the Truth, then their efforts peter out. Now they're not sure where they're going– if anywhere. Becalmed is the word for them.

Are you a human being, or just a human doing?

Maybe you recognize yourself as a joyless worker, or a non-starter, or one of the great becalmed. Or maybe you know there's something wrong with the way you are spiritually but just can't figure out what it is. In all cases I suggest you check to see if you have a being/doing problem. Are you aiming to *be* all that you can through delight and meditation in the Word?– or are you aiming to *do* all you can, and wondering why you don't seem to change for the better?

Remember also, that busyness can sometimes be a way of hiding from ourselves. We can fill our lives with things to do so that we don't have to face ourselves and notice that we're not being what we need to be. Occupation can mean avoidance. It's a reason why some people can't handle retirement from work. To cease from work is to come face to face with self. And if work is all they are, then they are nothing when the work stops, so they need to put off retirement for as long as possible. You might fear slowing down on work in the Truth for the same reason. You mistakenly believe that you are what you do. So, if you don't, you aren't!

The solution, as I've said, is to relegate *doing* into second place, and put *being* in first place. Cultivate the fruit of the Spirit and allow your spiritual activities to develop naturally from that. This is putting things in the correct order.

Eye-service

Alas, the pressures we put upon one another are in some degree to blame for our back-to-front thinking. There is a great temptation to eye-service in the Truth. How gratifying it is to do lots of the tasks that can be seen by our Christian colleagues! How easy it is to concentrate our efforts on high profile tasks to the detriment of our inner spiritual growth.

Not that we should shun leading Bible study groups, going on missionary travels, or other observable work, but rather that such work needs to be an extension of who we *are* in the Truth, not our preoccupation. All our work in the Truth is done as a good and natural outlet for our enthusiasm when we delight and meditate in the Word.

In fact, when we get being and doing in the right order, we don't even think of what we do in the Truth as work. We become totally free from the rat-race of spiritual performance. We will be doing what comes naturally, and enjoying it. And when we stand before Christ and he welcomes us into his kingdom, saying how he'd been hungry and we'd fed him, thirsty and we'd given him drink, naked and we'd clothed him, sick and visited him... and so on, we'll scratch our heads and say, "When, Lord, did we ever do all that?" We won't remember. It all came naturally from a Christ-like mind, from a mind in which the fruit of the Spirit had been nurtured. Those who have put doing before being are rejected. They will argue that they have *done* all manner of wonderful things in Christ's name. They've got a list as long as your arm. But Christ will say only, "Depart from me..."(Matt.25: 31-46).

Being is more important. This is what the fruit of the Spirit is all about. It's about the development of our inner lives through the development of love. The *doing* will take care of itself.

CHAPTER FIVE

LOVE: *(agape)*

D O WE appreciate that a wrong understanding of love can frustrate the very purpose of Christian life? Christian living is essentially about pleasing God. And if we want to please God we need to know, above all things, how to demonstrate His love."God is love", and He wants His children to be like Him. How can we do that if we don't know the love that God is?

The way we understand and practise the love that God shows us in His Word is a key factor in whether or not we please God.

We need to be clear about Christian love. It isn't what generally passes for love in the world. It's not the stuff of romantic fiction, or of simple emotional attachment, however fine and noble such attachment may sometimes be. While it's true to say that Christian love has a strong emotional content, there is *a lot more to it than that.*

Christian love is more than one-dimensional. It is a love that is at the same time both transcendent and practical. Like Jacob's ladder, the top rungs are in heaven, while the bottom legs are firmly on the ground. It is transcendent because it raises our thoughts to a level of harmony with the thoughts of the Almighty. It is practical because it provides a sound and workable approach to daily living. (Though it has to be said that from a purely human point of view this kind of love can appear alarmingly impractical!)

Which love?

In the Greek of the first century there were four words for love: *eros, storge, philia* and *agape. Eros*, as one might expect, concerns the physical passions. *Storge* is more concerned with family affections. *Philia* has more to do with affection and "falling in love" in the boy-meets-girl situation.

34

These definitions are an over-simplification, I admit, because the words do cross boundaries on occasions. But in the main this is what they mean. For a more scholarly examination of the words, one of the most readable sources is William Barclay's excellent book *New Testament Words*. (Well worth adding to your bookshelf.)

The fourth word, *agape,* is different from the other three. This is the word the apostle Paul used to begin his list of the fruit of the Spirit. And this is the word the Spirit chooses to represent Christian love in the New Testament.

Agape is different. It's the only kind of love that doesn't come naturally. While the other forms of love simply *happen* to us (are part of our natural make up: our family ties or our attraction to the opposite sex), *agape* doesn't happen to us at all unless we do something to make it happen. *Agape* is the one form of love that does not come naturally to the human heart. It is, in fact, *against* our instincts.

Defining *agape*

So, how do we define *agape*? One writer has actually written: "The Bible does not define love. It illustrates it." I believe the Bible does both. The same writer (John Sanderson in his book *The fruit of the Spirit*) also says that the Bible uses the different forms of Hebrew and Greek words for love indiscriminately—a word I would hesitate to apply to the Spirit's selection of words. If we cannot always follow the reasons for the Spirit's choice of words, or we cannot reconcile a seeming contradiction in the choice, that doesn't mean the Spirit has been indiscriminate. What it really means is that we don't understand why!

W.E. Vine in his *Expository Dictionary of New Testament Words* says that, "since the spirit of revelation has used [agape] to express ideas previously unknown, enquiry into its use, whether in Greek literature or in the Septuagint, throws but little light upon its distinctive meaning in the N.T." He's certainly not the only one I've come across to assert that *agape* is used in the N.T. to express ideas "previously unknown." But is that really the case?

Vine's mention of the Septuagint alerts us to the fact that the word *agape* and its derivatives abound in that Greek version of the Old Testament—a book which may have been a major preaching tool for First Century believers, the apostles themselves included. So the word wasn't the 'invention' of the New Testament writers; they found it ready-made in the 'Bible' of their day.

But was the Spirit *expressing* something entirely new when it used the word *agape* in the New Testament? Was this a new concept of love, previously unknown? Yes and no is the answer to that one. Yes—there was something new about it, because the Spirit took the *agape* of the Old Testament and moved it up a gear, so to speak. And no—it was not entirely new, because the essence of *agape* was already there in the Old Testament.

Old Testament *Agape*

Have you ever heard somebody say something like: "In a word, it was really good." It irritates me a little, because the person has said he would describe something 'in a word' and then proceeded to use *two* words: 'really good.' It's a fairly common error. But the apostle Paul, in Galatians 5:14 seems to have committed the 'daddy' of all such errors!

"For all the law is fulfilled in one word, even in this; Thou shalt love thy neighbour as thyself."

Paul's 'one word' turned out to be seven. So what was he thinking? The Spirit doesn't perpetrate blatant logical howlers. How can these seven words actually be one? Well, 'one word' here is actually 'one *logos'*—a familiar Greek word to Bible students from the oft wrangled-over opening words of John's Gospel. When Paul said the law was fulfilled in one *word*, I believe he was making reference to Deuteronomy 10:4.

"And he wrote on the tables, according to the
first writing, the ten commandments."

In this verse the Hebrew for 'commandment' is *dabar*,
which means 'a word'. So in Hebrew *the ten commandments*
can, in fact, be *the ten words*. The Septuagint actually uses
the word *logos* in Deuteronomy 10:4.

What Paul is saying, therefore, is that all the
logos/commandments of the law can be summed up in one
logos/commandment: love your neighbour as yourself.
'Agape' your neighbour, in fact. This is the underlying
message of the whole law given through Moses. Christ put
it perfectly when he said:

"Therefore all things whatsoever ye would that
men should do to you, do ye even so to them: for
this is the law and the prophets" (Matt.7:12).

Those words are the Bible's definition of *agape*. That's it
in a nutshell. And, as you can see, *agape* existed before
New Testament times. Even though the word itself doesn't
stretch back to the founding of the law, the concept of it
was there. But it goes back even further. If "God is *agape*,"
and always has been, then the concept pre-dates creation!

Israel, for the most part, failed to grasp the spirit of the
law and went to the extremes of either forgetting it
altogether, or of letting it tie them up in knots of their own
creation, adding hundreds of little self-imposed observances.

Love of one's neighbour should have characterised the
way of life of the people of Israel. They should have been a
shining example to the rest of the world. Their demonstration of *agape* was to have been a key part of their
witness as God's people. As it turned out, instead of Israel
being the envy of the nations because they had God's law,
Israel envied the nations because *they* didn't have the law!—
didn't have its burdens and restrictions!—many of which
they imposed themselves. What perverse creatures humans
are!

All this has a direct bearing on us today. When Jesus offered himself as the perfect sacrifice, he did *in reality* what all the sacrificial enactments of the Law of Moses had only expressed *symbolically*. The Law was God's way of associating His people with the saviour before the saviour had been born and before he had done his saving work. Else how were they to be saved before their saviour was born? When Christ's saving work was done, the Law had fulfilled its purpose. The enactments of the Law were no longer necessary. But the spirit of the Law—loving one's neighbour as oneself—that never ceased to be a requirement.

Moving up a gear

"God is love." He was love, is love, and surely always will be love. When Jesus came he took this *agape*-love which was at the heart of the law and he 'moved it up a gear'. He gave his disciples a 'new commandment':

"A new commandment I give unto you, that ye love one another; as I have loved you, that ye also love one another" (John 13:34).

That's what I mean by shifting *agape* up a gear. Jesus lived *agape* to perfection. He had (and *has*) the fruit of the Spirit in all its elements in perfect balance. He gave his disciples a living example of what *agape* means, and they with the Spirit's aid have captured that on paper so we can read for ourselves what it means. He made the ultimate sacrifice for all his 'neighbours', showing how great his love is. This is what God wants us to aspire to. This is how He wants us to understand and practise *agape*.

It's a whole lot more than simple good neighbourliness and brotherly kindness. It is joy, peace, longsuffering, gentleness, goodness, faith, meekness and temperance towards others. It not only involves us thinking, "How would I like to be treated?" when dealing with others; it goes higher to thinking, "How would *Christ* deal with this person?" Not only, "How would I like to be spoken to?" but, "How would *Christ* speak to this person?" That's the new dimension to *agape* which the New Testament gives us.

Who is my neighbour?

A question that needs to be asked when considering *agape* (the loving one's neighbour as one's self) is the question put to Jesus by a certain lawyer: "And who is my neighbour?" It's typical of someone hung up on the law to want to be this specific. Even love, in his eyes, had to be pinned down and properly organised! This exotic butterfly had to be killed, embalmed and mounted. One doesn't want to love the *wrong* person, after all! How terrible that would be!

But, in a way, it's a sensible question, because when *agape* was described in the Old Testament the term 'neighbour' was restricted to fellow Israelites.

> "Thou shalt not avenge, nor bear any grudge against the children of thy people, but thou shalt love thy neighbour as thyself: I am the Lord" (Lev.19:18).

Clearly the term 'neighbour' applied to those described as "the children of thy people", i.e. other Israelites. The lawyer probably wanted to know if that was Christ's view. As Christ was *quoting* Leviticus when he spoke of loving your neighbour as yourself, did he mean this love to extend only to fellow Israelites? Christ demonstrated what he meant by telling him the parable of the good Samaritan. He showed him that a man or woman who loves their neighbour in the true *agape* sense will not consider a person's national, religious or social background before offering help. Christ showed how incongruous such an attitude was.

Agape is not something you can turn on and off according to whom you're dealing with. If you have it, it's **there** and it's an integral part of you. You will react to circumstances the way it requires of you. If you can turn it off anytime you like, you haven't got it!

But what about Christ's new command to believers? Isn't that restrictive? It does resemble the love God required among fellow Israelites, doesn't it? Talking to his *followers*, he said we were to love one another (no-one else) as he had loved us. But if we believe that our love is exclusive to fellow believers, then we're falling into the same error as that lawyer. We might even become guilty of 'passing by on the other side', instead of being a 'good Samaritan'.

The truth is, Christ said the same about love as the law had said. Because the law said love your fellow Israelites, it wasn't correct to reason you therefore loved no-one else. The same applies to what Christ said.

A natural difference

Though it has to be said, a believer's love for other believers will naturally be of a higher order than his or her love for those outside the Truth. For undoubtedly *agape* is better expressed among fellow believers than it can be between believer and non-believer. It was an important part of Israel's witness to the world that they reflect a high level of the *agape* of God for all to see. The idea was that people would be attracted to it.

Agape should be the same among us. "As we therefore have opportunity, let us do good unto all men, especially unto them who are of the household of faith" (Gal.6:10). There must be a particularly strong bond of Christ-like love between believers. But this is not to the exclusion of expressing *agape* to all other people. It wouldn't only be an awful double standard; it would be *impossible* to have *agape* and to switch it off when dealing with people outside the Truth. As I said, if you can turn it off, it can't be real.

But there will naturally be a higher level of love among believers. **Our love for those who love the things we love will naturally be greater.** And we, too, need to be a reflection to the world about us of the *agape* of God, that people may be attracted to it. This is an important part of *our* witness. When Christ spoke of this new commandment that we should love one another as he loved us, he added: "By this shall all men know that ye are my disciples, if ye have love one to another" (John 13:35).

Let's ask ourselves if the level of love among us is so high that outsiders would notice it. They would notice how we always go out of our way to do good to one another, to help one another. They would notice how we always speak well of one another—always seem to prefer our fellow believers before even ourselves, always show such high regard for them, always think of them as such special people, always treat them as we imagine Christ himself would treat them. Is that the image that our community projects to the world outside? Are we a community reflecting the *agape* of God? Big question. It's up to us to see to it that we are.

James, the Lord's brother, described *agape* as "the royal law". It is the *chief*, the *king* among laws. It even makes a lot of other laws unnecessary: "Thou shalt love thy neighbour as thyself"—if we all *obeyed* that, the statute books would be slim indeed!

More specifically, in its outworking, *agape* is the full expression of the eight features of the fruit of the Spirit. As I hope to show.

CHAPTER SIX

NINE FRUITS OR ONE FRUIT?

IT'S not seriously important whether you believe the fruit of the Spirit is one or nine. I'm sure it will make little difference to the outcome whether you believe that love is the whole fruit, and that there are eight aspects of it (as I do), or whether you believe Paul describes nine separate fruits of the Spirit (in which case you will surely see them as complementary anyhow). Looking at the fruit either way, it still adds up to the whole spiritual personality.

But as I've touched on the subject a number of times, I really ought to give an explanation of why I believe as I do. The reason is partly the grammar of Galatians 5:22,23 and partly the inference of other Scripture.

It's just possible that you don't find grammar the most enthralling thing in the world. If syntax is not for you, then please don't get bogged down in this chapter. Pass quietly on to chapter seven. I understand perfectly, and there are no hard feelings.

Regrettably, I can't produce a single verse that says straightforwardly, "**Love** is the fruit of the Spirit." This chapter would be a lot easier if I could. It would be unnecessary! But I do feel there are enough pointers to it in the Scriptures to give the idea some respectability.

See what you think. If you disagree on having read this chapter, then I hope you'll nevertheless find the remainder of the book helpful in your quest to produce the Spirit's fruit. For, whether you believe the fruit is love, or that love is only a ninth part of it, the fruit of the Spirit remains unquestionably the vital ingredient in the truly Christian character. I say again what I said in the Preface that the fruit may well encompass all of what Christ will be looking for in us at his return.

One or nine?

The confusion over whether love is the whole fruit or only one of nine distinct fruits is due to the way the Apostle Paul describes it in Galatians 5. Here are the two verses again:

> "But the fruit of the Spirit is love, joy, peace, longsuffering, gentleness, goodness, faith, meekness, temperance: against such there is no law."

At first glance it looks as if the fruit is ninefold—that is, a single fruit made up of nine parts. A second look and you'll see it's also possible to take the meaning that there are nine *separate* fruits of the Spirit. But if the Apostle intended that, why did he say **fruit** (singular, it seems) and not fruits? (In fact, the grammar of verse 22 could well scupper both options. I'll come back to that shortly.)

To add to the confusion there is a third possibility to consider. This is the one I have already broached, and in which I have declared an interest. This is the view that the fruit of the Spirit is love (the first item on Paul's menu), and that the eight items following are various aspects of love. Though, perhaps, the least obvious of the choices, it does hold together reasonably well under scrutiny.

It may seem like quite a leap of the imagination (not to mention a downright liberty with the text) to say that the verse should be understood like this—

> "But the fruit of the Spirit is love, (comprising) joy, peace, longsuffering..."

—but there are some good reasons for putting the idea forward, not the least of which is that I believe it offers the most profitable line of enquiry from the available choices.

The Grammar: singular, plural, or collective singular?

The chief difficulty over verse 22 of Galatians 5 is that word *fruit*. Is it singular? Is it plural? Or is it a collective singular? The English word fruit can be any of these. I can say, "This apple is a fruit." I can say, "This apple and orange are fruit." I can also say, "This apple comes from a place where fruit grows." But more to the point the Greek word *karpos*, which is generally translated fruit in the New Testament, can also be any of these. The translators of the A.V. certainly thought so, because here are some examples which show the word in all three roles:

Singular "Now no chastening for the present seemeth to be joyous but grievous: nevertheless afterward it yieldeth the peaceable fruit [*karpos*] of righteousness unto them which are exercised thereby" (Heb.12:11).

Plural "They say unto him, He will miserably destroy those wicked men, and will let out his vineyard unto other husbandmen, which shall render him the fruits [*karpos*] in their seasons" (Matt.21:41).

Collective singular "And he prayed again, and the heaven gave rain, and the earth brought forth her fruit [*karpos*]" (Jas.5:18).

In some versions (e.g. NEB and Moffatt) the translators have sidestepped the problem of the uncertain quantitative value of *fruit* in Galatians 5.22 by substituting the word *harvest*. But this doesn't solve the problem; it only submerges it. *Karpos* is still lurking there for anyone who goes back to the original Greek. And there is absolutely no justification for translating *karpos* as harvest. There is a perfectly serviceable Greek word for harvest Paul could have used if that's what he'd meant to say.

So, which of the three options did Paul intend? Singular, plural or collective singular? We have some detective work to do.

The plural is quite easy to dispose of because the verb linked with fruit in Galatians 5:22 is without a doubt singular. "The fruit of the Spirit *is"*—this is the Greek *esty*, and in the verse it denotes third person singular. Which rules out fruit being plural because, as we learned at school, the subject of a sentence (in our case the fruit of the Spirit) must agree with its verb "is" in number—meaning that if the subject is singular so is the verb, and vice versa. That rules out the plural for the fruit of the Spirit because the verb is unquestionably singular. Which leaves two alternatives.

Singular or collective?

Most commentators tell us confidently that fruit in Galatians 5:22 is singular and that consequently the fruit is ninefold. Love is therefore just one ninth of the whole fruit. But it needs pointing out that the singular of fruit is an extremely rare event in Scripture. There's only one other occasion where *karpos* can be said with absolute certainty to be singular. That's in Luke 1:42, where Elizabeth says to Mary: *"Blessed is the fruit of thy womb."* That has to be singular. It refers to Jesus.

It's really not surprising that the singular of fruit is so rare in Scripture when we consider how infrequently we use the singular version ourselves in everyday speech and writing. Check it for yourself. On almost every occasion we use the word, we use it in the *collective* sense—and so do the Scriptures. This gives me serious doubts about the commentators' assertions that fruit is singular in our verse. They may sometimes mean singular collective, perhaps, but they don't say so, not the ones I've read. As almost all of the uses of the word *karpos* in the New Testament are collective, I think it's reasonable to conclude that this is also the case in Galatians 5:22.

Having narrowed the field down to the collective function for the word *fruit*, where does that lead us in the interpretation of the verse? We're nearly there. We have but one more step before we reach a conclusion. (And not before time, do I hear?). Again it involves a choice. This time it's a choice between the two ways in which a collective singular can be used.

1 Fruit, collective—meaning lots of one kind of fruit, as when we say, for instance, the fruit of a tree (all apples, all pears etc.).

2 Fruit, collective—meaning lots of different fruits, as in 'the fruit of the ground' (anything and everything).

If we apply version **1** to our verse in Galatians we get the following awkward comparison:

The fruit of the tree is apples.

"The fruit of the Spirit is love(s?)..."

For this to work (which clearly it doesn't), love needs to be plural (!) and the other eight items are redundant. (I accept that this model is rather clumsy, because, strictly speaking, tree does not equate well with spirit. Spirit is more fittingly the catalyst, the agent by which the fruit is generated, and might better be equated with the rainfall and the soil nutrients which cause the tree to thrive, rather than the tree itself. But the model still serves adequately to show that choice **1** is not right.)

If choice **2** is wrong, we've come an awfully long way for nothing! Let's see how it works out when we compare it with our verse:

(a) The fruit of the ground is (say) cereal, nuts, fruit, vegetables, herbs and so on.

(b) "The fruit of the Spirit is love, joy, peace, longsuffering" and so on.

That's more like it. Except for one thing. All the fruit in example (a) is plural, but qualities such as joy and peace don't have plurals in the accepted sense (unless you count the joys of Spring!) So the model is almost correct, but not quite. What if we make a slight adjustment to it, making the joy and peace equivalents singular, like this? —

(a) The fruit of the ground is cereal: wheat, rye, barley, maize, rice.

Now we have a result that matches our verse. And we notice that now all the items which follow cereal are items which are *collectively* cereal. Putting it into this form lines it up with our verse perfectly. And this is how I propose Galatians 5:22,23 should read with regard to love. The items following it are collectively love. Also bear in mind that the original Greek is not punctuated. So I would not be presuming too much if I were to add a dash (or colon) after love in the verse to set off the list of items.

I accept that any purist grammarians reading this might tear their hair out at my rude logic. But in my defence let it be said that while reading some of them on subjects like collectives, I've been close to tearing *my* hair out at times! And I can ill afford it.

If the reasoning seems a little contrived to get the end result I wanted, then I have to put up my hand as guilty. I have to admit that there is a little contrivance. But the element of bias that runs through the reasoning is not because I wanted to force an interpretation of my own on the verses, regardless. It's there because I have been trying to discover how the verses *could* be saying, grammatically, what other Scripture suggests they ought to be saying. And chief among that other Scripture is 1 Corinthians 13.

The Love chapter

The idea that there are eight aspects of love described in Galatians 5 does seem to be supported by Paul's more detailed description of love in 1 Corinthians 13. In that well-known 'love chapter' Paul sets out sixteen ways in which love can be expressed. They equate very well with the eight aspects of love, as you'll see from the table below. The temptation to make two expressions of love equal one aspect of love has not been resisted, as it strongly suggests itself.

Love (*agape*) Charity

Gal.5	1 Cor.13
JOY *(chara)*	"rejoiceth" "hopeth all things"
PEACE *(eirene)*	"beareth all things" "endureth all things"
LONGSUFFERING *(makrothumia)*	"suffereth long" "not easily provoked"
GENTLENESS *(chrestotes)*	"is kind" "envieth not"
GOODNESS *(agathosune)*	"rejoiceth not in iniquity" "thinketh no evil"
FAITH *(pistis)*	"believeth all things" "never faileth"
MEEKNESS *(praotes)*	"not puffed up" "vaunteth not itself"
TEMPERANCE *(egkratera)*	"behaveth not unseemly" "seeketh not her own"

Perhaps I haven't allocated them all precisely right. It could be argued that "envieth not" is a part of peace, or even faith, because a lack of envy denotes a certain peaceful satisfaction with one's own lot in life. It also betokens a modicum of faith that one has, and will continue to have, enough of whatever one sees as needful for one's life. "Not easily provoked" might better belong with meekness perhaps. But these little niggling doubts over exactly where to place some of the expressions of love don't detract from the general impression that the aspects of love of Galatians 5 mesh together more than coincidentally well with the broader description of love in 1 Corinthians 13.

In fact, there's more to it than meets the eye, because some of the reasons for the connections I've made aren't obvious at a glance. The link between *longsuffering* and *"not easily provoked"*, for instance, is better understood when you realise that *provoked* is a Greek word meaning *excited.* A *longsuffering* person is someone who doesn't easily get angry, as we'll see in Chapter 9. And the link between *gentleness* (kindness) and "envieth not" makes more sense when you know that *envieth* in the Greek is a word that connects with zeal. Zeal isn't always a good thing; it depends how it's directed. The man or woman with *gentleness* (kindness) will consider the feelings of others and not trample all over them with inappropriate zeal.

For a slightly different line up between Galatians 5 and 1 Corinthians 13 you might like to look at the chapter headed *Love: The fruit of the Spirit* in *The Genius of Discipleship* by Dennis Gillett. He gives his own brief reasons for how he connects the two lists.

There was one thing, however, that troubled me over the alignment of Galatians 5 and 1 Corinthians 13. At the close of 1 Corinthians 13 Paul writes of *faith, hope and love* as though they are quite separate things. If it's true that *love* is the eightfold fruit of the Spirit, then surely *faith* is a part of love, not separate from it. How can he write of *faith, hope and love* as though each stands alone? Well, I don't believe he does.

In verse 13, Paul writes: "And now abideth faith, hope, charity [*agape*], these three; but the greatest of these is charity." These three things that *abide* are in contrast to the three things of verse 8 which *won't* abide. "Charity never faileth: but whether there be **prophecies**, they shall fail; whether there be **tongues**, they shall cease; whether there be **knowledge**, it shall vanish away." So in contrast to these three things which shall fail, and which may be representative of the whole range of the Spirit gifts, there are three things which will abide—faith, hope and love.

It might be said that *faith* has supplanted the gift of prophecy in our day; that the hope of the true gospel alone has replaced the gift of tongues as a means of convincing the outsider that we are of God; and that "the word of knowledge" (Chapter 12.8) by which gift spiritual insights were gained, has been exchanged for delight and meditation *in* the Word of knowledge, by which love (the greatest of spiritual insights!) is nurtured.

And love is the "greatest" among *faith, hope and love* because it *contains* the other two and will go beyond them and outlive them in the Kingdom of God. For believers in the Kingdom the elements of faith and hope, as we know them now, will disappear from love. Faith will give place to sight, and hope to realisation. Therefore love is the all-important thing to develop now. Faith and hope on their own will not carry us into the Kingdom. These things will vanish at the Kingdom's door, leaving us empty-handed (or with oil-less lamps, more appropriately) if they're all we have. We see people around us who exhibit great faith and hope in their beliefs. But without *agape,* without the full fruit of the Spirit nurtured through delight and meditation in the Word of God, they will fall hugely short of what Christ is looking for. Let's not be carried away by a great show of faith and hope in Jesus that may appear to be love, but which is only a small part of it—and ultimately an unnecessary part! The real criterion is—how close to the Word are we? Real closeness produces love—the *full* fruit of the Spirit.

2 Peter 1

The Apostle Peter had much to say about *agape* among believers, and I believe he also connected it with the fruit of the Spirit in 2 Pet.1. Peter could not put *agape* more highly: "Above all things have fervent charity among yourselves: for charity [*agape*] shall cover the multitude of sins" (1 Pet. 4:8). "Love one another with a pure heart fervently" (1 Pet.1:22). "Love the brotherhood" (1 Pet.2:17). To Paul love was "the greatest", and to Peter it is "above all things".

In 2 Pet.1:5-7, the apostle mentions what appear to be seven steps through which *agape* is reached:

> "giving all diligence, add to your faith virtue; and to
> virtue knowledge; And to knowledge temperance; and
> to temperance patience; and to patience godliness; And

to godliness brotherly kindness; and to brotherly kindness charity."

What made me suspect that here was another version of the fruit of the Spirit was what Peter wrote immediately afterwards in verse 8: "If these things be in you, and abound, they make you that ye shall neither be barren nor **unfruitful** [*akarpas*] in the knowledge of our Lord Jesus Christ." If you lack these things you'll be unfruitful is another way of saying that *if you have them, you will have fruit.* This sent me rushing to a concordance to compare the original Greek words, to see if Peter's seven 'steps' are seven of Paul's aspects of *agape.* What a find that would be! What confirmation! But, alas, they are not the same. Well, some are, but most aren't.

But surely Peter must have had Paul's fruit of the Spirit in mind when he wrote those seven 'steps' and spoke of them, in effect, as fruit. He even mentions the writings of "our beloved brother Paul" at the close of his letter! So why doesn't Peter's list tally more closely with Paul's? I'm open to suggestions, of course. But maybe Peter is describing the best progression to love. I know there is a resistance to the idea that these items in 2 Peter 1 are meant to be taken as steps. But why not take them at face value? Could not the Spirit be giving us a clue as to the best order in which to develop the fruit of the Spirit?—that our delight and meditation would more effectively lead us to *agape* if centered upon these subjects and in this order?

If it is a progression, one thing upon another until the full *agape* is reached, then the Evangelical plunge straight into *agape* is very suspect. And we need not be troubled, either, about knowledge coming after faith and virtue. The case of Cornelius demonstrates it well. He was certainly showing faith and virtue before he came to a knowledge of the Truth. And personally I can recall (as you may) having faith in God and trying to live a virtuous life before starting formal instruction in the Word—certainly before finishing it. One might argue that we need a certain amount of faith and virtue in place to prompt a desire for real knowledge of Bible truth. The verses in 2 Peter 1 certainly read like a progression that we can't short-cut. To reach *agape* follow the instructions.

As with 1 Corinthians 13, I've lined up the fruit of the Spirit with 2 Peter 1, and here is the result:

2 PETER 1		GALATIANS 5
CHARITY *(agape)*	brings	LOVE
BROTHERLY KINDNESS	brings	MEEKNESS
GODLINESS	brings	GENTLENESS
PATIENCE	encourages	LONGSUFFERING
TEMPERANCE	(same word)	TEMPERANCE
KNOWLEDGE	brings (See 2 Pet1:3)	PEACE
VIRTUE	brings	GOODNESS
FAITH	(same word)	FAITH

JOY

Again, perhaps I haven't allocated them perfectly. But having tried all manner of computations, and bearing in mind the nuances of the Greek, this seems to be the best placement of the words. You may be wondering, as I did for a while, why Peter has only seven items on his list while Paul has eight. Joy, or its equivalent, is missing on Peter's list. I found that it does occur in 2 Peter 1, but the translators have obscured it. Peter didn't overlook it. He came to it later.

In verses 5-7 of 2 Peter 1 the words "add to" appear in connection with the steps towards love. The single Greek word translated "add to" is not common in Scripture, but one other place it does occur is in the eleventh verse of 2 Peter 1. We don't notice it because there it's translated "ministered unto."

> "Wherefore the rather, brethren, give diligence to make your calling and election sure: for if ye do these things, ye shall never fall: For so an entrance shall be ministered unto [added to] you abundantly into the everlasting kingdom of our Lord and Saviour Jesus Christ." (2 Peter 1:10,11)

Entrance into the kingdom of God is the final item 'added to' in Peter's list, and this surely equates with joy. Peter's final step is the joy of the kingdom, which we shall all reach by progressing through all the steps he mentions. Though let's keep it in mind that Paul points out in his list of the fruit of the Spirit that we must achieve joy *now* also as part of the fruit. The full realization of joy is future in Christ's Kingdom, but we need to carry the joy of that prospect with us right now.

Can it really be a progression?

The great drawback I see to Peter's list being a progression is the difficulty of knowing when to move on to the next item in the list. Each item is overlaid on top of another and we don't move on from each one to the next, leaving it behind: it stays with us. It seems to me a practical impossibility to know when you have enough virtue to add knowledge, or enough knowledge to add temperance. How will you ever know if you're ready for the next step? It's this objection (not usually the objection offered) that to me casts doubt on the 'step' idea.

It seems presumptuous to say, "I now have enough godliness so I'll move on to brotherly kindness." This would seem to kill any idea of a progression up the ladder of love. Perhaps we are more correct to see all the additions as contemporary rather than sequential: that we should be always in the process of adding all the things in Peter's list to our faith, not trying to move from one to another. This would be more in keeping with Paul's listing of the fruit of the Spirit, where no sequence is, or seems to be, prescribed. All the aspects of the fruit are nurtured simultaneously, it would appear, by delight and meditation in the Spirit Word.

Other appearances of the fruit

In addition to 1 Corinthians and 2 Peter being reflections of the fruit of the Spirit, I believe a good case could also be made for Colossians 3:12-16 (the items Paul tells us to *put on*), and Romans 12 generally, and 1 Timothy 6:11,12. But perhaps I can leave you to mull over these for yourself, rather than give more examples here. And let me say again that if you don't go along with the idea of the fruit of the Spirit being love with eight aspects, then I'm not insisting you do. Whether you do or don't, it should really make no difference to your attitude to most of what is covered in this book. At least, I hope not. To me the idea does have a certain fitness about it, especially when I consider that the eight-fold fruit of the Spirit characterizes the New Man in Christ, and the number eight in Bible numerology signifies a new beginning (the eight souls in the ark; the eighth day of the week on which Christ rose being the first day of a new week; and there are eight individual resurrections recorded in Scripture—see Bullinger's *Number in Scripture*).

CHAPTER SEVEN

JOY (chara)

THE first two aspects of love are really opposite sides of the same coin, the coin of security. Joy and peace are the active and passive sides of the coin. But, before we go any further, let me ask you something. If an angel were to appear to you tonight and say, "Fear not, you're on your way to the Kingdom. Keep it up, you're doing fine" (or words to that effect—I'm sure an angel would put it *far* better) how would you react? I know how I would. I'd feel a beautiful relaxed calm spreading all over me, mind and body. That sort of certainty would have me initially weeping for joy, and thereafter in a constant state of mild elation that would sometimes bubble up into the most exquisite joy. A feeling of perfect peace would settle over my heart.

I'm sure I'm typical of how most people would be in that situation. I would know a feeling of great security, and it would be characterised by joy and peace. But in the *absence* of an angel appearing tonight, how are you and I going to bring joy and peace into our hearts? How are we going to have these aspects of the fruit of the Spirit for ourselves? The answer, as you might expect by now, is **delight and meditation in the Word.**

We can find all the God-given security we need in the Word of God. Especially, we will find it in what the Word of God tells us to expect in our lives, moment by moment. Because through His Word we discover His care.

Let's not run away with the idea that delight and meditation is confined to periods of "study". Study is not an end in itself. You spend an hour or two shut away with a Bible, a concordance, and a Greek Lexicon, then emerge and get on with your real life! That isn't it. Nor should you be in a perpetual state of study. The character in Psalm 1 who meditates in God's law *"day and night"* isn't walking around

55

with a book on the end of his nose. He delights and meditates at *all* times, because his familiarity with the Word, gained from more intensive periods of study, makes him conscious of the mind of God throughout his waking moments. That familiarity also makes him aware of God's care in his life. And the knowledge and experience of God's care cannot fail to bring security. Hence, delight and meditation will bring the first two aspects of the fruit into your life.

Let's not be afraid to experience the care of God in our lives. It *is* Scriptural. Or would we deny what He does for us? We tend to generalise God's care for us rather than particularize it and see it in everyday events. We may feel it's safer to do this rather than presume too much, but are we, as a result, shutting God out of much of our lives?— and lacking the joy of security as a result, because we lack a sense of the reality of God's care? We'll touch on this again later.

What do the Scriptures mean?

Our concern in these pages is to understand *what the Scriptures mean* by each of the eight aspects of love. To do this we will need to look closely at some of the occasions in Scripture where joy, peace, longsuffering etc. are expressed or recommended to us. The context is generally a good guide to the true meaning. And once we appreciate the true meaning, we'll be better placed to cultivate and express the fruits more fully and appropriately in our lives. Our own concept of the fruit may well be faulty, or too limited, or too wide ranging. We need the Scriptures to tell us what *they* mean by joy, and the other items, rather than think that because we know what the words mean to us, we know what they mean in the Word of God. It doesn't necessarily follow.

Balance

Paul puts joy first when listing the aspects of love, while Peter (see previous chapter) leaves it till last. You'd have thought that joy *should* come last, following on from the other seven, the cumulative effect of them. But we're probably wrong to try and impose an order upon the aspects. Much as we do love to do this sort of thing, it isn't always appropriate. I don't see any significance in the way Paul lists them that might suggest an order of importance. The eight aspects are all, surely, of equal merit, all equal parts of love, because balance is so necessary when it comes to love. Over-emphasis on any one of the parts is not good. A love overloaded with joy may lack meekness. Too much emphasis on longsuffering will certainly be to the detriment of joy! A balancing of the eight parts is called for. Delight and meditation in the Word will bring all the aspects of love equally to fruition.

An attitude problem

All the qualities listed as fruit of the Spirit are attitudes. **They are the correct attitudes to life.** And we have more control over our attitudes than most of us care to admit. It's easier to blame circumstances for our attitudes than to accept that our attitudes often create our circumstances. It's easier to blame other people for our attitude than accept that our attitude may be responsible for how people are toward us.

For instance, we sometimes decide that certain people simply aren't our type, so we don't get on with them very well. But what would happen if we decided that they *were* our type? What would happen then? I've put this into practice, and I can tell you you'd be amazed at who your friends turn out to be! Our attitudes to other people and life in general make a lot of difference to our lives, for good or for ill. And we do have some control over our attitudes, and therefore our lives.

The best possible influence we can bring into our lives is that of the fruit of the Spirit. With attitudes which show that fruit, life is considerably different. But, as we noted in an earlier chapter, you can't simply *decide* to have all the aspects of the fruit in your life, as if they were your list of New Year resolutions. There is no quick fix, no instant love.

It takes time. But we do have the ability to initiate the right attitudes, once we know what they are, even though we know we can't sustain them by our own efforts. We can choose the right attitudes, the joy, the peace, and so on, even though we haven't got what it takes to keep them going for ourselves. Good old human nature—or rather, bad old human nature: 'the flesh', as we know it scripturally—gets in the way of progress. We keep losing ground because of the pull of the flesh. We can only suffer being longsuffering for so long, then something snaps, we go overboard and so does meekness and peace, and all the rest.

But all is not lost. It *is* lost if we try to do it on our own, or try the quick-fix resolutions method. All is not lost because we have at hand some great assistance. Yes, the Word of God, and that **delight and meditation** that I keep going on about, that will help us like nothing else can to hang on to those right, healthy attitudes—more than you might think possible. I say all this to highlight the fact that we do have the ability and the responsibility to *initiate* the right attitudes, once we know them. That much is in our hands. Application to the Word will supply what it takes to keep us going.

Attitude and joy

Christ's parables in Matthew 13 tell of the different attitudes people adopt to the Kingdom of God, and the results of those attitudes. And somewhere in what he said there's *your* attitude and there's mine, and there's the result of it. Please God we're all *"good ground"* in the words of the first parable, of the sower, and will one day *"shine forth as the sun in the Kingdom of* [our] *Father"*, in the words of the parable of the wheat and tares, rather than find ourselves wailing and gnashing our teeth because of the enormity of the mistake we made in our attitude to the Kingdom of God.

I don't say this in order to terrify anyone into a right attitude. That would be totally out of place. To be doing the right thing simply because you're terrified of doing otherwise is a wrong attitude if ever there was one! The man in the parable of the Talents made that mistake, you'll remember, by fearing God was a *"hard man."* That's never the right attitude.

So how do we test it? How *do* we check ourselves, whether we're good ground or shallow, whether we're wheat or tares?

Perhaps you test it by looking at the parable of the sower and going through a process of elimination. The seed that fell on the wayside was gobbled up immediately, so you say, "Well, I've been in the Truth five, ten, fifteen, twenty years. That can't be me." Move on to the next category: the seed that fell on stony ground. That seed was received with joy, but there was no root, so it lasted for a while and then died. Again, "That can't be me. Ten, fifteen, twenty years in the Truth!" Move on to the next one: the seed that fell among thorns. The thorns sprang up and choked it. "Ah, *sprang up.* That must have happened quickly, and here am I ten, fifteen, twenty years on, still in the Truth. Can't be me. That leaves only the good ground, so (Hey presto!) that must be me!"

Now, while I believe it's more spiritually and psychologically correct to believe and act as if we are the good ground, I also believe it's as well to check it a bit more thoroughly than we just did. Which is probably why Jesus immediately told the second parable in Matthew 13, of the wheat and tares, to write large that they'd be growing along together all the way to the Kingdom's door. It's not just the early drop-outs who are tares, is it? Length of service is no guarantee of a good reward. And so we come back to it— it's our *attitude* that matters.

You'll notice if you read Matthew 13 that there are some long parables and some brief ones. Jesus concludes the long ones by describing the separation of the righteous from the wicked. But in the smaller parables tucked in between the long ones, (the little, one or two verse parables), there is no mention of separation and judgement. These little vignettes have so much to tell us about attitude. There's a very good reason why there's no mention of separation in these little word pictures; it's because there's only *one* sort of person in them, and that's someone with the right attitude!

I'm thinking particularly about the parables of the treasure hid in a field (verse 44), and the pearl of great price (verses 45-46). These little parables tell us an awful lot about good attitude.

> "The Kingdom of heaven is like unto treasure hid in a field; the which when a man hath found, he hideth, and for joy thereof goeth and selleth all that he hath and buyeth that field."

> "Again the Kingdom of heaven is like unto a merchant man, seeking goodly pearls: who, when he had found one pearl of great price, went and sold all that he had, and bought it."

That's it. No judgement. No separation from anyone else. No losers, just winners. This is where we want to be, isn't it? And one of the two parables describes some believers—not *all* of them—and the other one describes the rest of them. How do I know that? Because here two different ways of coming into the Truth are presented to us. There is the man who seemingly stumbles upon hidden treasure, and in the other parable there is the man who is actively searching for the pearl of great price. As believers, you and I fall into one of those categories. Some of us just seemed to happen upon the Truth while not really out there looking for it. It seemed to find us. Others among us were out searching for it. We looked at this 'pearl' and that 'pearl' - this 'truth' and that 'truth'—and then one day, "Pow!—this one's really special!" and we sold/offloaded all the lesser and flawed 'truths' in order to have this beauty.

How true to life these little parables are. In both of them there is a gap between finding the Truth and actually obtaining it. Some might say that gap is what we're living through now, busily (or not!) trying to offload all the unnecessary stuff we have in order to make the final purchase in the last day. But I don't think it's that. I believe this is the gap between finding and accepting the Truth. For me, that gap was about two years. There's a period of assessment, of selling off what we don't need in order to obtain the truth for ourselves. It's in both parables. A period of unloading the things from our lives which are of less value in order to obtain what matters more to us. Only you can know how that applies to you.

So, to get to the point, what does the man who found the treasure have, and what does the merchant who bought the pearl have, that the weepers and gnashers of teeth don't have? Didn't they all find their way to the Kingdom in the first place? Yes, they did. So what's the big difference? The difference has everything to do with their attitude to what they found. And the difference is to be found in that little word *joy* that appears in Matt.13:44: "and for joy thereof goeth and selleth all that he hath."

But doesn't *everyone* who accepts the good news of the Kingdom do so with joy? Perhaps. Jesus said that those who were portrayed as the stony ground were those who received the word with joy, then problems came up and they didn't want to know any more. "Things are supposed to go right for me all the time! Isn't my life supposed to go right now that God's looking after me? How can I possibly keep this joy going if things keep going wrong?" So the joy withers and dies, and interest in the Truth of God dies along with it. The joy peters out in the face of the day-to-day mundane living of the Truth.

A question to all believers

I ask at this juncture, where is the joy you had when you first accepted the Truth? Where is now the glow inside that made you feel ten feet tall, and the rock-solid security you felt about your life, and your future? The longing for

61

Christ's appearance and the Kingdom? The avid, hungry reading of the Bible? The keenness to share the Word with everyone? Has bitter experience of sin and life's problems over the years knocked the spiritual stuffing out of you? Has the glow become a flicker, rather like a pilot-light that occasionally ignites you, but most of the time just keeps you ticking over?

At what level is your joy over the Kingdom of God? Is it the profound joy of one who sold all they had to purchase a treasure?—the joy of someone who knows a pearl of great price when they see one! Or is it a joy that fizzled out and went flat some time ago?

We probably have a good idea about the answers to that nasty barrage of questions. But to make a proper assessment, we need to know more about what joy actually is. To return to it, **what do the Scriptures mean when they talk of joy?**

Joy, in the Scriptures (NT) is generally the Greek word *chara*, and it belongs to that little family of words which includes *charis,* meaning grace, and *charisma,* meaning a gift. What a wonderful trio they make: *chara, charis, charisma: joy, grace, gift!* All related.

Tidings of great joy

A good point to start a closer look at the word *joy* is early in the Gospel narratives, because if there ever was an occasion for great joy it was at the news of the birth of Jesus. The angel of the Lord proclaimed the news to the shepherds in the field as "good tidings of great joy, which shall be to all people" (Luke 2:10). And the wise men who travelled from the East were among those touched by the joy of the event. (Incidentally, for a definition of *wise*, see Job 28:28, which shows these men from afar in the right light.)

You'll recall that they travelled from the East to Jerusalem, having seen Jesus' star. Then, having spoken to Herod and the chief priests and scribes, they set off for

Bethlehem as the most likely location for the birth place. And "when they saw the star, they rejoiced [chairo] with exceeding great joy [chara]." Jesus' star was plainly somehow different from the other stars in the heavens and easily recognisable to the Magi. It's evident from Matthew's account that for a time, certainly while the Magi were at Jerusalem, the star disappeared from view. It's not difficult to imagine them being concerned by this and wondering if they were doing something wrong. Maybe going about their search in the wrong direction altogether. Having journeyed this far they didn't want to fail to find the one they knew had been born King of the Jews (a title which must have meant far more to them than simply that! This was the King of Promise, the future King of the World, and they knew it). So, following the advice of the chief priests and scribes they set off for Bethlehem. Then the star reappeared! And this was their big occasion of great joy. It was the joy of doubt cast out, of certainty that they were on the right road, and, even more wonderfully, it was their joy that they would soon witness the babe whose birth would mean so much to the world.

The joy of the Magi was **the joy of certainty and of expectations soon to be realised.**

The joy that is a part of the fruit of the Spirit is precisely what the Magi experienced. *Chara* is the joy of doubt cast out, of the certainty of being on the right road, and of expectations soon to be realised. In a word: security. In a world where insecurity seems to darken almost everybody's path, we so need this *chara*. This is the joy that will be our own experience when we have love. There can be no real joy where there is doubt and worry. If we doubt that we are on the right road to the Kingdom, if we are unsure that our expectations of a place in the Kingdom will be realised— where will be our joy? If that sorry situation describes you, then your only moments of joy will be what you can wring from what this world has to offer, the rather shallow parody of joy that people generally use to mask a dreadful lack of the real thing. **And it does not have to be so!**

Why is it so difficult for many believers to look to the future with real certainty? It seems to be a part of our make-up (literally so, *doubt* having entered along with the curse in Eden) that we have to overcome. Certainty doesn't come naturally, even in the face of abundant grace. We're suspicious of certainty. It doesn't feel right. Perhaps because we see the over-confidence of some of those around us whose beliefs are different. We wonder that they can be so certain. We wouldn't want to delude *our*selves, would we?

In addition to this, we read God's Word and see the high standards set, and we know in our heart of hearts how far we miss the mark. Again we allow uncertainty about the future to take hold of us. All that talk of shame and punishment and outer darkness, weeping and gnashing of teeth!—don't you have good reason to be anxious! But why do we give so much weight to threats of punishment and shame, and not give equal and preferably more weight and attention to all the grace and goodness, mercy and forgiveness of which we read! And, it has to be said, the Sunday morning exhortation is sometimes not too helpful in this respect. Matters have improved in recent years, but there are still plenty of exhortations that err on the wrong side of the comfort/warning divide. I'm not suggesting that speakers should be so considerate as to leave us in ignorance of the spiritual dangers we face, but we shouldn't go home from the meeting feeling no good, and that we will *never* be any good. If we do, then the fault is with the speaker and not with ourselves. Such abuse of the exhortation period serves only to sap the certainty and security that is so necessary for joy to be part of our lives.

Good grief

It's easy for us to go into a downward spiral of guilt and depression over our constant failure to live the Truth at anything like the level of acceptability we feel we ought. Feelings of unworthiness can become chronic, an on-going state of mild (or even quite severe) despair. But we need never get this way. Feelings of guilt and unworthiness serve a useful purpose. They are to the heart what pain is to the body. We touch a flame and the pain warns us it was a bad move. On rare occasions, *thankfully* rare, a child is born without a natural pain response, and the problem is horrific. They might put their finger in a flame and watch with delight as it burns to a stub, not feeling a thing. These children generally become crippled through the stresses they unwittingly put on their joints. I recall the mother of such a child saying how wonderful it would be to see her child fall down, hurt itself and cry!

The consequences of not feeling pain are awful. Believe it or not, a toothache is a good friend, because it warns us that something is wrong so we can do something about it. I have a tooth from which the nerve was removed some years ago. This is the one my dentist keeps a special eye on, taking an X-ray picture every now and then, because it could go bad and I'd never know it, which could ultimately be more trouble than a mere toothache.

Guilt and unworthiness do the same job for our hearts, warning us that something has gone wrong so we can do something about it. These feelings, that we might wish we didn't suffer, actually perform the good task of leading us to repentance, confession and forgiveness. That's their job; that's why we have them. And when they've done their job, the emotional pain should go away. Once the recommended healing has been applied, the pain should subside. Any guilt remaining after repentance and confession is purely imaginary. It doesn't really exist. It's like the pain amputees say they sometimes get in limbs which have been amputated. They have no leg below the knee and yet their foot hurts, because the nerve receptors are still working at the brain end of the line, sending a false message that feels like the real thing. Our "guilt receptors" can do the same. We can confess and 'amputate' our sin but the old unworthiness record keeps on playing. The guilt feelings won't go away sometimes. Maybe we're not *certain* we're actually forgiven. Whenever this happens, we need to see the bogus pain for what it really is and let go of it. It's a false message. The guilt doesn't really exist. There's an excellent example of wrongly assumed guilt in the Old Testament. It was killing joy for the people of Israel.

"The joy of the Lord is your strength"

In the days of Nehemiah, the people of Israel were in the sorry state of seeing only the huge weight of their sin and neglect of God, while losing sight of the mercy of God. When Ezra the scribe read the book of the Law to the assembled people, and when other faithful men "caused the people to understand the law", the people went into great mourning. They were brought face to face with the dreadful fact of their own failings before God, individually and as a nation. The outlook seemed horribly bleak as they became aware of the awful chasm between what they should have been and what they were. But the people had totally misread the situation. Nehemiah, Ezra and the Levites had to reassure the people that this hopeless mourning was not what was wanted! "Do not mourn or weep," they insisted. "For all the people had been weeping as they listened to the words of the law." (Neh.8:9 NIV) Now take note of what followed.

> "Nehemiah said, Go and enjoy choice food and sweet drinks, and send some to those who have nothing prepared. This day is sacred to our Lord. Do not grieve, for the joy of the Lord is your strength" (Neh. 8:10 NIV).

The Levites actually had to go down among the people to reassure them, to tell them not to grieve over their past, but to be joyful. And eventually the people understood what the Levites were saying, the 'penny dropped', and the people went their way "to make great mirth" it says. When they understood the truth about the mercy and goodness of God, the burden of guilt and unworthiness dropped from their souls. Joy was the inevitable result.

We need more Nehemiahs on Sunday mornings. Not that the speaker needs to come down from the platform and reassure us when he sees the consternation on our faces! But the *grace* of God needs to be set more strongly against the *law* of God. Being sorry for our sins is needful (Israel were sorry), but to be continually sorry for them, having confessed them and while trying to overcome them, is more than counter-productive; it's wrong. It's a denial of God's grace and of His clearly stated willingness to forgive. And it will rob us of joy. It will make our love incomplete, lacking the necessary aspect of joy. And what strange vanity is this, to imagine that our sins are greater than Christ's atoning work could possibly cover! What nonsense.

The remedy for all despair

Nehemiah told Israel those lovely words: *"The joy of the Lord is your strength."* That word *strength* is the Hebrew word *moaz,* which carries the idea of a fort or stronghold. Do you notice how perfectly suited the word was to the occasion? The people had just completed building again the defensive wall around their city of Jerusalem, and no doubt they viewed that wall as their stronghold, their strength. But, *"No,"* said Nehemiah, *"The joy of the Lord is your strength."* Joy founded upon the certainty of God's love and mercy was their protection against the despair and hopelessness that the guilt of sin brings. And surely the Levites would have explained to the people, as they went among them, that this same joy had also been their defence against the physical enemy outside the city gates. God protected them while they joyfully and purposefully worked, building the walls under the baleful eyes of their enemies. They had no walls to protect them then; their safety came entirely from the Lord. And the truth of the matter was that although the city walls were now in place, their true safety *still* came from God. The people were no doubt made to realise and rejoice in that, and not be downcast because of the accusing finger of the law. God had, if they cared to think about it, already *proved* his mercy to them, preserving them while they worked. That was evidence enough that

God had not rejected them. So they could be joyful now, confidently trusting in Him. That was their strength.

And it's ours too. If you're ever cast down by the weight of your own sins, and feel rejected, then look back in your life. We all have somewhere in our past some evidence of the hand of God in our lives. Think on that. Did God do whatever it was for you because you were sinless? God was bothered with you then, and He's bothered with you now. Having been sorry, confessed and committed yourself to trying to do better, don't go on punishing yourself with thoughts of rejection; turn your mind to the love, grace and mercy of God. Think on His care for you till now, and know that it's still with you. Let that be *your* strength... and your joy.

Joy and sorrow

The direct opposite of joy is, of course, sorrow. The disciples were told that they were going to experience both these emotions because of what lay ahead for them. In John 16:20 Jesus told his disciples he must soon leave them. When that happened, he said, they'd weep and lament, though the world would rejoice (the Jewish world, no doubt, whose leaders were glad to be rid of him). "And ye shall be sorrowful, but your sorrow shall be turned into joy." It would be turned to joy because they would see him again, and their hearts would rejoice. "And your joy no man taketh from you."

The disciples were to experience a joy that no-one could take from them: a deep, inner joy that was unrelated to what was going on around them, not dependent on good circumstances. This is a joy that stems from deep-seated security, from knowing that despite all appearances to the contrary, all is really well and there is nothing to worry about. **That can only come from spiritual certainty.** And the disciples discovered it for themselves shortly after the anguish and uncertainty of the dark hours immediately following the crucifixion of their Lord. The realisation that Jesus was alive brought such gasps of relief and astonishment! Their hearts were lifted up, their spirits lightened, all because of renewed certainty. They had the joy of knowing their expectations were going to be realised after all. They were on the right road after all! Christ was alive! And it gave those ordinary men the extraordinary commitment and courage that was needed to establish Christianity in the First Century.

That's an indication of how *we* can feel about the fact that Christ is alive. It's an indication of the joy available to you and me because we know the Kingdom of God will be established. The possibility of being in it is great because of what Christ has done, and continues to do, for us. Don't even *think* about not getting there! That's called *unbelief* in the language of Hebrews 4:6. The Israelites who failed to reach the 'promised land' failed because of unbelief, not in a particular set of doctrines, but in the power of God to get them there! Don't follow their example, says the writer of Hebrews.

Be elated when you think about the Kingdom of God. Be like the merchant who's bought the pearl of great price. Take it out now and then just to drool over it because it's so gorgeous! That's the attitude that will benefit most. And we need that attitude of joy to keep us going through daily problems that can so drain our spiritual resources, and the sin and guilt that can deplete these resources more than anything. True scriptural joy makes us almost impervious to what seems like the "slings and arrows of outrageous fortune".

Leap for joy!

I'm reminded of a piece of advice James gave in his letter. Everyone calls James the most practical of all the New Testament writers, yet the very first piece of advice he has for us is this: "My brethren, count it all joy when ye fall into divers temptations" (Jas.1:2). It sounds like the most *im*practical piece of advice anyone ever handed out! But of course it isn't when we understand the true nature of joy.

And what James said is *mild* compared with what Jesus himself said. Jesus said: "Blessed are ye, when men shall hate you, and when they shall separate you from their company, and shall reproach you, and cast out your name as evil, for the Son of man's sake. **REJOICE IN THAT DAY, AND LEAP FOR JOY...**" (Luke 6:22,23 NIV, emphasis added).

Rejoice! Leap for joy! Yes, not just the more mild "count it all joy". How can we possibly take that attitude to being treated so badly, and when trying to cope with difficulties? Do James and Jesus tell us how? Well, yes, they do.

Jesus explained himself by adding (to "leap for joy"), "for behold your reward is great in heaven." And James must have had Jesus' words from the sermon on the mount in mind when he wrote his letter, because he lapsed into a little 'beatitude' of his own: "Blessed is the man that endureth temptation: for when he is tried, he shall receive the crown of life, which the Lord hath promised to them that love him" (Jas.1:12).

So, why, when talking of trial and temptation, should the subject of joy come up? Because joy is our best defence against trial and temptation, that's why. And joy comes not simply as a result of successfully coming through some trial or temptation, though of course, that's a joyful experience. James and Jesus point out that the joy needs to be present while you're *in* a problem. "Count it all joy **when** ye fall into divers temptations"—not afterwards when you put your feet up. And "leap for joy" **when** people are giving you a hard time, not later when the problem has gone away.

Because that's how you're going to overcome the problems, and survive the difficulties. Focusing on joy while you're in the trial or temptation is the answer. Getting the pearl of great price out of its little carrying pouch, and giving it a loving glance, and thinking to yourself, "Yes, that's why I sold all that other stuff. I certainly made the right decision there. It's absolutely beautiful!" Not putting the pearl in the mental equivalent of a safety deposit box, hidden away somewhere to be brought out, perhaps, only at moments of 'study'. That way we might even forget we ever bought it! Keep the pearl with you wherever you go. That's the secret of maintaining the joy you had when you first bought it. Remember -

(1) Keep the vision of your pearl clear (don't tuck it away)
(2) Keep the certainty of it clear (don't give doubt houseroom)
(3) Keep the expectation of it clear (don't let failure obscure your   view of grace)
(4) "*The joy of the Lord is your strength*"

A personal reminder

Do I still sense scepticism out there? Despite all I've said, is there still that little nagging voice inside that says, "How can I be really sure of my future? And surely it's going too far to say we ought to **expect** to be in the Kingdom of God? Aren't we presuming upon the grace of God?" Yes, in a way we are, in the sense that to presume something is to assume that it's true. What are we supposed to do with grace? Ignore it? Doubt it? Water it down? Limit it? Deny it for ourselves but not for others? What are the Scriptural grounds for all these negatives? That we *sin*? What's grace for, if not for sinners? That we just *don't measure up*? Again, what's grace for? Perfect people don't need grace! The only way we can miss out on grace is to turn our backs on it.

But still the concept of certainty is a problem for us, isn't it? If only we could have a sign from heaven that we're okay with God, like that angel we spoke of at the beginning of this chapter, appearing to tell us all's well. "Shew me a token for good", said one of the Psalmists. (Psalm 86:17— incidentally my favourite Psalm). People like Hezekiah were sometimes given big, dramatic signs. But us...?

Well, can you honestly say you've never in your whole life had an encouraging sign from God? Anyone with any appreciation of the reality of God in his or her life will have had signs, I'm sure. "Hold on there", I hear someone say, "this is getting a bit close to Spirit guidance." Well, yes. Of course there is unseen spiritual guidance in our lives. And unless we are aware of it, how are we ever going to know the security in our lives that is essential for joy and peace? The ways of providence work today. And we can observe them in action in our lives. We're not left struggling and alone, without the slightest hint of God's presence.

Consider for a moment, how are we supposed to understand this verse (Mark 11:24): "What things soever ye desire, when ye pray, **believe that ye receive them,** and ye shall have them"? The NIV says more correctly, "believe that you **have** received it and it will be yours." It doesn't appear to make sense, does it? Why would we ask for something we believe we already have? The sense becomes more clear when you remove the word *them* from the verse in the AV or the *it* in the NIV, which the translators have added to try to make more sense of the Greek. In this case they've helped to obscure the sense. Try it like this: "believe that you have received, and it will be yours." What it means is, when you pray, pray believing that you have received things from God in the past, and you *will* receive things now. This is what real prayers of faith are. They are prayers based on the belief that God has provided for you in the past, and so He will now, not in some general, vague way, but in specific ways.

Perhaps I can be specific now, and give a personal recollection. About five years ago (1991) I was running late for the office one morning and feeling bad with an illness that had laid me low for some time. I'd made it to the bus stop just in time to see my bus disappearing down the road. I felt awful, and I knew I had a long wait that I really could have done without. I was considering giving up and going home. So I prayed, as one does, when life gets bleak. I prayed that I might be helped in some way, with transport, or better health, or *anything*! I was startled out of my half-finished prayer by the noise of a car horn. I opened my eyes and found myself looking down at the roof of a car. A man I'd not met before, but who recognised me as he worked for the same organisation said, "Would you like a lift to work?" He brought me home that evening, too. And he did the same, morning and evening, for almost the next two years until he retired.

Just a coincidence? It could happen to anyone? I was wondering seriously about that a few months ago. I was walking towards a bus stop on a cold, dark evening on my way home from work, running over in my mind whether it really was a Godsend in the literal sense of the word. I was beginning to have little doubts, thinking maybe it could have been just a coincidence. These things do happen to people. And as I reached the stop and stood there still in my reverie, a car going the other way suddenly slowed, turned round in the road, and pulled up next to me. A fellow-believer just happened to be going down that way, not usual for her, she saw me and wondered if I would like a lift home!

I think I'm justified in believing that my angel wanted to let me know he'd organised it last time!

I'm sure we all have such events in our lives that we wouldn't dare say were *not* the hand of God. Like walking into an old country church to look round it one day while feeling a little low, and finding the big Bible on the lectern laid open at your favourite Psalm, the Psalm which always bucks you up. That's happened to me, too. This sort of thing must be happening to all who are in the Truth. But maybe we're not open to such things; we go around with our spiritual eyes shut. And we may lack joy as a consequence. As I said at the outset of this chapter, our delight and meditation when we read the Word doesn't supply all the joy we need. It's how we take what we read into our daily lives that makes the difference.

Our joy comes from our security in Christ. It's the joy of doubt cast out, and of knowing we're on the right road.

CHAPTER EIGHT

PEACE *(eirene)*

IF your name is Irene then you probably know it comes from the Greek *eirene*, which means peace. One of the aspects of the fruit of the Spirit is this *eirene*, so one of the characteristics of a believer will be peace. And, at the risk of sounding Eastern and mystical, it is *inner* peace that he or she will have. The fruit of the Spirit is an internal matter: all the aspects occur in our minds, in our hearts. And there's nothing particularly mystical about inner peace.

As we noted at the beginning of the last chapter, peace is the flip-side of joy on the coin of security. Peace is the more passive side of security. Whereas joy bubbles up and gives the sparkle to life in the Truth, peace provides a deeper, warmer glow of well-being. Peace is a product of security, and all the things we said about the need for God-given security in Chapter Seven apply equally here. Without God-given security there can be no true peace of mind. But there is more to peace than just security.

How many people have *real* peace in their lives? More to the point, how many even know what real peace is? No doubt most people have some idea of what constitutes peace for themselves. For some it's just the silence of being absolutely alone. For others it's a leisurely walk down an English country lane in early summer. Or maybe it's those precious moments when the children are finally in bed and asleep! Sitting on a riverbank with a fishing line draped in the water might be another person's peace. Alone with a favourite book, another's. You can doubtless add to the list with your own ideal scenario. And yet not one of these is *real* peace. None of them is the peace which the Scriptures speak of as part of the fruit of the Spirit.

The treadmill society

One of the major problems of this age is stress. A high percentage of illness today is said to be stress-related. And those who aren't actually ill with it are troubled by it to some degree. The very word disease is a joining together of the two components *dis* and *ease*, meaning lack of ease, or stress.

We in the West live in a society that promotes stress. The consumer society is the *treadmill* society. There are benefits, of course, and no-one is hurrying to swap it for a Third World economy! But there is also a downside—and that is stress. You get on the treadmill of *want*, and you have to stay on it to keep all the things that the treadmill society convinces you are necessary for your happiness. The whole industry of advertising is geared to convincing you that you need more and better. The result is stress: chasing the dream that is never quite fulfilled, always over the next hill. Or realising the dream, only to discover that the grass may be greener but it still needs cutting!

If you get off the treadmill, you become a 'dropout' and the stress of survival can be even more acute. And if you do so well for yourself that you can afford to stand aside from the treadmill, there is even the stress of success to deal with! It's also likely that the stress of making it to the top will have taken such a heavy toll physically and mentally that you can't enjoy the fruits of it when you get them. Stress counselling for all levels of society is a growth industry.

This generation even chooses forms of relaxation that are stressful. People actually 'relax' (or so they kid themselves) by watching murder and mayhem in their living rooms on the small screen!

Real peace is, I believe, a rare commodity these days. But the lack of it can surely be no new phenomenon. We seem to think we have just invented stress. Imagine living in the days of Christ and Paul. The Roman Empire extended a degree of peace throughout its regions, but life was precarious and hard for many of its subjects. Slavery and rough justice were the order of the day for the lower end of society. Getting too close to a fickle and often monstrous Emperor was your reward for climbing to the top of it! It seems to me that there can have been very few, if any, stress-free periods of human history.

But how should believers react to such a world? Christian counselling is also a growth industry. In some ways life can seem harder for a believer than it is for an unbeliever. The believer has not only the same everyday stress to contend with as everybody else, he or she has the additional pressures of trying to live according to Christian precepts. Let's be honest: the majority of believers seem no less stress-free than other people. We get 'tetchy' and miserable at times. We even get angry and confrontational. We get frustrated and snappy. We get depressed, and we get other stress-related conditions.

"The way of peace"

And yet Christ distinctly said, to believers: "Peace I leave with you, my peace I give unto you." (John 14:27). The gospel which believers believe and preach is called "the gospel of peace". And Paul says to all believers: "let the peace of God rule in your hearts" (Col.3:15).

And peace being part of the fruit of the Spirit, it will also be a part of the well-rounded Christian character. So, why isn't it always? The obvious answer (which also happens to be the *wrong* answer) is that we're all different, and some cope better with life than others. Some are more capable of peace than others. How unfair, then, of Paul to say that peace will be a part of the true Christian character, when many can't manage it! (For that matter, what about *longsuffering, gentleness, goodness,* and the other parts of the fruit?) The Scriptures don't make allowance for our different personality types, do they, when it comes to the fruit of the Spirit? They hold up one version only of the true Christian character, with no options to allow for temperament. It may seem dreadfully unfair that habitually troubled souls are expected to exhibit peace, but **the underlying message is that everyone is capable of it**, no matter what their temperament, no matter what their circumstances. And that's a message of hope! It's possible for every believer to have peace.

Peace and circumstance

Probably the biggest misconception about peace is that it all depends on circumstances. Too many people (believers among them) live with the illusion that their inner peace is totally dependent upon what goes on outside of them. For instance, they may wake up in the morning feeling okay, then the breakfast toast gets burned, or an unexpected bill hits the doormat, and their okay mood goes up in smoke, just like the toast. Their peace of mind is shattered. They get agitated. Something outside of them has taken away their inner peace. It's as if they had no control over what went on in their own head. I'm sure many people believe that to be the case, and they go through life as victims of everything that happens to them. Their peace is entirely dependent on good circumstances. That's not *real* peace. The peace that is of the fruit of the Spirit doesn't evaporate over a red hot temper!

If you are a believer and your peace is controlled by what happens to you, or how people treat you, or whether it's raining, then the peace you have is counterfeit. It is not the peace which is a part of the fruit of the Spirit. Remember that the qualities that make up the fruit of the Spirit become *constants* ingrained in the very character of the believer. They are *part* of him or her, having been nurtured in the heart of the believer by constant delight and meditation in the Spirit Word. He or she will naturally slip out of character once in a while under pressure, but it will be exactly that: *out of character*. Their normal state is peace.

Stephen was able to retain his inner peace, even while being stoned to death. He died with forgiveness for his killers on his lips. Habakkuk also qualifies as one of the heroes of peace:

"Though the fig-tree does not bud and there are no grapes on the vines, though the olive crop fails and the fields produce no food, though there are no sheep in the pen and no cattle in the stalls, yet I will rejoice in the Lord, I will be joyful in God my Saviour" (Hab 3:17,18 NIV).

It's beyond the comprehension of most people that Habakkuk could be untroubled amid all those serious problems. I'm sure this is what makes "the peace of God" the kind of peace "which passeth all understanding". And yet this is what God holds out to all. It's so radical that most people can never go right out on that limb and trust God as far as He invites us to trust Him. How different, and how remarkably peaceful our lives could be if we took to heart and practised exactly what the Bible recommends.

This is what Paul recommends through the Spirit. Weigh every word as you read it here from the New International Version. Dwell particularly on the words in bold.

"Rejoice in the Lord **always**. I will say it again: Rejoice! Let your gentleness be evident to all. The Lord **is near**. Do not be anxious about **anything**, but in **everything**, by prayer and petition, with thanks-giving, present your requests to God. And the peace of God, which transcends all understanding, will **guard** your hearts and minds in Christ Jesus" (Phil.4:4-7).

That's the secret of real peace. It transcends our understanding. It goes beyond what is naturally reasonable for us to "rejoice in the Lord **always**"—to praise the Lord in whatever circumstances we find ourselves, knowing that God is in control. When we learn to praise God come rain or shine, we have found real peace. When we know and trust that our *whole* lives are ordered by God, we learn to see Him even in the 'bad' events, not only the good. To complain about the 'bad' is to complain about what God is doing to bring us closer to Him.

Can you seriously envisage losing your health, or your job, or your house, or your reputation, or even a close family member, and yet still trusting God enough to feel peaceful within? It doesn't seem possible, does it? And yet in truth it is. That's the place you get to when you "let the peace of God rule in your hearts." To trust that even in the direst circumstances God is working for your good—when you can't even pretend to see an ounce of good in what has happened, that is the acceptance of a peace which is beyond understanding. Of course calamity will cast us down, but it can't *keep* us down if we have *eirene*.

Real peace is practised by maintaining inner calm and absolute trust in God during the smaller everyday crises of life. The Bible tells us that "all things **work together** for good" for us, not that all things "*are* good". Some of those things working together for our good won't appear at all good in themselves. So even the 'bad' events that might make us 'go to pieces' must be viewed in the context of God guiding all the events in life to a good outcome. The truth of the matter is "there shall no evil happen to the just" (Prov.12:21).

Mind the gap

How does the real peace described above compare with the peace you feel inside yourself? There is a certain level of peace of mind that being in the Truth affords us, that doesn't go all the way to *real* peace. There is what I call *The Gap* that we can fall into if we don't watch our step.

On one side of *The Gap* there is a mind filled with trouble and confusion, a mind devoid of spiritual relaxation, called the natural mind. On the other side of *The Gap* there is a mind filled with real peace, called the spiritual mind. In the middle, in *The Gap* itself, there is a no-man's land where neither true peace nor real confusion reigns. And this is where you might easily get stuck. It's easy to get stuck here because it gives the illusion of being the real peace that we seek. But the absence of war is not necessarily peace.

Cold war

Peace of mind may seem like a passive quality in many respects, but that does not mean it is negative. Peace is not simply the absence of war. It is a quality in its own right which actually *replaces* conflict within us. You may not feel especially troubled in your mind about the way your life is going, you may even be pretty happy about it, but that doesn't necessarily mean you have the real peace of mind that comes from God.

The absence of war is not always peace. Just think of the state that existed between the Americans and the Russians after the Second World War and up to the late 1980s. They weren't at war, but neither by any stretch of the imagination were they at peace! Someone came up with the term *cold war* to describe the peace that was not peace. One cynic has described peace as a period of cheating between two periods of fighting. And you and I know that even at an inter-personal level when someone takes a dislike to us for whatever reason, they may not physically or verbally abuse us but their conduct towards us can hardly be described as peace.

It's possible to have your own personal inner cold war in progress. This is what happens when you're part way between war and peace: when you're not overtly troubled, and seem quite at peace with yourself and with God, but it doesn't take an awful lot for hostility to come shooting to the surface, or for doubt and complaint to start circulating inside. This is what it's like to be in *The Gap*. It's not sufficient for us simply to move away from being troubled in mind, easily provoked and downcast; we have to move right across *The Gap* to a positive state of peace. It's not enough simply to "resist the devil and he will flee from you"; we also have to "draw near to God and he will draw near to you" (James 4:7,8 RAV).

Sometimes we "resist the devil" but we don't "draw near to God" in the process. We move into *The Gap* instead. We allow the pendulum to stop in the middle, at the lowest point, instead of letting the momentum of resistance to evil carry us right over to God.

Observe yourself the next time you *resist* the urge to do something un-Christian, like responding rudely to the rudeness of a colleague at work. Test to see what you feel. Does it leave you feeling frustrated, impotent, and secretly wishing you had reacted angrily? Or, just as bad, does it give you a glow of self-satisfaction that tells you how much better you are than that rude person? Both these reactions are *Gap* reactions. Anyone with real peace inside will actually be *thankful* for the experience and "count it all joy". For them it will be as much a part of God's hand in their lives as the early morning sunshine (or rain!) that greeted them when they stepped out of the house that morning.

Take the Joseph point of view about the events in your life. There's no record of him moaning about the cruel treatment he had from his brothers, or from Potiphar's wife. What he went through was enough to make anyone bitter. But he simply said, "God meant it for good." Joseph knew real peace of mind. He may have been in prison undeservedly, but he wasn't in *The Gap*.

Spiritual judo

To be reminded of God every time something goes wrong for you, however trivial, is a perfect way to stay focused on the Truth. It's during the little daily 'disasters' we most need to remember God. And this is a sure way to overcome that tendency we all have to *complain* about the things God is doing to help us strengthen our characters in readiness for the Kingdom of God. Every complaint about our lot is a criticism of God. And we are supposed to be *praising* God, not criticising Him! Seeing a reminder of God in each little 'set-back' of the day is what I call **spiritual judo.** Because the trick of judo is that you use your opponent's strength *against* him. You use his own body weight and motion to accomplish what *you* want to do with him! If you can learn to see the hand of God in things which would normally defeat you, you will have mastered the art of spiritual judo.

Seeing God in even the 'bad' events of our lives is not being critical of God. We are simply acknowledging that God's hand is in our **whole** lives. When things go wrong, press the *praise* button, not the *panic* button. It sounds radical I know, but a revised attitude to problems, and a recognition of God in *all* of your life changes your life for the better. It brings real peace. "Be not overcome of evil, but overcome evil with good" (Rom.12:21). Paul wrote that in the context of recompensing "to no man evil for evil" and in the context of "avenge not yourselves, but rather give place unto wrath." He surely didn't mean that we should walk away from injustice fuming inside, and stressed-out. That's what we do when we're stuck in *The Gap*. God's way is infinitely better. As Paul said in an earlier verse in that same chapter of Romans: "Be not conformed to this world: but be ye transformed by the renewing of your mind, that ye may prove what is that good, and acceptable, and perfect, will of God." The practical outcome of all this is peace. All that God commands us to do is for our own benefit.

We show our love of God by keeping His commands. "For this is the love of God, that we keep His commandments: and His commandments are not grievous" (1 John 5:3). **What we discover when we keep those commands is that God is showing His love to us *through* them.** In the keeping of the commands we will find all that we could possibly want for ourselves that is truly good for us. God isn't just telling us to do what He wants in order to gain some selfish pleasure from having power over us, like some earthly tyrant who wants his every whim obeyed, *or else.*

"God is love." And because He is love, the things He commands us actually enable us to experience that love. God created us, and He knows exactly what we most need to function well, and His commandments are designed to give us exactly that in the keeping of them. "He that getteth wisdom loveth his own soul" (Prov.19:8). So if you want what is truly best for yourself, be wise to what God asks of you.

The same can also be said of the commandments of Christ. Christ said, "If ye love me, keep my commandments" (John 14:15). But he might equally have said: "If you want to see my love *for you*, keep my commandments."

Perfect inner peace is obtained by finding the will of God through delight and meditation in His Word, trusting in the Lord with all your heart, leaning not towards your own understanding, and in all your ways acknowledging Him so that He can direct your paths (to paraphrase Proverbs 3:5-6). Nothing can destroy a peace which is governed by this Biblical approach to life.

The Laodicean GAP

The Laodicean condition is an excellent example of *"The Gap"*. The members of the Church at Laodicea were told that they were lukewarm (Rev.3:16), neither hot nor cold in their attitudes to the Truth, and to Christ. But it's not so much in this that they showed a Gap mentality, but rather in the fact that they were described as *naked*. They thought they were splendidly clothed. They were "rich, and increased with goods and had need of nothing," in their own eyes. But Christ knew them better than they knew themselves, and said, "thou art... poor, and blind, and naked" (Rev.3:17). So, what could they do about that? The answer to nakedness is, of course, to put on some clothes. Which is exactly what Christ told them to do: "white raiment, that thou mayest be clothed, and that the shame of thy nakedness do not appear."

What sort of clothes were these? Not actual *material* clothes, of course, because Revelation is a book of sign and symbol. The nakedness of the Laodiceans wasn't physical nakedness; it was spiritual. So, what sort of clothes did they need? I believe that the answer to that is to be found in Paul's letter to the Colossians. Significantly, this letter was also sent to the Laodiceans at Paul's request: "And when this epistle is read among you, cause that it be read also in the church of the Laodiceans..." (Col.4:16). I'm certain that when Christ mentioned, in Revelation, the nakedness of the Laodiceans, and their need to put on some sort of spiritual clothing, he was harking back to Paul's earlier letter to the Colossians, which also applied to them.

In Colossians 3 Paul mentions all the items of spiritual clothing that believers should put on:

> "Put on therefore, as the elect of God, holy and beloved, bowels of mercies, kindness, humbleness of mind, meekness, longsuffering; Forbearing one another, and forgiving one another, if any man have a quarrel against any: even as Christ forgave you, so also do ye. And above all these things put on charity [love: *agape*] which is the bond of perfectness. And let the peace of God rule in your hearts, to the which also ye are called in one body; and be ye thankful" (Col.3:12-15).

(Pause for a moment here, before we carry on talking about spiritual clothing. Notice that these verses are a restatement of most, if not all the aspects of the fruit of the Spirit. And notice particularly that love is described in verse fourteen as the thing to be put on *"above all these things"* and that it is the *"bond of perfectness"*—not only because it unites brethren and sisters in Christ, but also because it unites all the aspects of the fruit within itself).

These 'clothes' in Colossians 3 are the equivalent of the *white raiment* that Christ wanted the Laodiceans to put on in Revelation 3. They are the spiritual clothing (fruit of the Spirit, in fact!) that will cover their spiritual nakedness.

But we should not miss the fact that Paul also tells believers in that same chapter of Colossians what clothes they need to *put off* before they can put on the spiritual attire: Having already (v.5) told them to put off sexual immorality, he goes on to say:

"But now ye also put off all these; anger, wrath, malice, blasphemy, filthy communication out of your mouth. Lie not to one another..." (Col 3:8,9).

Let's turn the spotlight upon ourselves for a moment, before we consider again the Laodiceans. How would you answer this question? What do you think you are now wearing, spiritually? It's a tricky question because there are *three* possible answers. It's not just a matter of the clean, white garment of the Spirit, or the dirty garment of the flesh. There's a third possibility.

First of all, can you honestly say, hand on heart, that you now have on the pure white garment, "unspotted from the world" of the elect of God? Remember it consists of things like holiness, kindness, humbleness, meekness, longsuffering, and above all, love. Maybe when you look at this list you feel you don't quite have that good a raiment—not quite your style! Yours is a bit ragged and muddy from your passage through life.

But now consider the other garment. It's not just a little bit muddy, is it? It's absolutely filthy! "Fornication, anger, wrath, malice, blaspheming, filthy communication, lying." Well... no, you surely don't have one like that on, do you? Surely *none* of us is wearing that!

But if you're not wearing the filthy one, and if you don't quite see yourself wearing the clean, white one; if you think of yourself as something in between—then what are you?

Naked is the answer!

The Laodiceans weren't wearing either the filthy garment or the white one. So they were naked. They weren't malicious or blasphemers, or liars. Oh, no. But neither were they humble, or merciful, or longsuffering (in a word, loving) towards one another. They were neither one thing or the other, and so they were naked.

They were in *The Gap*. They had moved away from the mind dominated by the flesh, but they hadn't moved all the way towards a mind dominated by the Spirit. If they made that move, they would have clean white garments, not the ugly red-blotched garments of sin. For "though your sins be as scarlet, they shall be as white as snow." Every time we seek and obtain forgiveness for our sins, every time we seek to walk in love, Christ whitens our garments for us. That doesn't happen in *The Gap*, where we have no clothes to be whitened.

Simply   putting off the old, filthy garments is not enough. Once the negatives are ousted, there must be the positive action of putting on, or we will be left in *The Gap*. There are two things to be done: "resist the devil" **and** "draw near to God". These are not one and the same action, but two separate and complementary actions that will together lead us to and keep us in a state of peace. "To be spiritually minded is life and peace" wrote Paul (Rom.8:6).

Confusion and peace

When Paul wrote to the Corinthian believers about the haphazard way in which the gifts of the Spirit were being employed in their ecclesia, he chided them with the words: "For God is not the author of confusion, but of peace..." (1 Cor.14:33). The Greek word for confusion in that verse is *akatastasia* which conveys the idea of instability, the rocking back and forth of a boat on water. (AV margin also says *tumult* or *unquietness*). It also conveys what I mean by *The Gap*. *The Gap* is a mental state of confusion, instability, tumult. God is certainly not the author of *The Gap;* **we** are. He is the author of our peace, if we will allow Him to be.

A double minded man

When you're in the gap you're looking both ways at the same time, like the mythical Roman god Janus who is represented with two faces, one on the front of his head and one on the back. Our month of January is named after Janus, because he was thought to stand at the gate of the year looking into the past and into the future. But the believer stuck in *The Gap* could be depicted in the same way, confused between the mind of the flesh and the mind of the Spirit, trying to blend the two and not getting anywhere because the two just don't mix. He certainly doesn't have peace of mind.

James talks of this sort of person as "a double minded man" (though of course there are double minded women also!) James says that "A double minded man is unstable in **all** his ways." (Jas.1:8) **All** of them! **Everything** he does! That word *unstable* is the Greek *akatastatos* and it's a variant of the same word Paul used when he said that "God is not the author of confusion". A double minded man is unstable and confused about all he does because his mind is in conflict. He wants to go two different ways, live two different lives. He won't commit himself one way or the other, and so he has no peace of mind.

The only way for the double minded man or woman, stuck in *The Gap*, to find real peace is to bring an end to the inner confusion by fully committing to the way of the Spirit. Draw near to God. Especially turn to Him in praise for *everything* in your life, and look more closely into His Word for *everything* you need to help you.

"Teach me thy way, O Lord; I will walk in thy truth: **unite my heart** to fear thy name. I will **praise** thee, O Lord my God, with **all my heart:** and I will glorify thy name for evermore" (Psalm 86:11-12).

Those verses express the perfect frame of mind for anyone seeking real peace of mind. A **united** heart is what we need. Above all we need to be able to praise God with our **whole** heart. This is the way of peace. It is the way of praising God for everything in our lives, because it is all working together for good. "In everything give thanks: for this is the will of God in Christ concerning you" (1 Thess.5:18).

There's an apposite reference in the Old Testament. It concerns those men who pledged their allegiance to King David in Israel. David is a type of Christ, therefore we can view those who choose to follow him as typical of believers. In 1 Chronicles 12:33 we read the following amid the list of families who threw in their lot with David:

"Of Zebulun, such as went forth to battle, expert in war, with all instruments of war, fifty thousand, which could keep rank: they were not of double heart."

And just look in the AV margin against that phrase *not of a double heart*. It gives the literal Hebrew rendering as: "without a heart and a heart." Doesn't that express it perfectly! Those who followed David from Zebulun were not the sort to have two hearts, or to be in two minds about it. Their hearts were united to follow him in literal war, exactly as our hearts must be united to follow the Captain of our Salvation in spiritual war. Paradoxically, being an "expert in war, with all the instruments of war" will bring us the only real peace available. As the Psalmist expressed it, "Great peace have they who love your law, and nothing can make them stumble" (Psalm 119:165 NIV).

Peace like a river

In the days soon to come when the Kingdom of God is established on this earth, Jerusalem will be the capital city. Isaiah spoke of those days saying, "For thus saith the Lord, Behold, I will extend peace to her like a river, and the glory of the Gentiles like a flowing stream..." (Isaiah 66:12). It's a beautiful simile, isn't it? and one which is picked up in the final chapter of the Bible, where the Kingdom is described for the last time:

"And he shewed me a pure river of water of life, clear as crystal, proceeding out of the throne of God and of the Lamb [in the new Jerusalem]. In the midst of the street of it, and on either side of the river, was there the tree of life, which bare twelve manner of fruits, and yielded her fruit every month: and the leaves of the tree were for the healing of the nations" (Rev.22:1,2).

This is a symbolic glimpse of a time of unparalleled peace on earth. Did you notice anything familiar about that picture of a tree by a river bearing bountiful fruit with healing leaves? It takes us back to Psalm 1 where the truly righteous man is pictured. He is the man who develops the fruit of the Spirit from the water of life which is in God's Word. He is "like a tree planted by the rivers of water that bringeth forth his fruit in his season." (Psalm1.3). His leaf shall not wither. In fact, his leaves shall be for the healing of nations, because the righteous ones will teach the nations the Truth. Such people, who delight themselves in meditating upon God's Word, will be in the New Jerusalem, when "the meek shall inherit the earth; and shall delight themselves in the abundance of peace" (Psalm 37:11).

But we don't have to wait until then to experience a good measure of inner peace for ourselves. Real inner peace is part of the fruit of the Spirit we are to develop now. Christ will be looking for it in you and me when He comes.

"We, according to his promise, look for new heavens and a new earth, wherein dwelleth righteousness. Wherefore, beloved, seeing that ye look for such things, **be diligent that ye may be found of him in peace,** without spot, and blameless" (2 Pet.3:13,14).

Above all, don't forget that real God-given peace (the only sort worth having) comes from being thankful for everything in your life in Christ. "And let the peace of God rule in your hearts, to the which also ye are called in one body; **and be ye thankful**" (Col. 3:15).

CHAPTER NINE

LONGSUFFERING *(makrothumia)*

FROM the start I sensed that this chapter was going to be a difficult one. Longsuffering doesn't especially appeal to anyone. The very word puts us off. None of us wants to suffer long if we can help it. If we have to suffer, then *please let it be over quickly!* That's my view, anyway.

Our English word longsuffering is self-evidently the joining together of two words. And coincidentally the Greek word for longsuffering in the New Testament is also a combination of two words *makro* and *thumeo*. *Makrothumia* means literally slow anger, or long temper. Sometimes it's translated patience. And, annoyingly, newer versions (such as the NIV and NEB) give patience in Galatians 5 as part of the fruit of the Spirit. I believe the translators are wrong here, because they fail to maintain a necessary distinction between patience and longsuffering. There is a difference, and it's worth hanging on to because one is a fruit of the Spirit, and one isn't.

The impatience of Job

The scriptural difference between patience and longsuffering is best shown in the character of Job. Job is proverbial for his patience, but he is not proverbial for his longsuffering! And the record of his life is a powerful illustration of how far God will sometimes go in order to encourage a man in some vital part of the fruit of the Spirit which is lacking.

When James wrote, "Ye have heard of the patience of Job," he didn't use the word *makrothumia* (longsuffering), he used the word *hupomone*, the more usual word for patience in the New Testament. Nothing remarkable about that, you might think. But the point is that James suddenly switched from the word *makrothumia*, which he'd used four times in the previous five verses, and used a different word to describe Job! You wouldn't know this from reading the Authorised Version (or many other versions) because the word *patience* is used in all cases regardless of a change in the original Greek word.

It has to be significant that all the while James was talking about the sort of patience it takes to develop fruit, he used the word *makrothumia*:

> "Be patient therefore, brethren, unto the coming of the Lord. Behold, the husbandman waiteth for the precious fruit of the earth, and hath long patience for it... Be ye also patient..." (Jas. 5:7-8).

But when he turned his attention to Job, he changed the word:

> "Ye have heard of the patience (*hupomone*) of Job, and have seen the end of the Lord; that the Lord is very pitiful, and of tender mercy." (James 5.11)

Logically, James should just have carried on using the same word. But the Spirit that moved James's hand directed otherwise, and for good reason. James was trying to impress upon his readers (us!) that we need more than *hupomone*. Because the 'end of the Lord'—that is, the final outcome towards which the Lord was steering Job through his trials—was that Job should learn *makrothumia*. Those trials were perfectly tailored to teach Job precisely what he needed to learn: an aspect of love that was missing from his character.

I'm not denying that Job was an exemplary character, or that the patience he exhibited under extreme trial was of a very high order. But he still had a lesson to learn, and I believe that lesson concerned a lack of longsuffering. Some further thoughts on the Greek word will bear this out.

William Barclay, in his excellent book 'New Testament Words' describes *hupomone* as "one of the noblest of New Testament words," because it represents a form of patience that relates specifically to tribulation. So, of course, James chose his word well when he related *hupomone* to Job. *Hupomone* is not a passive sort of patience, that sits around and lets the world go by. This is an **active** patience. It's the patience by which we can bear things with a blazing hope! It's not a quiet, stoical endurance, grimly hanging on in there because things just might work out better in the end. It's a patience which radiantly **expects** a better dawn to break soon, even from within the blackest clouds of misery.

That was Job all over. He had the capacity for standing back and seeing the whole picture, maintaining his faith; knowing that no matter what was going on, God was good and God was in control, therefore only good could ultimately come out of it. There is no denying the excellent qualities of Job. To achieve and maintain *hupomone* as he did was no mean feat.

Having said that, though, there is undoubtedly another side to Job's character that comes out when we read his conversations with his three friends. Job wasn't so patient in another sense of the word. He wasn't particularly patient towards his friends. At times he appears quite exasperated with them because of their inability to understand and sympathize with his situation (and, one might add, who can blame him?) "No doubt you are the men who know all," he said to them, (and not without sarcasm, surely?) "and wisdom will die with you. But I have brains as well as you; why, anyone knows all you say!" (Moffatt) "Plaguy comforters" he called them. And he asked when their windbag speeches were ever going to end!

He wasn't particularly patient in this way, was he? He wasn't especially good when it came to the other sort of patience which is *makrothumia*. As we said, the word means long-tempered, or slow to anger. The fault in his character was of being short-tempered with his friends. It's not difficult to see why James didn't apply *makrothumia* to Job, but opted for another word. But by the end of the matter, Job had learned to be longsuffering. He finally prayed for his three friends, instead of snapping at them. Interestingly, James goes on to speak of prayer: "Is any among you afflicted? Let him pray" (Jas.5:13). And in the verse immediately following his mention of Job (v.12), James warns against the evils of swearing—something to which the *short*-tempered are especially prone!—they just let fly without thinking.

"Swear not at all"

Originally, swearing was confined to taking God's name in vain: uttering an oath you have no intention of honouring, merely using His Name or Jesus' name to add force to what you're saying. It's a way of saying, "I really do mean this!" But it is both displeasing and dishonouring to God to call upon Him to lend weight to our petty opinions, commitments and feelings. Jesus warns us not to swear at all; not to commit ourselves to anything we may afterwards be unable to follow through. **Certainly not** to treat swearing as an habitual literary device for underlining what we say! This latter use of swearing is common today. Nowadays 'swear-words' need not refer to God or Jesus, but can be any word thought crude enough to add emphasis or show how 'big' the speaker is. What great company for the names of God and Jesus!

It could also be pointed out that there are many expressions where the names of God and Jesus are being used, probably without the user being aware of it. Phrases like "My Goodness", "Good Gracious", "Good Heavens", "Crikey" seem innocuous, but are they really? And sometimes initials are substituted, as in "Giddy Aunt" (God Almighty) and "Jiminy Cricket" (Jesus Christ). "Gosh" and "Cripes" don't fare too well, either. (But don't heap guilt upon yourself because you suddenly realize what you've been saying all these years! Ignorance is not an excuse, but neither is it unforgivable. Under the Law of Moses provision was made for sins of ignorance. No one can seriously doubt that a similar provision exists under the present High Priest-ship of Christ.)

It's often said that swearing covers for a lack of vocabulary, but the problem is worse than that. If it were simply lack of vocabulary, then the educated wouldn't swear. You know as well as I do that they can be as bad if not worse than the uneducated. What is lacking in the habitual swearer is not generally a decent vocabulary but the ability to express *feelings* adequately. People feel they must swear in order to show they are upset or happy. It is their *emotional* vocabulary that is sparse. This is what needs addressing. When a believer falls into the habit of swearing, as can happen, it's as well to look for this emotional deficit. Do you think that people will take you seriously *only if* you add some 'reinforcement' to your talking? Is swearing the only way you have of communicating that you're really angry over something? Or that you really *mean* something? Perhaps it's even a sign of suppressed anger? (We'll look at that in a moment.)

Of course, swearing is often just *caught*, like a cold. It's a social disease. People do it because everyone around them does it. It's difficult being in the same workplace, school, college, or home environment with those who swear without catching the disease yourself. Standards in the media have dropped, too. But believers need to resist it. It's not a matter of being a prude, or out of touch with today's more down-to-earth approach to living. There's *always* been swearing. And the reasons for believers not doing it have always been the same. First and foremost, it displeases and devalues God. Next it involves crudity and sometimes shows an unbecoming preoccupation with sex and bodily functions. Added to these, it's a sign of emotional immaturity. It can indicate the lack of ability to express strong feeling in any other way. For instance, we shouldn't have to swear just to convince others we are passionate about something. Added to which there's usually a strong social-acceptance factor in swearing. It's generally done to make you feel one of the boys, or girls—so insecurity plays a part. In contrast, a believer needs to be God-pleasing,

God-honouring, clean-speaking, emotionally mature, and have God-given security. Only a fool would say that a believer is prudish and out of touch by not swearing. The believer is very much in touch with what truly matters. And his life is better for it. Swearing really is 'down to earth', as people sometimes say in its defence, but that's not a good direction for a believer's thoughts.

Slow anger, not no anger

Once we realise that longsuffering means long or slow anger, we're well on the way to understanding this aspect of the fruit of the Spirit. God Himself is described as being "slow to anger" (Neh.9:17), so it's appropriate that His children should bear the family likeness. Incidentally, that other word, patience (*hupomone*), is never used of God, doubtless because God can't be said to endure tribulation in the same sense that we do. But we do read of the longsuffering of God. The Apostle Peter mentions it in relation to the time of Noah, "...when once the longsuffering of God waited in the days of Noah, while the ark was a preparing, wherein few, that is, eight souls were saved by water" (1 Pet.3:20).

Slowness to anger is a characteristic of God for which we can all be extremely grateful. Peter actually says in his Second Epistle that we should "account that the longsuffering of our Lord is salvation." He bears with us in our folly every day of our lives. He restrains Himself from dealing with us as our sins deserve. He is very slow to anger with us. In Noah's time He could easily have miraculously held Noah and his family aloft and dry while He brought the flood on the earth. Instead of which He waited all those long years while Noah built the ark and preached righteousness to the world in the hope that more would be saved. And you have to consider that God foreknew that only seven other souls would be convinced, the rest of Noah's immediate family—so God waited all that time for only seven people to come to their senses!

God is the same towards this last generation. He waits while the preaching goes on. But He'll not wait forever. His longsuffering will come to an end. Slow anger is not no anger at all. God *will* ultimately vent His anger upon the incurably godless of this world. The flood came, and so will this world's judgement—exactly the point Peter made in his Second Epistle (2 Pet.3:6,7).

To a lesser degree the same is true for believers with regard to longsuffering. It is God's prerogative to rid the world of ugliness (vengeance is His, not ours), but we all need to keep in mind that slow anger is not *no* anger. Or we may do ourselves some harm.

It's not possible for us to experience no anger whatsoever. **What matters is how we express the anger we sometimes feel.** Also what matters is that we do express it, or release it, in some way.

A lot of psychological damage can be traced to unexpressed, repressed anger. Counsellors dealing with emotionally disturbed people often find unexpressed anger over past events the root cause of present problems. The hidden damage works its way to the surface. It is necessary that we give vent to, or release our anger, but in acceptable ways. It's not acceptable to express the anger we may feel in ways that are physically or emotionally damaging to other people. I'm sure I don't need to marshal any scriptural proof for that.

The very opposite of slow anger is quick temper. The unacceptable face of anger is the quick temper. Everyone hates being around the time-bomb personality. And such personalities do far more harm to themselves than encourage a scarcity of friends and high blood pressure. Such people are in deep Spiritual trouble. Nothing is more plainly not a part of love—not a part of the fruit of the Spirit—than quick temperedness; the short fuse, the acid tongue, the angry glare: these were never products of love.

Bible Psychology

But to get back to the point: we do need to express and release the anger in our lives. It's evident that longsuffering is slow anger, and not the total absence of it. That is not to say that when something angers us we spend our time fretting and fuming underneath, slowly coming to the boil. We don't want to be like the man who slowly counts to ten and then socks the other fellow on the jaw! It's not the postponement of anger we seek, but the resolution of it. It's not the denial or suppression of anger that we seek, but the healthy expression or dissipation of it.

Regarding anger, the Bible and modern psychology are in general agreement. In fact, there are many points of agreement between the Bible and today's psychology. It shouldn't really surprise us that the professors who study the workings of the human mind sometimes come to the same conclusions as the God who created the mind. It would be the more astonishing if the two didn't agree sometimes. Believers should not shy away from psychology, as if it were the next best thing to witchcraft!—but treat it as they would any branch of science, taking from it the good and helpful, and rejecting the bad and unhelpful.

It should also be borne in mind that before the *science* of psychology came along (not that long ago), psychology was the province of the church. *Psyche* is a Greek word familiar to Bible students which means *soul*. Psychology is literally the study of the soul. Helping troubled souls was traditionally the church's business. The recent hi-jacking of psychology by science should neither make us suspicious of *all* 'soul-study', nor make us forget that it is *still* the province of the church.

The advent of the Christian psychologist is a fairly recent phenomenon, but not unexpected as some branches of psychology move ever closer to the wisdom of Scripture. Much of the work of Christian counsellors is based on the findings of Christian psychologists, and carried out by them. And it's good to see that the psychology, in this case, has become Bible-based, drawing its conclusions from the Bible, rather than attempting to fit Bible data to existing psychological dogma. Bible statements, such as "A merry heart doeth good like a medicine" (Prov.17:22) and "as [a man] thinketh in his heart, so is he" (Prov.23:7), are good, sound psychology, telling us of the effect of attitude upon health and life generally. Some psychologists are, in fact, discovering the proofs for these Bible truths through their own observations. And *so can we*, through our own experience! Some might say it's just good common sense that how we think and feel affects how we are. But, as the saying goes, "common sense isn't so common." Common sense is usually the label we attach to self-evident truths after someone has pointed them out to us. The Scriptures abound with such truths.

Let's now have a look at some Biblical 'common sense' about anger.

"A fool gives full vent to his anger, but a wise man quietly holds back" (Prov.29:11 RSV).

"Be ye angry, and sin not: let not the sun go down upon your wrath" (Eph.4:26).

"Be ... slow to wrath: For the wrath of man worketh not the righteousness of God" (Jas.1:19,20).

Looking at those verses we can see that the Bible doesn't mince words over what we are if we allow anger its full reign. We are fools! The idea that it is better to let off steam and not bottle up anger is not supported here. It's not an excuse for inexcusable behaviour, which is how the idea of letting off steam is usually put forward. However justified we may feel, a fit of explosive temper is not the Bible's answer. A literal translation of the second part of Prov.29:11 is "but a wise man calms it back." Anger is like a beast that wants to run amok, pawing the earth and snorting, and that needs restraining and calming by its owner. The wise man holds on and calms it back. How does he do that? We'll come to that in a moment.

One of the easiest things to do when angry is to sin: to attack another person verbally or even physically, or to think hateful thoughts about them and start a grudge festering away inside us. We might even say that we **couldn't** help our response, or the way we feel. Which just isn't true. We do have a choice about how we act and feel. Much as we might believe we're out of control, to vent our anger unacceptably is a choice we make, and a habit we get into. It is not something we are forced to do. There is a better way. Which we'll come to in a moment.

The sun should not go down on our wrath. That's the greatest piece of advice we'll ever find anywhere on the subject of anger.. Wouldn't it be great if we never let our anger last for more than a day! That whatever bad thing happened to us, we let it go before we put our head on the pillow! There would be no carry-over anger, no simmering hatred, no build-up of suppressed anger working its way to the surface one day as free-floating guilt, or neurosis, or physical illness. Letting go of anger quickly is an important step on the road to Spiritual, emotional and physical health. But how do we manage it? We'll come to that in just a moment.

In the third of the above quotations, James tells us that we need to be longsuffering because "the wrath of man worketh not the righteousness of God." And it's rather important that we **do** achieve something of the righteousness of God, isn't it? Because, if you remember, it should be one of the primary concerns of us believers that we *"seek first the Kingdom of God **and His righteousness."*** When we do this we don't have to worry about all the necessities of life, because these things will be added to us (Matt. 6:33), as we discussed in Chapter One. But if we're allowing ourselves to vent our anger destructively (souring relationships or breaking noses!) or letting anger become chronic (the festering grudge), then we can forget all about the righteousness of God in our lives, and consequently any ideas we may have of God looking after our necessities.

The lack of just this one element of the fruit of the Spirit—longsuffering—can have that big a negative impact on our lives! But don't let that frighten you; let it motivate you. Fear is best used as fuel for motivation. The same can also be said of anger in some of its forms. If we can get worked up about something, we might be motivated enough to do something about it. So there is a positive side to anger. It's positively helpful at times! So long as we *use* anger and are not used by it. In general, though, our anger needs to be dealt with effectively by letting it go, calming the beast back. There is a simple Bible remedy for anger that really works, and is a pleasure to use when we get the hang of it. But we'll put off talking about that for just a little longer, until we have thought about the root cause of anger.

Anger is a response to loss

What causes anger? If you think about it, I'm sure you'll have to agree that it always involves some sort of **loss.** Try these examples:

1. LOSS of basic needs/security (anger at injustice)
2. LOSS of possessions by theft
3. LOSS of possessions by carelessness
4. LOSS of possessions by foolishness
5. LOSS of health
6. LOSS of a loved one
7. LOSS of a relationship
8. LOSS of a pleasure
9. LOSS of self-respect (mistreatment from others)
10. LOSS of self-respect (through sin)

Anger seems always to be a response to loss. We want to hit back somehow at something or someone - and sometimes even at God, though we might not be aware that's how we really feel, or want to express it quite so directly.

The first time the word *anger* appears in Scripture is when Esau was furious with his brother Jacob over the loss of his birthright (Gen.27:45). Esau's anger certainly wasn't achieving the righteousness of God for him! He felt cheated at his loss of family possessions and honour (probably in that order, too), and his only thought was for revenge. Many suns went down on his wrath.

The first time the word *wrath* occurs in Scripture (AV) is Genesis 4:5,6, and it's another brother problem! This time it is Cain who is angry with Abel. Cain lost his acceptability before God because he presented the wrong offering to Him. Cain wanted to do things his own way, and he vented his anger at being rejected on his brother who had done the right thing. That's one of the perverse things about anger, isn't it?—that we sometimes direct it not at the supposed offender, but at an innocent bystander, especially if the offender is big and powerful. Or we resent the man who did it properly when we fouled it up! There's the fellow who has had a bad day at the office. His real grievance is with the boss, but he arrives home to bark at the kids. And when things are going badly for us we can begin to feel annoyance towards those who are doing well and whose lives seem to be running much more smoothly (though they're probably not!).

If you look again at the above list of things we can lose that might lead to anger, you may recognize that each of the items on this list is also on the list we gave in Chapter One, on the very first page of that chapter. I didn't contrive this. I realised what was happening part way through composing the new list. That earlier list, you may recall, showed us ten items which add up to, in many people's minds, a satisfying and fulfilling life. It was mentioned there that we don't actually have to concentrate on acquiring those things—in fact, it's better that we don't do that. All we need to do is focus on our Spiritual life, and all that is necessary for us will come our way. But in order to test our Spiritual muscle we are tested through the lack (or loss!) of one or more of these items. Now, when that happens, *and it will*, the most *in*appropriate reaction we can have is anger. And yet anger is the most likely response!

The inescapable conclusion I draw from this is that whenever a believer gets angry, he or she is actually getting angry at what God is doing in their lives! They get angry at some particular circumstance in their lives (usually a loss of some kind) which God has brought to them. Anger is therefore a criticism of God. It may be indirect—we may say we're angry with a certain person who let us down or was rude to us—but it is still a criticism of the One who engineers all things to work together for good in our lives. The idea is that we should **praise** God, not criticise Him!

The gourds of life

Remember the story of Jonah? He got angry about going to preach to the people of Nineveh. He didn't want to go and preach to them because his own people of Israel saw the people of Nineveh as a threat. The Israelites would have been pleased if God were to destroy Nineveh for its wickedness. The thought of a prophet going to turn them from their wicked ways and bring the blessings of God upon them would not appeal to a man of Israel. It certainly didn't appeal to poor Jonah as the prophet chosen for the job! He would be seen as a traitor by his fellow countrymen, fraternising with the enemy. So he took a boat going somewhere else instead of Nineveh, and God had to put him back on course by having him unceremoniously dumped overboard and swallowed by a huge fish. The fish deposited him on the sea-shore, and the reluctant prophet got on with what he now saw as the inevitable task of preaching to the people. And, woe upon woe! the people of Nineveh took notice of him and repented in their thousands! His worst fears had come true.

> "It displeased Jonah exceedingly, and he was very angry" (Jonah 4:1).

The Hebrew is quite strong there in the original. Jonah even asked for his life to be taken from him, fearing he no

longer had a place among his fellow Israelites. For him to be
the cause of great blessings upon Nineveh was unthinkable.

"Then said the Lord, Doest thou well to be
angry?" (Jonah 4:4).

There's no recorded answer from Jonah. Instead it says he
went out of the city into the desert to sulk. These people in the
Bible are so real, aren't they? They are real people for certain
when they get the hump and go off on their own to sulk!

And God caused a huge, leafy plant to grow up and shade
Jonah from the hot sun, and Jonah was glad of it. Let's just stop
at this point to note how longsuffering God is in all of this. We
hear sometimes that the God of the Old Testament appears to
be an angry and vengeful God, quite unlike the God of the
New Testament. Some people almost think of them as two
different Gods. But no, it is the same God of love all the way
through the Scriptures. It's the Old Testament which first
reveals God to be slow to anger, and that slowness is certainly
evident here in His dealings with Jonah.

But then God sent a huge worm-like creature to eat up the
leafy plant, so it withered and died, and Jonah lost his
sunshade. More than this, God made it extra hot and
uncomfortable the next day! So Jonah was angry again because
his shady gourd had died. It was then that God put the same
question to him again: "Doest thou well to be angry...?" (Jonah
4:9).

God had given Jonah the shade of that plant to enable him
to sit in some comfort to consider his situation, to reflect upon
his anger and come to his senses. That gourd was a visible
evidence of God's providential care of Jonah. If only Jonah
could recognize *that,* he would see that he really had nothing to
be so worked up about. Why should he fear for his life when
the providence of God was so obviously working for him? He
would have been better occupied rejoicing in the salvation of
Nineveh rather than stewing in his own misery.

There is a parallel in the story of Jonah for all
believers. Jonah unwittingly acted out a little parable for

all those believers who ever get angry (and who does that leave out?). We all experience the gourds of life that God produces for our shelter and which make life reasonably comfortable for us. We have to appreciate that these things are from God. Be thankful for them and don't take them for granted. When we know for certain that all we have is from God we shouldn't worry; we can trust Him to look after us. We don't need to fret and fume like Jonah. If we choose to go through life anxious about the future, we are doubting God's future care for us, and we are doubting God's present care.

If we truly believe that God controls all we have, we have no worries about the loss of anything because it's all in His hands. God can send along a 'worm' at any time He chooses to gobble up the sheltering gourds in our lives. And He may not only remove the shelter from us, He may also make the day a lot hotter than it was before! Not because He is cruel and likes to see us sweating and struggling, but because He has our best interests at heart. He wants us to learn to trust Him. If we haven't yet learned to rely on God in our day-to-day lives, if we haven't yet taken on board the reality that "all things work together for good" for believers, then God will bring something into our lives that will be designed to wake us up to that reality. I doubt, though, that many of us will see it as God *bringing something into* our lives; it will seem more likely that He's taking something out! It will be the loss of something. And if we're not careful we will be angry at that loss. Do we do well to be angry? Of course not. "The wrath of man worketh not the righteousness of God." God is trying to instill His righteousness into us when He tests us, and our anger will stand in the way of that righteousness. We do well to be slow to anger—longsuffering—in order that we might, over time, soften the anger and learn to trust God. How do we do that? The time has come to reveal the amazingly ordinary answer.

The answer is simple

What is the secret, then, of de-fusing anger? What is it that lies at the heart of longsuffering, **and makes it possible?** It's very simple really. It's one of the most basic elements of Christian love. It works to allay all kinds of anger, from the sudden burst, to the long-running seethe, to the hidden angers that knot us up inside when we're not even aware what's really 'bugging' us. Someone once wisely said,

> ### TO FORGIVE IS TO SET A PRISONER FREE AND DISCOVER THE PRISONER WAS YOU.

The answer to all anger, and thus the secret of longsuffering, is quite simply the act of forgiveness. Okay, we all knew that, it's Christian ABC! **But how well do we know it, and how well do we do it?**

Forgiveness is so easy. Anyone can do it. There's absolutely nothing to it. Is there? If only it really were that simple. If only we all understood it and practised it as well as we think we do! And for the sake of our own emotional, and even physical well-being, it is essential that we do. Though, primarily, we don't forgive for emotional and physical reasons, we do it for our spiritual health. The emotional and physical advantages are a spin-off from focusing on the spiritual. Which is always the case. When we address the *"one thing"* which is needful, other benefits will follow.

It does us more harm than others when we don't forgive them. Firstly, it puts our relationship with God in jeopardy. For, "If ye forgive not men their trespasses, neither will your Father forgive your trespasses" (Matt.6:15). Nothing could be more serious than that. To be unforgiving is to throw away the Kingdom! Make no mistake about it.

Secondly, not forgiving others causes a sort of emotional blockage that puts tensions inside us that can have physical repercussions. Psychologists have learned that deep emotional problems which began even way back in childhood and youth can be dealt with by an act of forgiveness. Emotional disturbances later in life have been traced to underlying and often unacknowledged anger at a parent, or teacher, or brother, or sister, or some other authority figure in our lives who either wilfully or unintentionally mistreated us. The anger of unforgiveness simmers away over the years. And the best way to resolve it? Forgiveness, plain and simple. Not necessarily going to the one, or ones, who made you angry because of their treatment of you, because they may not even be alive or accessible now, but bringing them to mind and what you believe they did, and from the heart freely and honestly forgiving them. When you don't know what's knotting you up, when it's a case of free-floating anxiety, I suggest you delve back and you may well find the emotional blockages and physical tensions of unforgiveness.

Forgive everyone, everything. Hold nothing against anyone. Even if *they* won't forgive you, even if they go on being unpleasant to you - forgive them. Let it go! "Love your enemies, bless them that curse you, do good to them that hate you, and pray for them which despitefully use you, and persecute you; That ye may be the children of your Father which is in heaven..." (Matt.5:44,45). Be longsuffering like God. Turn every occasion for anger into an opportunity for forgiveness.

Forgiveness needs practice. Like all the things that don't come naturally to us, forgiveness needs to be worked on until it becomes a habit. The man who flares up at almost every opportunity and claims he can't help it, and tells you, "That's the way I am," is really telling you *that's the habit he's gotten into.* It took years of practice to get like that, the nurturing of lots of grudges and the labour of building a sizeable chip on his shoulder. He's spent a lot of time getting like that, reacting badly to the slings and arrows of life. It didn't just happen overnight. But it's still a choice to *stay* like that, whatever he might believe. All it requires is the acquiring of a new habit.

The more we practise forgiveness in our lives the better we get at it. It starts in the small everyday things like mentally forgiving the person who pushed in front of you in the queue instead of fuming and wanting to give him a piece of your mind. You just let it go, calm it back, take the opportunity to practise forgiving. Let forgiveness be a way of life for you in all things, however small or great. Then you will have learned to express (not hide and suppress) and resolve your anger in a positive and healthy way. Looking right back over your life from your earliest memories to now, do you have **anything** against **anyone**, any hints or lumps of bad feeling towards them? However small, however large, be it friend or enemy, neighbour or work-fellow, family or acquaintance—**FORGIVE THEM**. Set yourself free from the bondage of anger and unforgiveness. It's your prison, not theirs.

'Forgiving' God

There is even a kind of forgiveness that we can direct towards God. We can get angry with God, even if we dare not admit that's how we feel. Our anger at circumstances, as I've said, is really indirect anger at God who brings about our circumstances. We may feel that living as a Christian makes unreasonable demands on us—that, in fact, *God* makes unreasonable demands on us. So we can't cope and it's God's fault. Though we may shrink from saying it like that. Jonah's anger was this sort of anger, which is perhaps why he never responded to God's questioning about it. If we ever sense that that form of anger is part of our lives, then we need to start looking at our lives from a broader point of view—*God's* point of view. Putting ourselves in another's shoes always makes forgiveness easier. In many cases it will make us realize (certainly in the case of anger towards God) that there really was nothing to forgive. We have simply misjudged the situation, failed to see the whole picture. In truth it is we who are responding wrongly and not the other person who is acting wrongly. God wants our total trust in Him, and sometimes He will make us very vulnerable (as

Jonah in the unshaded heat) in order to get us to that place. It is not ours to be angry (unforgiving) but to learn the lesson of trust—to learn the reality of God's care rather than continue, oblivious and heedless, to our own eventual destruction. We do *not* do well to be angry at God.

Forgiving yourself

Probably the most difficult form of forgiveness we ever have to practise is the forgiveness of ourselves. We have to realize that the anger we sometimes direct towards ourselves is no less bad than the anger directed towards others. We seem to think that we *own* ourselves and therefore can mistreat ourselves as much as we like. We're not hurting anyone else, so that's all right. Not so. We were bought with a price, remember, when we became followers of Christ, and for that reason we ought to matter to ourselves. Added to this there is the matter of loving our neighbour **as we love ourselves.** The Scriptures assume that we will have a certain healthy regard for ourselves, and that is not wrong.

The very essence of love is that we love our neighbour as ourselves (Matt.19:19). It has often been said (by me certainly) that if some of us loved our neighbours as we loved ourselves, they'd be in for a hard time! How many of us, I wonder, have prayed for forgiveness for a sin and yet have not **felt** forgiven afterwards, though we sincerely sought it. Is it because God hasn't forgiven us? Of course it isn't. Where does God tell us in His Word that He won't forgive us when we ask Him in all sincerity? Where does He tell us of the limitations on His forgiveness in such circumstances?—"No. You've done this before a few times and I forgave you then, now this is too much." If you don't feel forgiven even when you've pleaded for it with your whole heart, then it's possible, not only that you don't fully believe in the willingness of God to forgive you, but also that you haven't forgiven yourself. You're still angry at yourself. You see your "perfect" image of yourself forever tainted by failures, and think you are no good. You can't forgive yourself.

But are we greater than God that we cannot bring ourselves to do what He is willing to do? We really must be *longsuffering* towards ourselves - especially if we hope to have any success in being longsuffering towards others. If we're over-critical and chronically angry with ourselves, we're not going to project an entirely different attitude towards our neighbours. At least we won't be able to keep it up. As time goes by, the strain shows, and we eventually appear in our true, bitter colours. As the Word says: "As a man thinketh in his heart, so is he."

Go easy on yourself, or you'll find it impossible to go easy on others. **You cannot give away what you don't have yourself.** You may put on a good show of loving your neighbour while hating yourself, but you're building up a big weight of emotional and physical problems for yourself, and one day the dam may burst—inevitably, I would say.

The trouble is that certain verses of Scripture tend to feed our self-condemnation. Probably because we're over-sensitive when we read them. I would say that most, if not all such verses are not intended for the repentant and conscience-stricken individual, but for the proud and hard-hearted. They don't apply in your case! Or, sometimes, we quite simply misunderstand what is written. Take 1 John 3:20 for example:

"For if our heart condemn us, God is greater than our heart, and knoweth all   things."

The next time you read those words don't say to yourself, "Oh no! If my heart condemns me, God is greater than my heart so He condemns me even more: He knows everything, so He knows more than I do how bad I am!" Say to yourself, rather, "If my heart condemns me, God is **greater-hearted** than I am. He takes all things into account." That's what it really means. Have a look at some alternative translations and you'll see what I mean. We sometimes *forget* that God is love. He is *agape,* and has the fruit of the Spirit in no small measure. He is more longsuffering than you might imagine.

We're often wrongly hard on ourselves, and wrongly imagine God to be even harder. That isn't to say He takes a soft line on our failings, but it *is* to say that He lends a more ready ear to our confessions of those failings than our over-sensitive consciences sometimes allow. What are we trying to tell ourselves anyway?—that by being harder on ourselves than is necessary, by being afraid to accept the forgiveness of God and to enjoy a clear conscience, we stand more chance of entering the Kingdom of God? Do we believe that God is actually going to be pleased with us for doubting Him and blighting our own lives in the process! This 'hair shirt' mentality must surely be abhorrent to the God of love.

We will never have the fruit of the Spirit all the while we fail to be longsuffering and forgiving towards ourselves. Fail to be longsuffering to yourself and you will fail towards others. Fail to be longsuffering towards yourself and you will fail at joy and peace also. All the parts of the fruit overlap and interlink, as you may have noticed from what's been said so far. To borrow some words from the side of the jigsaw puzzle box: they are *fully interlocking*. The lack of one part of the fruit will generally mean shortages in other areas. Towards the end of the book we'll look at how all the parts of the fruit combine to make the complete and wonderful, truly Christian (Christ-like) character. The puzzle of how to live the Christian life will be solved. At least in theory. The practice is up to us.

CHAPTER TEN

GENTLENESS *(chrestotes)*

C*HRESTOTES,* the Greek word for gentleness in Galatians 5:22, is more often translated *kindness* in the AV New Testament, and we will better understand this fifth aspect of love if we think of it as *kindness.* (*Gentleness* is a word best applied to aspect seven which appears as *meekness.*)

So it is kindness that we are going to look at now. It seems such a *petty* thing, doesn't it? and yet it holds equal rank with joy, peace, and all the other elements that go to make up the character of a believer. But kindness seems so low-key, so ordinary, that it hardly merits a mention. It's just, well... er... kindness, that's all. So maybe there's more to it than we think.

What *do* we think of as kindness? We probably think of it as an act. We may think of an act of kindness like the "cup of cold water" that should be offered to a thirsty disciple, according to Christ (Matt.10:42). It represents the least we could do for another believer. So again we notice how insignificant the act appears—merely a cup of cold water—re-confirming our notions of the smallness of kindness. Kindness seems like just the little everyday things that anyone would do for anyone. Certainly there is that form of kindness, which is a kindness forced upon us by the constraints of society. We are all generally *nice* to one another, because that's what's expected of us. It's a civilised way to behave. If we want to keep our friends, our jobs, our families, and keep our lives running reasonably smoothly, there is a certain acceptable level of kindness at which we must operate. When we fall below that level we are thought rude and unfriendly. We're made to feel guilty and we can get a rough ride from others.

Basically, most of us are kind because we like to be liked. We don't like to be thought of badly. That, I believe, is the motive behind most of the kindness that passes between people. It's purely a social kindness. And that's why we think of kindness as such a small thing. We equate it with everyday niceness, which we sense is more often engaged in for convenience than because people care! So, how can such an everyday ploy for getting on with people be raised to the lofty heights of being part of the fruit of the Spirit! Surely social kindness *isn't* part of the fruit?

Don't get me wrong. I don't mean to sound cynical and dismissive about social kindness. It's really not that bad. It serves a useful purpose in the present human condition, keeping people from one another's throats. It is much to be preferred to social *un*kindness. Imagine *that* being the norm!

But it must be obvious by now that the kindness Paul mentions as part of the fruit of the Spirit has to be something different from mere social kindness. It has to be something a lot better. And, indeed, it is.

As I said, we tend to think of kindness as an act, like proffering the cup of cold water. But we have to remember that the fruit of the Spirit is essentially about **being** rather than **doing**, and the proffered cup of water (or whatever simple deed that may represent) is an act. What concerns us more is the quality of mind that would cause us to proffer the cold water in the first place—the internal quality of kindness, not the outward manifestation of it. Because it is possible to proffer the cup and yet not have the right quality of mind. The deed need not spring from kindness at all.

If we perform an act of kindness with gritted teeth because we really don't want to, or don't have enough time to, or would rather be doing something else far more interesting, then we're not engaging in an act of true kindness. We are doing what we feel we must do, because at that moment we can't get out of it. That's not at all how we'd expect the fruit of the Spirit to affect us, is it? I cannot believe that Christ will be patting anyone on the back for offering "a cup of cold water" in that spirit.

Unfortunately some (maybe even a lot) of what passes for Christian kindness is of this order. A perfunctory kindness, no better than social kindness. A kindness carried out through a sense of obligation rather than as the natural product of a kind heart. Or maybe just good old social kindness, wanting to be liked. *Chrestotes* (mostly translated kindness), and the related word *chrestos* are only ever used in Scripture to describe a **genuine kindness of heart**, of the sort that mirrors the kindness of God Himself (Luke 6:35) and of Christ (1 Pet.2:3).

More than half of the uses of *chrestotes* and *chrestos* in the A.V. New Testament are references to the kindness of God.

"the riches of his goodness."	Rom 2:4
"the goodness and severity of God."	Rom 11:22
"if thou continue in his goodness."	Rom 11:22
"the riches of his grace in his kindness"	Eph 2:7
"the kindness and love of God."	Titus 3:4
"the goodness of God leadeth thee to repentance."	
	Rom 2:4
"He is kind to the unthankful."	Luke 6:35
"Be ye kind...tenderhearted...forgiving... as God."	
	Eph. 4:32

The verse among these which best conveys the nature of the kindness of God is Ephesians 2:7. Here it is together with the following two verses from that chapter.

"That in the ages to come he might show the exceeding riches of his grace in his kindness toward us in Christ Jesus. For by grace you have been saved through faith, and that not of yourselves; it is the gift of God, not of works, lest anyone should boast" (Eph. 2:7-9 RAV).

God's kindness is shown here to be inextricably bound together with the "exceeding riches of his grace."

His kindness is one of the ways—I would suggest the *principal* way—that God shows us His grace. This being the case, we're going to take a short excursion into the meaning of grace.

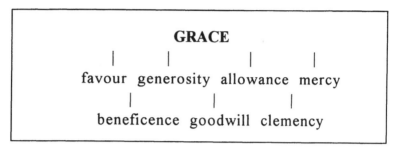

GRACE

favour generosity allowance mercy

beneficence goodwill clemency

Grace has a number of synonyms, all of which help to define it, and all of which carry some flavour of God's kindness towards us. Of them all I must say I prefer *allowance*. That God makes *allowance* for us sums it up perfectly for me. God sees and knows exactly what we are, and knows just what we are personally and collectively capable of. He is fully aware that we are insufficient of ourselves, and that by His standards we are suited for somewhat less than immortal glory. But though He might quite justifiably extinguish us for our spiritual ineptness, He bears with us. Though He could easily remove the unthankful and the evil at a stroke, He bears with them! He is actually kind to them, said Jesus (Luke 6:35). I recall a business colleague of mine saying that if he were ever called upon to defend the human race before God, to give some good reasons why it should not be annihilated, he would have no defence to offer. We were weighed in the balances and found wanting as far as he could tell. It's not difficult to understand what he felt, and from that standpoint to marvel at the kindness and mercy of God for giving houseroom to this sin-infested little corner of His universe!

God tells us that He is "angry with the wicked every day" (Psalm 7.11). **But He bears with us. He makes**

allowance. We are not destroyed. Neither are we looked down upon from some cloud-decked Olympian height and rebuked out of hand, or barely tolerated for our sin-prone behaviour. We are *loved* and we are *understood*. And grace contains that idea of being understood, too, doesn't it? Allowance is made for us, and we are understood. "For he knoweth our frame; he remembereth that we are dust" said the Psalmist (Psalm 103:14). And that doesn't mean God bears with us only because He knows our bodies are rather feeble dust-machines in comparison with His. The word the Psalmist used for *frame* is actually a Hebrew word that means *imagination* or *thought*. It's so easy to miss the point of this verse, which is that God is telling us He knows the way we *think*—**He understands us**—and therefore He makes allowance for us. He knows the way we frame our thoughts.

Jesus is shown to be the same in this respect. We are told that Jesus "needed not that any should testify of man: for he knew what was in man." (John 2:25). There are many references to his knowing the precise thoughts of the people around him. That was while he was on earth, but the same is true, and more so, of Christ now he is in heaven in the role of High Priest. As High Priest he is someone who is touched "with the feeling of our infirmities", we are told (Heb.4:15). We have a High Priest through whom we can approach God in prayer with confidence. That fourth chapter of Hebrews concludes: "Let us therefore come boldly unto the throne of grace, that we may obtain mercy, and find grace to help in time of need." There can be few more encouraging words in the whole English language! How approachable God is shown to be here. Going before the throne of a great king would normally be done to the accompaniment of knocking knees and much hand wringing, especially if we're seeking a pardon for some wrong committed against the One who sits on that high and powerful seat of authority. But that simple, elegant phrase, *the throne of grace*, changes the whole picture, and takes away all the worry. We go boldly!

The Spirit encourages us to go boldly before the throne of grace in the sure knowledge that we will not be dealt with unsympathetically, but mercifully and with great sympathy. Grace will be expressed in His kindness toward us. Allowance will be made for us.

Manifold grace

God shows His grace in so many different ways. In fact, Peter made mention in his first letter of "the **manifold** grace of God" (1 Pet. 4:10). Manifold means numerous and various, of diverse kinds. Those of you who are inclined to look under motor car bonnets will know that an important part of the engine is called the manifold. This little device delivers a mixture of petrol and air to the cylinders. It sends out the mixture in various directions to however many cylinders the engine has.

God's grace toward us is expressed in many ways. It is varied because we believers vary in our need for His grace. Helpfully, Peter uses that word *manifold* twice in his first letter, and each use explains the other. On the first occasion he refers to his readers as being "in heaviness through manifold temptations" because they were going through a particular time of trial (1 Pet.1:6). The trials to their faith were many and various—manifold. The second time Peter uses the word is to talk of "the manifold grace of God". Do you see how the two references complement one another? The manifold temptations are met by a manifold grace. We all face varying problems of varying intensity in our probationary walk, but the manifold grace of God is there to meet them all. That's what Peter is saying. God understands us each in our differing needs, and His judgement of us takes everything into account, especially our weaknesses. He knows "our frame", remember.

I found over thirty aspects of the grace of God mentioned in the New Testament, of which the following is a selection:

> Kindness	Eph 2:7
> Power	Acts 4:33
> Justification	Rom.3:24
> Election	Rom.11:5
> Knowledge	1 Cor.1:4,5
> Revelation	Eph.3:2,3
> Edification	Eph.4:29
> Speaking kindly	Col.4:6
> Consolation	2 Thess.2:16
> Good hope	2 Thess.2:16
> Help	Heb.4:16

His grace is truly numerous and various, as is the kindness through which He expresses it. And surely that particular expression of His grace "in his kindness to us in Christ Jesus" is the one that stands out above all the rest. The allowance God makes for us because of Jesus is the greatest kindness anyone will ever do us. And that kindness is a part of the *agape* of God. The same kindness is to be found in all true believers as part of the fruit of the Spirit. It may not be fully formed as yet, but it will be slowly and surely developing in their hearts as they delight and meditate in the Word of the Spirit. I seriously doubt whether any of the aspects of the fruit can be *fully* developed by anyone before Christ comes. Perfection is not for the likes of you and me right now. But it *is* within our capabilities to be always advancing, however slowly, towards perfection; learning the lessons that life hands us (or, rather that *God* hands us), so that even apparent setbacks are transformed into moves forward. Christ will then be happy to give us the perfection we long for. Our present state will always be one of hungering and thirsting after righteousness and never being fully satisfied. But, as Christ said in the fourth Beatitude (Matt.5:6), "Blessed are they which do hunger and thirst after righteousness: for they shall be filled." It will come, if only we can keep moving, however painfully slowly, towards it.

A little sympathy for the human condition

Having spent a little time considering the kindness of God, now it's time to turn the spotlight on ourselves. Having seen some of the principles at work in God's kindness, we now have an idea of what to expect from ourselves.

If our reading of the Bible is having the right effect on us—if it is developing the fruit of the Spirit—we should be developing a greater sympathy for people. That is how our kindness will manifest itself. We will find ourselves making more allowance for people, understanding them more. We will direct the same grace towards others as God directs towards us. The example set by the Father and the Son shows us the way to true kindness. Reading in the Bible about the sad reality of the cursed human condition should help us to feel genuinely sympathetic to all our fellow creatures on this earth. For man, even at his very best state, "is altogether vanity," "a vapour" (RAV), says the Psalmist (Ps.39:5). He has no substance and walks the earth like a shadow. His life is emptiness and loneliness which he must by all means disguise from himself, blot out from his mind.

Shakespeare's lines from *Macbeth* come to mind:

"Life's but a walking shadow, a poor player / That struts and frets his hour upon the stage / And then is heard no more: It is a tale / Told by an idiot, full of sound and fury, / Signifying nothing."

We all know something of this from personal experience. No one can be wholly immune to the occasional intrusion of thoughts on the futility of life. But for believers the burden of this experience is greatly lightened by the kindness of the One who has shown us how to put substance into these lives of shadow. We can live lives of purpose and fruitfulness, and we're hugely grateful for that.

Most people are not living the truth; they are living a lie. In order to make this shadow-life more tolerable they have to convince themselves that life outside God's truth really does have purpose. They may tell themselves they are bound for eternal bliss at death, even believing that the God of the Bible promises it; though not many will check it thoroughly for themselves. Or they may believe the depressing lie that this short life is all that's on offer so they'd better make the most of it (though most of them don't seem to, I've noticed). Others believe they are in a cycle of death and rebirth. All of these deceptions are designed to create some meaning from the otherwise meaningless. Those who choose them are lost souls. The overwhelming majority of them *will* not be helped. Many of them will lose themselves in all manner of diversions because they so desperately need to prevent themselves from facing the reality of the nothing they possess, and which will eventually possess them.

This sad scenario should not evoke the believer's contempt (or, worse still, superiority); it should evoke his compassion. The secret of genuine kindness lies in having true sympathy for others, which can only come from knowing and appreciating what others may be going through. It can only come from knowing and appreciating the needs of other people— how they 'tick'—and from treating people in a way that shows you believe they matter. Kindness is not being patronising and condescending; it is empathising with people.

Kindness begins at home

Kindness, like charity, begins at home: meaning that it should find its fullest and best expression among fellow believers. It is inevitable and right that believers should feel more strongly towards their fellows than they do to non-believers. The explanation for it is simple. Both God and

Jesus are said to be in any believer who is doing his best to be Godlike and Christlike. It follows that if a believer's greatest love of all is toward God and Jesus, that love will be significantly greater toward those people who are Godlike and Christlike, namely other believers.

The Bible tells us to love our neighbours as ourselves, it even tells us to love our enemy, but where a believer's relationship with other believers is concerned, it goes one giant step beyond both of these: **"Let each esteem others better than himself"** (Phil.2:3 RAV). Esteeming others to be *better than* ourselves really brings kindness into play. It indicates the high level of grace we should direct towards others of the faith, the high level of allowance we are to make for them, the understanding we are to have for them.

How seriously do we take this matter of esteeming others better than ourselves? Is it something we practise?— or has it fallen into disuse among us? And has kindness fallen into disuse as a consequence? Exactly how do you and I put this promotion of others into practice? (Kindness is not something you can leave in the theory stage.) The big problem I'm sure all believers encounter is that it's so easy to be partial when it comes to esteeming others. Some people make it easy for us to admire them. Their good qualities are obvious. Other people? Well... they'd be all right *if only*—if only they were tidier... more punctual... less talkative... more considerate... less interfering, etc. What's happening here? Why the reservations that probably most of us feel towards a good number of people—fellow believers, no less! Can you honestly say, hand on heart, that you esteem all other believers above yourself? Is it something you've ever seriously practised? Or, when reading Philippians 2:3 have you always plunged into the next thought very quickly, not wanting to stop and dwell on the implications? Somehow verses 4, 5, and 6 seemed to be pressing for attention!

And incidentally, let's not get this *totally* wrong. I'm sure there are some who turn the idea completely on its head and make the verse say what it doesn't. There are some who read it not as "let each esteem others better than himself," but rather, "let each esteem himself [or herself] **worse than others.**" It is *not* reversible in this unhealthy fashion. We cannot use the verse to put the Divine seal of approval on our own inferiority feelings. That's not what it's telling us to do. There is a world of difference between seeing others as better than yourself and seeing yourself as worse than others. Seeing others better than yourself, you delight in their good qualities, but seeing yourself worse than others, you simply despair at the bad qualities of yourself. The spirit of the verse is that we exalt others, not depress ourselves. Exalting others actually works in a positive way upon yourself. We actually feel better about ourselves when we see the good in others. It has the effect of making others feel and act better towards us, which in turn makes us feel better. We get into an upward positive spiral rather than a downward negative one. As always, the Spirit knows best. Trust it.

So, to get back to it, how *do* we show kindness to our fellow believers? The answer is what I've been saying all along. By passing on the grace of God. By making allowance for others, treating them with sympathy and understanding. Whenever we *don't* esteem another as highly as we could, it's because we have failed to make allowance for them. We've done the very opposite, and homed in on the very things about that person that we *should* be making allowance for. We have failed to understand what makes them that way—what makes them 'tick'. We lack sympathy towards them and finish up being unkind. As a general rule our lack of kindness will make itself known in the way we talk to them, and about them. It's no accident that one of the key passages in which c*hrestos* appears concerns what we say.

> "Let no corrupt communication proceed out of your mouth, but that which is good to the use of edifying, that it may minister grace unto the

hearers... Let all bitterness, and wrath, and anger, and clamour, and evil speaking, be put away from you, with all malice: And be ye kind [*chrestos*] to one another, tenderhearted, forgiving one another, even as God for Christ's sake hath forgiven you" (Eph.4:29,31,32).

Being kind to one another is shown as the result of putting away all the bad uses of the tongue. Our mutual kindness, or lack of it, has a lot to do with what we say to and about one another. If you think about it, most of our dealings with one another are through language: most of what passes between us is verbal. So it is in *this* area that we can do the most good, or the most harm, to one another. And it's a first-class indicator of what's going on inside us, "for out of the abundance of the heart the mouth speaketh." (Matt.12:34). The kindness within us, or lack of it, will be known by what we project to others. Paul says that we should use our mouths to edify one another, that we "may minister grace unto the hearers." That's a lovely phrase, isn't it?—'ministering grace' by what we say to one another: making allowance for the other person when we speak. Not bulldozing our way through the conversation, shovelling aside anything they might feel or want to express. Not really listening when they talk, only waiting to get back in with our 'better-reasoned and far more interesting point of view'—which also happens to be the only right way of looking at it!

The old saying is a good one, that we were given two ears and one mouth and should use them in that ratio! The man or woman whose opinions override all others cannot be esteeming others better than themselves. They believe they are usually right and others usually wrong when they differ. (Of course, I'm not talking about first principles of Scripture here. We all have a right to argue the correctness of Scripture, without giving ground. But we do need to be sure that what we argue *is* a first principle, and we're not elevating something peripheral to a first principle in order to get our way!) When we esteem others highly we take notice of what they say. It must also be said that we don't abuse the fact that they in their turn should esteem *us* highly—which will most likely have the reverse effect! When you *truly* esteem others highly, you can't do other than speak kindly to and about them. Nobody said it was going to be easy.

Kindness can be very expensive!

There is a saying that goes *Kindness costs nothing*. But I'd argue strongly with that. I believe kindness can be very expensive. The saying is usually trotted out when someone has failed to be kind in some way, and the gossips are a-huffing and a-puffing and saying indignantly, "Well it wouldn't have hurt him to [do whatever it was]. Kindness costs nothing." Evidently the subject of this juicy piece of gossip felt that it would have cost him something or he'd have done it. Kindness does have a cost. Which is probably why we don't see too much of the genuine article. It can cost us our time. It can cost our energy. Our money. Our pride. Our safety. Our convenience.

But one of the many good things about all the elements of the fruit of the Spirit is that when we have them we are not overconcerned about the cost. As the spirit of kindness develops, it gets easier to apply it. All the parts of the fruit are like this. If we considered them long and hard before we started producing them, we might decide they were beyond reach. From the outside looking in, they can appear too difficult to produce. But in fact, they're very like the cold swimming pool, which takes some effort to get into, but the water's lovely once you're in. We don't count the cost of kindness once it has become an everyday part of our Christian character. Walking the extra mile, giving more than someone asks or expects, becomes second nature. And we're like that towards believers, neighbours, and enemies alike when kindness is part of our love.

What frightens some people about kindness, though, is that it can make them feel vulnerable. That's why I listed 'our safety' when I mentioned some of the things kindness can cost us. There is the worry that 'If I'm too kind, too giving, too helpful, too friendly, then people will take advantage of me.' Do you ever have that thought, and so you hold back?

I quoted from Shakespeare's *Macbeth* earlier, on the futility of life, but there's a line from that same play, about being overkind. In the play Lady Macbeth voices her opinion that her husband is "too full o' the milk of human kindness." She felt he had too much kindness for his own good. People would take advantage of him. If he lent someone something, he might not get it back. If he helped someone, they may not appreciate it; or worse still, they might lean too heavily upon his help and become too demanding. If you're too kind you can easily be fooled, because you're reckoned to be a 'soft touch.' "Don't worry, Muggins will do it," they may say behind your back. The answer, though, to any such misgivings is quite simple. All we need to do is leave it in God's hands. He leads us down this path of kindness. It is His will that we take this direction, so He won't abandon us along it to the whims of others. Once again we return to the theme of that most vital of requirements for a believer—trust in God. All the parts of the fruit of the Spirit demand our trust to some degree or other. Where kindness is concerned we may have to suffer ourselves to be defrauded (1 Cor.6:7) because of our generous nature. We may find that we're 'put upon' rather too much, but when what we have is the *genuine* fruit we are not greatly troubled. When such problems come we remember it's only God trying to strengthen our kindness-muscle by giving it a work-out. Like all muscles, it can be toned up with a little exercise. Never allow the milk of human kindness to go sour for you. It stays fresh if you keep drinking it and don't let it stand around unused!

Regarding that famous phrase from Shakespeare, I strongly suspect that the bard was making an oblique reference to Scripture. There's a passage of Peter's from his first letter from which I think Shakespeare took his idea of the milk of human kindness:

"As newborn babes, desire the sincere milk of the word, that ye may grow thereby. If so be that ye have tasted that the Lord is gracious [*chrestos*— kind]" (1 Pet.2:2,3).

In this verse the kindness of Jesus is said to be experienced by tasting the sincere milk of the Word. So it was Peter who first brought the ideas of milk and kindness together, not Shakespeare. Out of curiosity, I checked back to see whether the Bibles of Shakespeare's day (pre-1611 AV) actually translated *chrestos* as kind in 1 Peter 2:3, thus leading Shakespeare directly to his famous phrase. But the Geneva Bible (1599) gave *'bountiful'* and the Tyndale (1536) gave *'pleasant'*. It makes one wonder if Shakespeare's grasp of New Testament Greek was a match for Tyndale's!

Mind reading

Kindness will be almost second nature to us if we read the Word constantly with delight and meditation. We will taste the sincere milk of the Word, and know the kindness of Jesus. When we are fully citizens of the Kingdom of God, kindness will be manifest perfectly in us. We will be able to empathise fully with others, even as the Father and Son do now. They are able to read and know every thought and feeling. I believe that will be the case for all the immortals in the Kingdom. The barriers will be down. I shall "know even as also I am known." (1 Cor.13:12). And it won't be an intrusion to have our minds open to our brothers and sisters, and theirs to us; it will be the end of what philosophers have called existential loneliness—the loneliness of existence. We all suffer from it, because no matter how many friends we may have, how close we may get to them, in the last analysis we are each alone with ourselves, our own thoughts, inside our own head. Everyone else is out there, and we are alone.

One of the things I look forward to in the Kingdom of God is the end of existential loneliness. I look forward to having an open mind in this other sense. This is one of the things that has always interested me about the concept of a 'multitudinous Christ' at the time of the end—the unity of mind and purpose of Christ and the saints, which will continue throughout the Millennium. At the end of that thousand years the indications are that yet another and even more awesome barrier will come down: the barrier between the mind of man and the mind of God. It's already down, of course, from God's direction. Our minds are fully exposed to Him. But we are told that at the close of the Millennium God will "be all and in all". That cryptic phrase I take to mean that in some sense, at some level, there ceases to be a difference between us and God. It is toward that staggering finale that the development now of the fruit of the Spirit (the full *agape* of God) is leading us. It's a journey that makes everything else in this world seem rather bland by comparison. **There is no comparison!**

CHAPTER ELEVEN

GOODNESS: *(agathosune)*

GOODNESS is very like kindness. Both seem so unspectacular that they hardly merit devoting time and space to. They seem even the sort of qualities that truly spiritually dynamic believers would have left behind with the milk of the Word in spiritual Kindergarten. Kindness and goodness appear genteel and old hat to this thrusting and self-assured world. They are qualities seen as belonging only to gentle, elderly people who move slowly and smile a lot (not that I have anything against such people!). The young and newly middle-aged don't talk much of goodness. To call somebody 'good' is not to pay them the highest of compliments. They'll probably assume you think them such bland characters that 'good' is the best you can say about them!

I hope the last chapter dispelled some false notions about kindness. The purpose of this chapter is to do the same for goodness. Goodness isn't a bland, low-key characteristic—it's one of the most invaluable and dynamic forces we can have in our life. It's a quality which, probably more than any other, helps keep us on the straight and narrow. And, what's more, it adds sparkle to life!

Four appearances

The Greek for goodness in the New Testament is *agathosune*. The good news is, it appears only four times so we can indulge ourselves a little and look at each appearance of the word—something we weren't able to do for previous aspects of the fruit because the words appeared too many times. But, more good news, scarcity of appearances need not be a problem when it comes to determining the meaning behind a Bible word.

127

We'll take the appearances of *agathosune* in the order they come in Scripture. The first is Romans 15:14:

"And I myself [Paul] also am persuaded of you, my brethren, that ye also are full of goodness, filled with all knowledge, able also to admonish one another."

The verse doesn't give away a lot at first glance about the nature of goodness. But the clues are there. Paul mentions that his Roman brethren are "full of goodness." He had already praised them for their faith (Rom.1:8), which he said was "spoken of throughout the whole world"—by which I'm sure he meant the whole world of believers, not the entire population of the globe, many of whom would have been perfectly indifferent toward the faith of the Roman believers. Paul also praised them because their "obedience is come abroad unto all men" (Rom.16:19)—again I'm sure the word *all* is meant in a restrictive sense. Not everybody in the whole world knew of their obedience, but the Christian world did. And now in Rom.15:14 Paul credits his readers with being "*full* of goodness" and "having *all* knowledge" (italics added). Again the apostle applies superlatives to the Roman believers, and again we have to be careful about the superlatives. Just as their good qualities were not known and admired throughout the entire world, it's not likely we are meant to believe the Romans were completely full of goodness and knew *all* things. In fact, if they already knew all things, Paul was wasting good parchment and ink writing to them; and dear sister Phoebe, who is thought to have carried the letter to Rome, was wasting her time and energy taking it.

Absolutes rarely, if ever, apply to humans. Even Christ refused to be addressed as "Good Master" saying "there is none good but one, that is God" (Matt.19:16,17). Christ was there making it clear to someone who thought goodness could be earned by keeping the law, that in the final analysis only God was good. Human beings do not attain such perfection. Even Christ, Trinitarians should note, did not equate himself with God in absolute terms. God may choose to *impute* goodness on His own terms, but that's another matter; it's not inherent or earned goodness.

The Apostle Paul writes as he does in Romans 15:14, about *full* goodness and *all* knowledge, because he is winding up his remarks and giving his reasons for writing. He writes to the Romans not because they have full goodness or all knowledge in the impossible absolute sense, but because he is convinced they have sufficient goodness and knowledge to be able to comprehend and practise what he is telling them. Otherwise there was no point in writing. It's not that they were perfect in goodness and knowledge, but that they were perfectly able to know and effect what he was telling them. They had *enough* goodness and knowedge.. And what is ever more needful than enough? It's as good as a feast, as the saying goes. So it was in a sense 'full', and it was *all*, for Paul's purpose. With such goodness and knowledge they would be perfectly able to "admonish one another" from Paul's letter to them, and lead one another along the right road, away from the false doctrines and unChristlike practices Paul was warning them against.

If only

If only believers could always have enough goodness and knowledge when dealing with unchristian doctrines and unChristlike practices. The knowledge part is relatively easy to come by, but the goodness often needs working at. Sometimes, one feels, this precious aspect of the fruit of the Spirit is sadly lacking when it comes to the business of admonishing one another. Both the admonisher *and* the admonished can have a short-fall in the goodness department. The admonisher may wag the finger and take a haughty 'I know best' attitude, while the admonished smarts and takes up a defensive and rebellious stance, probably as a direct result of the attitude of the other person. And the two parties move ever further apart, adding reason upon reason for their differences. All for the lack of a little, simple goodness! Which is why I believe goodness is not so little or so simple. Before we comment further on the nature of goodness, let's look at the next two verses that include the word. First Galatians 5:22:

"But the fruit of the Spirit is love, joy, peace, longsuffering, gentleness, **goodness**, faith..."

A familiar verse! This is where we came in, isn't it? This is the verse which picks out goodness as a fruit of the Spirit, and in doing so alerts us to the fact that there must be more to this quality than we generally give it credit for. Goodness is one of the eight qualities which combine to produce love, and consequently combine to produce the whole, balanced, spiritual personality of a believer. And in the next of our four verses, the importance of goodness as an aspect of the fruit of the Spirit is highlighted.

"(For the fruit of the Spirit is in all goodness and righteousness and truth)" (Eph:5:9).

Here's a verse to pause over and ponder! If this were a Psalm, the word *Selah* would surely appear. It's actually a parenthesis, hence the brackets, and was never meant to stand on its own. We have to see it in its natural habitat of the surrounding narrative to appreciate what it means. It's an important and helpful aside on Paul's on-going argument.

In the previous chapter of Ephesians, chapter four, Paul lists all the good things we need to "put on" when we become a believer, and all the bad things we need to "put off." Becoming a believer gives the soul a change of clothing. Then in chapter five he changes the metaphor to a familiar one of light and darkness, day and night. He opens the chapter by telling us, "Be ye therefore followers of God, as dear children; And walk in **love,** as Christ also hath loved us..." Then he lists many of the evils of which we are all capable, and in the midst of making comparisons between our opposing good and bad inclinations, Paul says:

"For ye were sometimes darkness, but now are ye light in the Lord: walk as children of light: (For the fruit of the Spirit is in all goodness and righteousness and truth;) Proving what is acceptable unto the Lord. And have no fellowship with the **un**fruitful works of darkness, but rather reprove them" (Eph.5:8-11).

The Apostle was telling the Ephesian believers that their chief source of defence and strength against the unfruitful works of darkness was the fruit of the Spirit. And the only aspect of that fruit he mentions explicitly is goodness. (Though righteousness and truth are found in aspects of the fruit.) But what stands out the most to me in this narrative is the way in which **goodness works in "proving what is acceptable", and in reproving the "unfruitful works of darkness."** This proving and reproving is the effect of goodness. This is the important work it does, and why it is such an important part of the fruit of the Spirit. Do you see the link with the first verse we looked at from Romans 15, where we read of goodness supplying the ability to admonish one another?

It must be significant that the only two verses which show goodness in a context that could help us understand its nature, show it in relation to admonishing and reproving. What is that trying to tell us? It's telling us that *goodness* must be at the back of any reproving that goes on. It makes perfect sense, because only from the vantage-point of genuine goodness can any *acceptable* admonishing or reproving ever take place. Only those who have some goodness themselves can possibly reprove others for their shortcomings. Otherwise we have hypocrisy.

We'll come back to this all-important point about the nature and application of goodness in a moment, after we've looked at the last of our four references:

"Wherefore also we pray always for you, that our God would count you worthy of [this] calling, and fulfil all the good pleasure of [his] goodness, and the work of faith with power" (2 Thess.1:11).

This verse obviously caused the translators some problems. Although they put "his (God's) goodness" in the verse, there is some ambiguity in the original language over exactly *whose* goodness is meant—whether God's or the believers. Some other versions (NIV, NEB, Diaglott, Good News, Weymouth, for instance) impute the goodness to the believer rather than to God. *The Speaker's Commentary* cites four alternative renderings of the verse by different scholars. So the AV rendering is open to dispute. And I believe that in view of what we've discovered about goodness and its connection with reproof and admonishment (and in view of where that will lead us in a moment), it is doubtful that the goodness of God is meant here. It must be the believer's. When you read through 2 Thessalonians chapter one you find that the chapter is chiefly about the differences between those who "know not God" and who "obey not the gospel of our Lord", and who are consequently heading for destruction, and "all them that believe" (and who "stand fast"—2 Thess.2:15) who are heading for salvation.

It's quite evident that the believers of Paul's day were going through a time of much reproving, and proving what was acceptable, and much admonishing of one another in order to keep themselves from going the way of destruction. And only spiritual *goodness* would equip the true believers adequately to deal with the troublesome ones. So I suggest that the verse should be read as follows:

> "Wherefore also we pray always for you, that our God would count you worthy of calling and fulfil all the good pleasure [all the delight and desire] of [*your*] goodness and the work of faith [*yours* again, though unstated] with power."

In a nutshell: The fulfilment of their delight in goodness would be their salvation. I believe it's as simple as that.

But where is all this leading? What exactly *is* the quality of goodness? Are we any nearer to understanding another aspect of the fruit of the Spirit? Certainly.

Stating the obvious?

Maybe it sounds like stating the obvious, but: Goodness is that quality of character in a believer by which he or she is able to combat badness—evil. He or she can direct it towards other believers who are in error, using it to strengthen and validate the admonitions and reproofs. It's certainly not a quality which anyone can come by naturally, of themselves. We can only obtain it from the Spirit Word, which is what makes it a fruit of the Spirit. It can only come to us from the sort of familiarity with the Word that we gain from delighting and meditating in the Word. But let's not take away the idea that goodness is *only* a gladiatorial quality, to be marshalled as part of our weaponry against erring others—a sort of higher moral ground from which we can more easily pick off the enemy! True, as we've seen from the verses we've looked at, having goodness does give us credibility when trying to straighten out an errant believer, but that's not its primary function. Its more important role is what it does for *us* inside our own heads and hearts, not how we employ it out there dealing with others.

Being and doing—again

We need to remind ourselves that all the aspects of the fruit of the Spirit are about *being* rather than *doing*. They are all qualities of character, not things to do. Actions flow *from* the fruits, that's inevitable, as we've already discussed in an earlier chapter, but the fruits are not the actions. There are numerous mentions of good works in the New Testament—and 'good' is *agathos,* a close relative of *agathosune*—but I've steered away from them in order to keep to the point: **Goodness is the quality of character that lies behind, and must precede, all truly good works.** It is also, as something of a by-product, that particular quality of character which equips us to admonish one another, and to reprove the erring.

Talking to yourself

As a quality of character, goodness works something like a conscience. As a matter of fact it most likely *is* the conscience of a believer. It is the inner voice of the Word which is reproving and admonishing us. This is how the Word should affect us, and it is precisely how the Word was *intended* to affect us. Its readers or hearers in Old Testament times were told as much. This is what the Law should have done for all those who delighted and meditated in it day and night. The Proverbs tell us: "When thou goest, it shall lead thee; when thou sleepest, it shall keep thee; and when thou awakest, it shall talk with thee" (Prov.6:22). This is a reference to the inner dialogue that the Word will establish in our hearts/heads if we give ourselves sufficiently to it. The Psalms tell us the same: "Thy word have I hid in mine heart, that I might not sin against thee" (Ps.119:11). This is not hiding the Word so it cannot be found!—this is to lay it up in your heart like a prized possession. Back to the Proverbs for the full explanation:

> "My son, if thou wilt receive my words, **and hide my commandments with thee**; So that thou incline thine ear to wisdom, and apply thine heart to understanding; Yea, if thou criest after knowledge, and liftest up thy voice for understanding ; If thou seekest her as silver, and searchest for her as for hid treasure; Then shalt thou understand the fear of the Lord, and find the knowledge of God" (Prov.2:1-5).

We all talk to ourselves, don't we? It doesn't mean we're mad. Not usually. We all have a constant stream of words and sometimes pictures passing through our minds. Much as we might wonder whether some people have anything at all going on in there, we all have something going on. One epitome of laid-backness once said "Sometimes I sits and thinks, and sometimes I just sits." But it's actually quite difficult to 'just sit'. Numerous meditational disciplines have been devised for the very purpose of trying to stop the flow of thought and clear the mind for a time, because this can be beneficial; it's supposed to help relaxation. We are naturally thinking beings, talking to ourselves the whole while. Just try to stop thinking for as long as you can and you'll see what I mean. After a few seconds (if you make it that far) you'll start wondering how you're doing, and, *zap!* you're out.

The nature of our self-talk is extremely important to our spiritual and mental well-being. For most people—that is, those whose minds are untouched by attention to the Word of God—the nature of their stream of consciousness is determined almost entirely by other people, by society. Their self-talk is governed by, "What *should* I think about this or that?" "What *should* I do?" "How *should* I feel about this?"—it is largely determined by what society has conditioned them into believing is acceptable for them. This came about mostly over their formative years through input from parents and other family members; teachers and other authority figures; friends and role models; and it continues down the years through bosses, governments and associates. All these influences have combined to determine what is 'right' for most people. This mishmash of influences procures the general haphazard morality by which most people live their lives, and which rather loosely holds society together.

Any *goodness* such people may have is not the real thing, not a fruit of the Spirit. It may appear to be genuine Biblical goodness, but it isn't. Ask the majority of 'good' people in the world why they would not steal or murder, and they would answer 'because it's wrong', or 'because I believe it to be morally wrong,' but they will rarely say 'because God tells me in His Word it is wrong.' That's the difference, isn't it? The goodness which God wants from us and which is a fruit of the Spirit argues from an understanding of what the *Word* of God says, not from what 'I think'. The self-talk of the believer is marked by the gentle but firm inner reprovings and admonitions of the Word of God. This is what it means to have the mind of the Spirit, or the mind of Christ. Our devotion to God's Word puts a new voice in our heads. "When thou awakest, it shall talk with thee," as the Proverb says. This is the presence of goodness challenging the old society-induced and flesh-induced voice of evil.

"In the beginning"

In the beginning mankind was made "very good" (Gen.1:31). Adam's and Eve's inner dialogues were with the unsullied voice of goodness. Evil had not occurred to them. They had only the godly counsel of the angels to affect their thinking, no knowledge of anything else.

When they were deceived by the serpent, what they did was to eat of the tree of the knowledge of good *and* evil (Gen.2 & 3). That changed everything for them. That disobedience introduced a new voice into their heads. Their inner dialogue changed. And the new voice was loud and strong, and it spoke to them of doubt and fear (making them want to hide from God); it spoke of anger, lust and all kinds of evil. And the original voice of goodness became overwhelmed, weaker, smaller and quieter, and in need of constant reinforcement to prevent it from disappearing entirely in the face of this brash but subtle inner voice of evil. The Word of God became a 'still small voice' indeed in the thinking of mankind (1 Kings 19:12). Now only the applied influence of the Word of God can help this desperate situation in which we find ourselves as the heirs of Adam's disobedience. There is no other remedy. From the good influence of the Word we can develop the fruit of the Spirit, an important aspect of which is the godly voice of *goodness* reproving and admonishing the natural evil voice of our hearts.

Experiment

What's the inner voice in your head telling you most of the time? Is it, do you think, predominantly the voice of goodness or the voice of evil? Try the experiment of keeping track of your inner dialogue for a while. Check how much of what is going on in there can be traced directly to the influence of the Word of God, and how much of it is attributable to another source. Perhaps, even as a believer, you are still conditioned in your thinking by the influences of society, living according to its conventions more than by the Word of God. Is there any evidence in there of the voice of the Word reproving and admonishing the natural voice of your mind? Any sign of the goodness that is of the fruit of the Spirit? Or has goodness been put to silence by your own way of thinking? As I say, try the experiment.

Jesus had this goodness, without a doubt. He could always produce a "thus saith the Lord" to handle the natural promptings of his mind. He did it during the temptations in the wilderness. He so strongly committed himself to knowing the mind of God that he overcame the mind of the flesh *completely*— he admonished and reproved it out of existence! We won't achieve his total domination of the mind of the flesh, but if we use his method we can go a long way towards it. He is the role model for us, one who really applied himself to knowing what "saith the Lord". And that, as the saying goes, was the secret of his success. And it can be ours, too, if we're intent on making ourselves Christlike—as in *Christians*.

Positive and negative

Now, I said at the beginning of this chapter (rashly, you may have thought!) that goodness is one of the most dynamic forces in our lives, and a quality which, probably more than any other, helps to keep us on the right road. I even went so far as to say that goodness adds some sparkle to life! Hopefully, you can now see that some of those claims are true. Goodness is characterised by the indwelling of the Word of God in our hearts, put there and held there by our constant recourse to that Word in a spirit of delight. All of which has surely to be a major factor in keeping our feet firmly on the straight and narrow! But what about adding some sparkle to life!?

The Word of God is a totally positive force, "having promise of the life that now is, and of that which is to come" (1 Tim.4:8). Even the Ten Commandments are framed as double negatives (don't do the bad) which turns them into positive statements even though most of them begin, "Thou shalt not." So the incorporation of godly thinking into our minds is the way to achieve the purest form of positive thinking available anywhere! Goodness is, in fact, a form—the very *best* form—of positive thinking. Our own natural mode of thinking tends to be negative in its tone, and certainly in its outworking. It leads to death, and you can't get any more negative than death!

Positive thinking was always traditionally and rightly associated with *religious* thinking. Norman Vincent Peale, who is probably responsible for bringing the phrase 'positive thinking' into current use by his best-selling book, *The Power of Positive Thinking*, was a Methodist minister. He died only recently, well into his nineties, active to the last, and one of the best advertisements for his own book you'll ever find. His book leans heavily on Bible quotation and on the godly life being the positive life.

Over the years, positive thinking has lost a lot of ground (probably because it isn't as easy as many of its advocates made it sound), but it still pops up in other guises as the stuff of motivational speakers and writers. Nowadays the religious content tends to be sifted out of it and the result is generally an odd blend of humanism and mysticism. Yet it still *works* for people. In so far as people are employing Scriptural concepts, even though they are not *aware* they are Scriptural, there is bound to be some success. Of course it's better to go to the undiluted Source for our guidance on positive thinking, but other writers, like Peale, can be uplifting. A most amusing, and telling criticism I heard of Norman Vincent Peale was when someone compared him with the apostle Paul, and said, "I found Paul appealing and Peale appalling!" But, to be fair, such writers, when they are setting out helpful Scriptural principles of living in an easy-to-assimilate way, can be helpful.

True and valuable positive thinking is Bible-based. It's basically the inner goodness that constant recourse to the Scriptures will generate inside us. It is the good Word of God in our head and heart, admonishing and reproving the old negative man of the flesh.

Admonishing and reproving *isn't* a negative procedure, although it sounds like it. Something advising us what is right and good for us over what is wrong and bad for us can never really be negative. Our natural way of thinking will lead us *away* from our own highest good if we let it. It will tell us that living the Christian life is too difficult for us; that we are never going to live it well enough to make the Kingdom. It will tell us all sorts of negatives about ourselves and our hopes, and it will drain our spirit if we let it. It will try to convince us that bad things are actually good for us. But the introduction to our thinking of *Bible-based positive thinking*—the voice of what is truly good and right—will change us from hopeless to hopeful, from aimless to purposeful, and from fearful to confident. That's what this aspect of the fruit of the Spirit will do for us. And if you should ever doubt that positive thinking is a bona fide Christian concept then you should read what I call the Positive Thinkers' Charter which is found in Philippians 4:8:

"Finally, brethren, whatsoever things are **TRUE**, whatsoever things are **HONEST**, whatsoever things are **JUST**, whatsoever things are **PURE**, whatsoever things are **LOVELY**, whatsoever things are of **GOOD REPORT**; if there be any **VIRTUE**, and if there be any praise, **THINK ON THESE THINGS**." (My capitals).

This is positive thinking with a vengeance! So you see, it's a very scriptural phenomenon. It isn't, as many would say, an unrealistic and Pollyanna-like approach to life. If 90% of what we worry about never happens (which is reckoned to be the case), then which is the realistic approach? *Negative* thinking is the unrealistic approach to life. Being positive is far more real! How well does that charter for positive thinking represent what goes on in your head most of the time? It would certainly add some sparkle to your life if you could let your inner goodness admonish you into thinking along these lines, wouldn't it?

The Emperor Philosopher

Marcus Aurelius, the Roman Emperor philosopher who lived AD 121-180, wrote in his Meditations: "our life is what our thoughts make it." He certainly struck a golden nugget of truth there. What a pity it didn't lead him to discover the best possible use of his own thoughts by allowing the Word of God to enter and steer them. His thoughts would then have made his life incomparably better. His thoughts would also have made the lives of many good believers a lot better, for he was unkind toward the believers of his day. History calls this Stoic Philosopher a good man in spite of his mistreatment of believers. He demonstrates how men can be when they possess a goodness which is not the fruit of the Spirit, but a ghastly parody of it. But what he said about our life being what our thoughts make it is worth bearing in mind. He stumbled on a Scriptural truth. Sadly, as Sir Winston Churchill once observed, most men who stumble upon truth will simply pick themselves up and carry on their way.

The French Philosopher

In more recent history the French philosopher René Descartes (1596-1650) made a memorable statement on the subject of thinking. Philosophers are, so they tell us, after the underlying truths about the nature of all things. And in a valiant attempt to come up with an *absolute truth*—a statement that he could say without fear of contradiction was absolutely, positively, undeniably true—he arrived at this:

"Cogito, ergo sum"

—better known to non-Latin speakers, like myself, as:

"I think, therefore I am."

Why this Frenchman should lapse into Latin to make his supposedly immortal statement, I don't know. It's rather like Shakespeare's Julius Caesar lapsing into Latin when his conspiratorial colleagues began hacking him to death: "Et tu

Brute". One can only assume it was thought to add a little scholarship to a hopefully profound statement.

In my view, Descartes' statement, 'I think, therefore I am,' just stops short of being useful to a Bible believer. For us the statement needs finishing off with just one more word to make it an *absolute* truth about us.

There are two ways of thinking, as we've discussed. There is natural, sin-prone, negative thinking in which the majority of people engage all their lives, and by which they will attain at best a false goodness as a reaction to the demands of society. Or there is the kind of thinking that is influenced by the Spirit Word—Biblical positive thinking in which so few engage and which will lead to the genuine, life-enhancing goodness of the fruit of the Spirit.

To extend M. Descartes' pronouncement into one which will ultimately prove absolutely true for everyone, I give you either

"I *think*, therefore I am ... evil";

or

"I *think*, therefore I am ... good."

Which of these absolute truths does your thinking tell you is the most likely true of you at the moment? Do you have the mind of the flesh or the mind of the Spirit? But don't be too hard on yourself. If in doubt, make the attempt to be positive from now on. Delight and meditate in the positive Word and let it talk with you throughout the day. It will bring you true goodness.

As a P.S. to this chapter, you might consider that Descartes' ultimate truth should not have been "I think, therefore I am," but rather: "I think, **therefore God is.**"

CHAPTER TWELVE

FAITH: *(Pistis)*

FAITH is the only aspect of the fruit of the Spirit that is actually defined for us in Scripture, because Hebrews 11:1 tells us: "Now faith is the substance of things hoped for, the evidence of things not seen." All the work appears to have been done for us. This could prove to be an extremely short chapter! We don't have to do any delving to discover what faith means; the answer is lying right there on the surface for all to see. So, what now...?

Now we should look to see if we really know what the meaning *means*. This is not just me being perverse, or grabbing at straws in order to have something to fill this chapter. It's the recognition that we can all too easily *think* we understand a passage of Scripture when in fact we don't, or we understand it only in part. Or maybe we don't fully know *why* we understand the passage the way we do, even if we're right on target about what it means.

It's always useful to look more closely at familiar verses, to check our understanding. Even if we only confirm what we already knew, the experience is nonetheless rewarding. Digging a little deeper under the surface is never a waste of time when it comes to God's Word. His Word is like the rest of His creation. The closer you look, the more you find. Take a microscope to a flower petal and the revealed structure is as entrancing as the flower. Take an inquiring mind to the Scriptures and the underlying patterns are as entrancing as the simple truths.

And if by closer study you arrive at a new and better understanding of some familiar verses, or find some unexpected connections with other parts of Scripture, then so much the better! Perhaps that's what you'll do now with Hebrews 11:1. Let's look at it more closely. Let's take the key words in that seemingly simple statement about faith and see what they each mean, then put the whole thing back together again and see if we still have the same package we thought we had when we started. And hopefully, like many a *failed* attempt at fixing something by pulling it apart and re-assembling it, we won't have any pieces left over at the end.

THE EQUATION

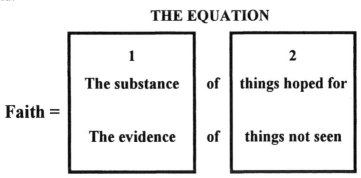

What we have in Hebrews 11:1 is an equation. Faith equals two things, as you can see in the illustration. And if, as I have, you add boxes to the right hand side of the equation, you can see that the two things that faith equals are parallels. The **substance** and the **evidence** are ideas that match one another, and so are **things hoped for** and **things not seen.** It seems to me that Paul, under Spirit guidance, has evoked the pattern of Hebrew poetry (such as we find in the Psalms) where two lines will rhyme in meaning or thought, rather than in sound. It isn't surprising, either, that Paul, being a Hebrew scholar, should use such a device. Spirit inspiration did leave the writers of Scripture free to be themselves—or David would never have been permitted to pour out his heart under inspiration; neither would Job and his three 'comforters' have been allowed to be so obviously themselves—so much so that we have to be wary of quoting from the book of Job lest we find ourselves parroting a wrong opinion! It's a pity that many people should see this individuality of the human writers as evidence against the Divine inspiration of the Scriptures. They don't believe that an all-powerful God has the power to express Himself perfectly through fallible humans. But clearly that is exactly what He has chosen to do in the Scriptures. Even man's failures have been harnessed to produce Divine perfection!

In Box 1 we have the words **substance** and **evidence** brought together. What do we generally mean when we speak of the substance or the evidence of something? In concrete terms, a thing that has substance is a thing we are able to detect with one or more of our five senses. We can touch, see, hear, smell or taste it. The book you're holding in your hands has substance in this concrete sense. Whether it has any substance in the *abstract* sense is quite another matter! For it to have substance in this sense means that the book contains ideas which are meaningful, useful, and grounded in reality. Sometimes what we read does not have any substance.

But enough of what we might take the word to mean for ourselves. What does the Bible word for substance convey? The Greek word is *hupostasis. Hupo* is a prefix meaning mostly *of, by* or *under. Stasis* is a word which has moved unchanged directly into our own language as *stasis,* and slightly changed as *state. Hupostasis* means literally *of state,* or *of standing.* **It's something you can stand on**—it's a solid base. The Emphatic Diaglott actually reads: "Faith is a basis of things hoped for," and Schonfield gives: "faith is the solid ground...". We can see what it's driving at. The Greek word also implies the idea of confidence.

Faith is a chunk of good solid ground; it's a firm base; it's a place where you can stand with confidence. *Faith* is the sort of place where you could build a lighthouse, knowing that whatever the sea and the weather threw at it, it would still be standing in the morning. That's *hupostasis.* And in our New Testament piece of 'Hebrew poetry' we saw that it was equated with evidence (**Box 1**).

When we think of *evidence,* our minds generally link it up with thoughts of courts of law. Which is a very good connection because the word in Greek does have something to do with conviction! In court it is evidence that often leads to a conviction. So it is with faith. Faith is not just an airy-fairy feeling. It is not a rather general belief about a vague possibility. Faith is solid, and it carries conviction: meaning that it is something you are convinced about, not something you feel is sort of likely. It's something you feel so strongly about that you act in accordance with it. That's why James said "Faith without works is dead" (Jas.2:20). Because when you have something solid in your life, about which you have conviction, it simply *must* make a difference to your life. If it doesn't affect the way that you live, then it can't be real for you. You're kidding yourself. This is why Paul wrote "The just shall LIVE by faith" (Rom.1:17—my capitals). Faith is a way of life.

Faith is the perfect model for what I've been saying all along about the fruit of the Spirit. When you have the fruit it will outflow into your daily life, and the *doing* of good and right things must follow as night follows day. When any part of the fruit is in your being it will consequently be in your doing also. It cannot be any other way.

Faith and works

James wrote, "Yea, a man may say, Thou hast faith, and I have works: shew me thy faith without thy works, and I will shew thee my faith by my works" (Jas.2:18). So elementary. Not, as some have suggested, a doctrine of salvation by works, but a doctrine of salvation by faith (among other things) that inevitably *leads* to works. The works are not the goal. The fruit of the Spirit is the goal, and the works are the outcome of the developing of the fruit—especially faith, because faith is the solid foundation, the unshakable conviction that God and His purpose are real.

Works are not the goal. If you have only works then you will have only the phoney fruit we spoke of before. It has all the appearance of the real fruit (good works that spring from humanistic or selfish or legalistic motives look convincingly like the real thing), and it may convince others or fool even ourselves what fine people we are, but it doesn't fool the One who looks directly into our hearts, not for one moment. God looks at our being, not at our doing. The two need to be in harmony. And not only for our future well-being in the Kingdom of God, but also our present well-being. It is stressful to live a lie, to live a life of works that is not consistent with your inner self. To spend your time putting on a show may have short-term benefits, like making people think you are good, or it might save you the aggravation of having to deal with criticism or rejection from those you live alongside, but in the long term it will breed anger and resentment and emptiness. That's what going for works without faith will bring—a bitter harvest, and not the fruit of the Spirit.

Works without faith are no good. On the other hand, *faith without works* is, I believe, impossible. It cannot be done.

The reluctant violinist

James also wrote, "by works was faith made perfect," (Jas.2:22). By definition, faith without works is imperfect (so imperfect it's dead!). Faith must have an outlet in works. It cannot and will not abide being locked up inside us, unexpressed.

Imagine for a moment having a total belief in something and yet trying to live your life as if it were not true, denying it at every turn. You'd go off 'pop' with exasperation, I should think. For instance, imagine going through life with the knowledge, with the *absolute conviction*, that you were a wizard on the violin or piano. World class! But every time someone asks you to play, you deny you can really play at all. You say, "No, not me. I tinker a bit, but not seriously." And all the time you know in your heart of hearts that you're the best and you could make that instrument sing. But you never do. And you never will. Could you, or anyone, really go on living your life like that? The ache to express what you knew to be true would be so persistent and so demanding that eventually the truth would break through. You could not contain it forever, could you?

Now imagine something similar. Imagine living a life of faith in which you are fully convinced of God, that He is the greatest thing in your life. That He guides and protects you, and has made great promises to you. Could you go on living as if God didn't exist?—as if His message to the world had never been written? Could you go on living, once you had believed for certain in God and His Word, without changing the way you live in any way at all? Impossible. Again, I say, I believe you'd go off 'pop' from trying to bottle it up! Real faith produces works, without exception. It's a law of the universe—and it's God's universe.

An antidote to phoney fruit

Faith is a great antidote to phoney fruit. Anyone motivated to do works for any of the *wrong* reasons—people-pleasing, guilt, legalism, or whatever—can easily change to doing works for the *right* reasons by getting a firm hold on faith. Get back to the roots of belief. Be fully convinced by the Word of God of the solid ground on which you stand when you believe in the Word. "Delight" and "meditation" again! Once that conviction takes a hold of the heart you'll *be* a believer instead of just acting like one. Real fruit—*faith*—is the result. And that leads to good works that are not only good for others but good for you too. Because if you're doing works that have no faith behind them, only wrong motives, you really are being good for nothing!

Box 2

Before we run on ahead too far, let's go back to our equation of faith. We haven't considered the second of the two boxes yet. **Box 2** contains the second set of parallel ideas, which are these: **Things hoped for** and **Things not seen.** Fairly straightforward this time. Because the things we hope for are by very definition the things we can't see at the moment. As Paul wrote: "hope that is seen is not hope: for what a man seeth, why doth he yet hope for?" (Rom.8:24). Extremely logical. You can't hope for something you already have. Things hoped for *are* things not seen.

In particular, the things a believer hopes for that he or she cannot see at present are:

> 1 The return of Christ
> 2 Resurrection of loved ones
> 3 Their own immortality
> 4 The Kingdom of God, and all that it entails

These are things that none of us can now see. They are things hoped for. And our faith gives substance and conviction to our hopes. Our faith turns these things which are not yet reality *into* reality for us. So much so that we are to consider ourselves even *now* to be citizens of the Kingdom of God: "fellowcitizens with the saints, and of the household of God," wrote Paul in Ephesians 2:19. He also wrote, "For our citizenship is in heaven" (Phil.3:20 NKJV). The spiritual passport we carry says "Kingdom of God."— not United Kingdom or Canada or wherever. Future things are *that* real to us when we have true faith. We live as if we are already in the Kingdom. We "set [our] affection on things above"—Paul again in Colossians 3:2. This is how living *in the world but not of it* works. We consider ourselves now citizens of the Kingdom of God, and we *act* accordingly.

I believe it is wrong, and maybe dangerous, to think that we shall all be oh-so-different in the Kingdom, leaving the transformation of our characters to the miracle power of Christ at his return. We should think of it as Christ *confirming* our citizenship when he comes rather than bestowing it. The Spirit power in that day won't be making our *characters* fit for immortality; it will be making our bodies fit for it, if our characters are already suitable! So, now is the time to become citizens of the Kingdom of God. And the only way to achieve the transformation is by developing a true faith in the things which we cannot see, as yet. Live now, insofar as is possible, how you think you'll live in the Kingdom. In essence that's what will happen with the ripening of the fruit of the Spirit. You'll begin to live now as if you were there. Our old friends "delight" and "meditation" in the Word of God will produce this kind of life—this kind of faith.

A quantum leap of faith

We know from another famous verse of Scripture that we cannot please God unless we really do have this faith in the future which so changes the present for us: "But without faith it is impossible to please [God], for he who comes to God must believe that He is, and that He is a rewarder of those who diligently seek Him" (Heb.11:6 NKJV).

I especially like this verse because it tells us not only to have faith in God, *but also in our own reward.* The verse doesn't mean that we should have faith in God *generally* as a rewarder of people. How would it please God if we believed He existed, and had great faith in Him as a rewarder *of other people*, but not of ourselves?

Probably the greatest leap of faith we are ever called upon to make in our lives is a belief in our own personal salvation. But think on the fact that it is impossible to please God without that belief.

It's easy for us to believe in Believer A's or Believer B's salvation, because they are so good. They always seem to do the right thing. But our own salvation? Well... that's another matter!. The funny thing is that if you went to Believer A and Believer B and asked them about *their* salvation they'd most likely suck in air through their teeth, begin staring over your shoulder into the middle distance and musing on the unlikelihood of it! They don't see themselves as you see them. More than this. They're actually strange enough to believe that *you* are doing all right!

The problem here is that we all know *ourselves* only too well, and other people hardly enough. As I see it, if you knew the *real* me you probably wouldn't be reading this book! And if I knew the real *you* maybe I wouldn't want you to! We're all too aware of what is sometimes called our shadow selves. This is the bit of us that isn't for public display, but which we are woefully aware cannot be hidden from God. And yet you and I are expected to have faith in our own personal salvation! It really is a quantum leap of faith!

Of course I'm not suggesting we're all out-and-out rotten. We're all trying to overcome our rottenness and eject our shadow selves. We're all trying, I'm sure, to make that area of our heart that is occupied by the shadow self as small as possible, and the area occupied by the fruit-of-the-Spirit self as large as possible. And we all have different mixes, different balances of flesh and Spirit inside us according to our progress along the spiritual path. And, let's face it, no matter how much progress we make, there will always, in this life, be areas we cannot win for the fruit of the Spirit.

But because *we* tend to focus on these unconquered areas we think that God is doing the same. No matter how much progress we make, even maybe to ninety per cent of the territory of our heart, we still imagine God staring at the other ten per cent and shaking His head that we could be so unspiritual.

With most of us He doubtless has a greater area than ten per cent to look at.

But what we often fail to appreciate is **how pleased God is with *whatever* percentage we've gained for the fruit of the Spirit!**

Never mind the current situation. Never mind the current position of the borderline between Spirit and flesh in our heart. What matters to God is that we're *working* on it. What matters is that through delight and meditation in His Word we are attempting to move the border back millimetre by millimetre.

We can't expect to win the whole war in one or two skirmishes. (We'll *never* win the whole war in these flesh-and-blood bodies.) This is a mistake I'm sure many believers make. I certainly have. And it's the cause of a lot of despondency, feelings of failure, and of giving up entirely. We imagine we're going to meet sin head-on and cast it right out of our life. I know I did when I was baptized. I hung on in there gritting my teeth, keeping myself perfect, or so I thought. But it couldn't last. It never does. I remember when I fell from my supposed position of purity (God probably remembers an earlier date!), feeling that I'd lost the Kingdom. Others I've spoken to have related similar stories about this 'walking-on-eggshells' period that immediately follows baptism. Eventually we put a foot wrong and there's yoke and white everywhere! And we can be extremely downcast if we don't learn the right lesson from our collapse.

The pipe-devil

There's a very wise old saying (theologically adrift, but wise all the same) that goes: You can't throw the devil out the front door: he must be coaxed down the back steps one at a time. I remember a much respected believer (now asleep in Christ) once telling me about his own father, who until he was baptized was a great pipe smoker, and had been for years. Upon baptism he felt that pipe smoke defiled his body and that smoking was a disgusting habit. The day of his baptism he threw away the rack of pipes that had stood for years on the mantelshelf in the living room. He wasn't going to defile his body any more. No, not him! His body, however, had other ideas. A short while later a new pipe appeared on the mantelpiece. He realized that he was going to have to take this 'pipe-devil' down the back stairs one at a time. It was a great lesson for him to learn—and to pass on to his son—so early in his life in the Truth.

How many believers still have that lesson to learn? We tried the front door method with our sin. It failed. So we concluded that *we* were failures—and that was that. As a result we now have great difficulty seeing God as our personal rewarder. Therefore it is impossible, in our eyes, to please God. We believe that He exists, and we believe that He is a rewarder of those who diligently seek Him, but we don't put ourselves in that last category. Our shadow selves lurk behind the masks we wear. And they tell us we've failed and we're not good enough.

But this impasse is all of our own making. It doesn't come from God.

If some besetting sin that we failed to throw out of the front door is robbing us of our faith in our personal reward from God, the solution is not to despair and give up on ourselves. We might mistakenly think that's the only decent thing to do—as if our despair and self-rejection is somehow the most appropriate response to our failure. It isn't. Guilt and unworthiness lead us to repentance and renewed hope, *not* into a permanent state of guilt and unworthiness.

Poor Johnny One-Talent

If what I've said describes you, then please bear in mind the lesson of the one-talent man of the parable of the talents (Matt.25:14-30). The lesson shouting out to all the self-styled failures of the Christian world is that success is well within reach. The only true failure is to believe you have no hope. It comes from believing that somehow Christ is a *hard* man who expects more from us than we can possibly deliver. He wants our perfection, and all we can offer is our incompetence. So we reason we have no hope.

I firmly believe that the "weeping and gnashing of teeth" of the rejected ones at Christ's return is in many cases because they suddenly understand how *easily* they could have succeeded! But they missed the point; they gave up on their hope. Maybe not outwardly—their mask was intact—but inwardly they felt they'd lost it.

They'd seen the Truth as a huge mountain they had to climb, and they'd not noticed the escalators marked *grace, mercy and forgiveness.*

The one-talent man of the parable had only to put his talent out to usury—to invest it by lending it out at a decent rate of interest. Have you ever wondered exactly what that means? Have you ever tried to translate that into a way of living the Truth? It's safe to assume that the talent each parable-man was given from God is intended to represent the gift of the knowledge of the Truth. God gives us that when He calls us. Some people's appreciation and capacity for living the Truth seems greater than others at the outset. They seem to have been given five or ten talents to work with. They have a more natural inclination towards spiritual things. Of them we are clearly told that more is expected. "For everyone to whom much is given, from him much will be required" (Luke 12:48 RAV). What a relief it is not to be one of them!

But the downside is that poor Johnny One-Talent has it in his mind that God unjustly expects him to multiply his mere one talent ability into the incredible twenty talent version of his more gifted spiritual colleagues. God would be delighted, of course, for it to happen (and I'm sure it does sometimes), but to say that He *expects* it is quite another matter.

God's only expectation of us is that we do *something*—something positive with our gift, not something negative like burying it. Burying it is akin to saying to ourselves, "Well, I'll never amount to anything anyway. Too much is being asked of me."

When money is put out to usury it means the money is loaned out for interest. Once you've loaned it out you don't actually have to do anything. The money does all the work for you. And to put this in the context of the parable, it *isn't even our money*! It's God's money we loan out (He gave the talent), so that He can get it back with interest. How much easier can it get for us! We're even handed the money.

But what is it that we have to do in our lives that corresponds with the actions of the men in the parable? If

153

the talent we are given is to be "traded with" or loaned out to accrue interest, how is that going to happen?

The talent is the gift of the knowledge of the Truth. How can we trade with that or lend it out to accrue interest for God? What is the most, and what's the very *least* we can do? Well, if you recall some of what we've covered so far about *being* and *doing*, you'll probably realize that asking what we can *do* is the wrong question. The one-talent man needed not to *do* anything; he needed to *be* something. He needed to be different!

If ever you feel helpless and hopeless about what Christ will be expecting of you at his return, what you need is a shift in your thinking, not in your acting. It requires a shift away from seeing yourself as a no-hoper and a small-faither, doubtful of acceptance. The reality of your situation is only that way if you choose to see it that way. Thinking that way *leads* us that way! A simple shift in thinking can change the whole picture.

The truth is, one-talent man or woman has as much hope of spiritual success as ten-talent man or woman. All it takes is a rational appraisal of what God expects. We have to appreciate how pleased God is when, in spite of all our failures, we *still* see Him as our great rewarder. It *must* please God when we do this because it demonstrates to Him that we understand something of His character. And it shows Him that we really do believe what He says about love, forgiveness, mercy and grace. If you fear God, and if it worries you that you are desperately hoping for the mercy of God, then have a look at Psalm 147:11: "The Lord taketh pleasure in them that fear him, **in those that hope in his mercy.**"

To be believers we have to be believers

To be believers we have to be believers. Now there's a truism for you! But think about it. Because it's perfectly possible to continue thinking of yourself as a believer long after you gave up believing. Faith has to be two-pronged. It must involve a belief in God *and* in His reward for you. So, are you still a believer?

And never forget that 'believer' starts with that important little word **be**. It's also worth noting that the second half of the word—*lieve*—shares a common root in English with the word **love**. So one might say that to be a believer is to be **one whose *being* is associated with *loving!***

Win/win/Win!

As soon as we see ourselves as people with real faith in our own future we become different people. We cease to be brow-beaten by our shadow self and we have a positive outlook on life. And that attitude inevitably makes us *traders* with our talents. Those who believe in God and in their own future are entirely different people from the negative, doubting people. True believers interact differently from people who doubt themselves. A person of faith affects all those around them in positive ways. And so it is that the talent is traded, the gift of the knowledge of the Truth is shared. A person of faith naturally makes it his business to go and trade with the world. Those in the parable with five and ten talents went out and did this. They dramatically increased what was given to them. God's gift was doubled in them. Meaning, not only did the people they traded with benefit, *they* benefited also. They shared the gospel, and enhanced their own faith in the process. This is what is called in business terms a win/win situation, when both the giver and the receiver come out of the arrangement with profit. The spiritual version, though, is a win/win/Win situation, because God also receives profit from the good stewardship of His gift. Souls are influenced and won for Him.

But what should the less dynamic one-talent person do who doesn't feel competent to go out into the world and trade? What can you do if you don't feel you can cope with direct preaching? What's the *least* you can do? The least you can do is put the talent out to usury. Lend it out rather than trade with it. Preach *indirectly*—that's what it means.

You have to enter the Jewish mind to understand this aspect of the parable. Remember the parable was delivered to a Jewish audience. Under Jewish law (God's law given through Moses) the people of Israel were not allowed to lend out money for interest to their brethren, their fellow Jews. They could exact usury from foreigners (Gentiles) only. Christ's telling the one-talent man he should have put his talent out to usury should be seen in this light.

What it means for one-talent people is that the talent *can* and should be used. It means that God accepts we may not have it in us to go out with Bible in hand and preach to the world in a dynamic way, but there's no reason to do the opposite and deny our religion to the world, keep it timidly to ourselves, bury the talent: we can still preach *indirectly*, passively, simply by *being* who we are. Simply by living the Truth in the world we can have an effect upon it. And interest will accrue for God when people take note of our way of life, when they see we are quietly assured people with faith in God and in our future.

I know exactly of what I speak. I was 'brought into' the Truth by a brother who never directly preached to me. As a work colleague he simply went about his day being just who he is: a man of faith, excited by what he knows and at the prospect it holds for him. Any person in the world who is called by God and exposed to such contact for any length of time cannot help being drawn to want to know more about the man's beliefs. It is possible to be quietly dynamic!

God expects no more of us than we can reasonably give Him, bearing in mind what He gave us in the first place! The one to whom much is given, of him or her much is expected. It follows that the one to whom less is given (I avoided saying *'little* is given' because the gift of the knowledge of the Kingdom can never be called 'little'), of him or her less is expected. Take heart all one-talenters: God doesn't expect to reap where He hasn't sowed. Just don't hide who you are from the world, that's all He asks.

Extra interest on account of our faith

But, of course, a person living with an attitude of faith benefits not only the unbelievers, helping them to wake up to the Truth; he or she benefits believers, too. Being men and women of positive faith we naturally do a little trading and investing of talents among one another. When we let other believers know how good we feel about the present and the future, and help them to see that they can feel that way too, if they don't already, then we're sharing our faith. If we can lift someone out of their spiritual doldrums by communicating our positive feelings about life in the Truth, we are letting our talent earn a little extra interest for God. After all, it is His talent, not ours. We trade or invest with it: He gets the profit—and we don't exactly lose out on the deal, do we? It's win/win/Win, remember! If we, by loaning out our God-given attitude of faith, turn someone away from their 'God is a hard man' mentality, then God undoubtedly gains interest on the loan. So never bury your conviction that God and His reward are true for you. Unlike the Jews under the Old Covenant, we Christians under the New Covenant can lend to our own kind with profit for all.

Faith now

One more thing to note about faith is that the 'things not seen', of which faith is our evidence, are not exclusively future things, like the Kingdom of God and the return of Christ. There are three other matters of faith to consider. One is the hand of God in our lives *now*, another is His hand in the affairs of present nations, and a third is the hand of God in the past, none of which we can see, except by faith.

The hand of God in our daily lives is unseen, only 'visible' sometimes in its outworkings. His hand in world affairs is unseen, again only 'visible' in its outworking, and usually only by hindsight. As for the miraculous, direct intervention of the hand of God in the past, we have only the Biblical record to go on, not sight or experience. We need a rock-solid conviction about all these if we are to please God. And we do want to please Him!

To be believers we have to **believe,** as I said earlier. Being a believer means having a personal belief and not an institutional belief. By which I mean that our faith in His existence, His reward for us, His hand in our lives and world affairs, His deeds in the past—our faith in these things should exist independently of the group of believers to which we belong. We must have faith of ourselves. The Truth is not an institution, or some club we can join and go along for the ride, thinking that because *it* is headed for the Kingdom of God then so are we. *It* isn't. People are. You are, I am, he is, she is! It's not a party ticket; it's all of us as individuals on the road to the Kingdom, on the spiritual path.

I'm not denying that we each have a measure of responsibility for one another. But we are never going to be able to take on that responsibility if we don't look first to our own spiritual welfare. We can't help others to grow strong in the faith if we're not doing it ourselves—now.

Faith in then

Finally, to go back to it, we need a strong faith in God's hand in the past. Faith operates in all three tenses. It covers faith in what the **future** holds, faith in Divine help **now**, and faith in what God did in the **past**.

When it comes to believing in God's hand in the past, we recognise first and foremost that our whole faith is founded upon an event in the past. The death and resurrection of Jesus Christ is the foundation of all our hopes. Salvation. And if we are to have faith in our God as our own rewarder, we need also to *personalise* salvation, that is to think of Christ dying for us as individuals. That's surely the way Christ himself saw it. He saw himself saving individual men and women with all their peculiar needs, doubts, hopes and fears; not a huge amorphous, anonymous blob of mankind.

When you look at a photograph in a newspaper you get the illusion that the area of the picture is completely covered in newsprint. But if you take a magnifying glass to it you'll see that it's made up of thousands of tiny dots of printer's ink. Together they make up the picture. Sometimes we need to take a mental magnifying glass to the notions of salvation and the Kingdom of God. Instead of treating salvation and the Kingdom of God as big concepts, grand ideas taking in the broad sweep of humankind and making individuals seem insignificant, take a look more closely and see that these big concepts are populated by people like you and me. Thousands of us make up the big picture. All playing an important role in the finished product. Without those dots there is no picture.

The Kingdom of God will be populated by the people who believe in it

So have this aspect of the fruit of the Spirit called faith. Believe in God and salvation—*your* salvation. It will make your own life better. It will improve the lives of those around you. *And* you'll please God. What could be better than that? Everybody wins.

CHAPTER THIRTEEN

MEEKNESS: *(praotes)*

EVERY writer or speaker I've ever read or heard on the subject of Biblical meekness has had to stress that this form of meekness *is not weakness.*

We don't use the word *meek* very much in general conversation, and when we do it's rarely a compliment. What we're usually implying is that the *meek* person is a bit wishy-washy, doesn't have much force of character.

But here is meekness as a part of the fruit of the Spirit. Something is definitely wrong here. Alarm bells should be ringing. It cannot be one of the goals of believers to develop a lack of personality! Are we really expected to make weakness of character one of our aims? That's what you'd think if you took meekness at face value. But, as with all the aspects of the fruit, there is more to being meek than our general understanding of the word allows.

Praotes, the Greek for meekness in Galatians 5:23, doesn't signify timidity, it means **CONTROLLED STRENGTH**. We have it when we have great strength but contain it. It's when you know you have a lot in your favour but don't flaunt it. It's having power without abusing it. In fact, as you'll see, *true* meekness is possible only for believers. It arises from the strength and security we have from trusting God.

William Barclay in *New Testament Words* says that in classical Greek *praotes* means *gentle* when applied to a thing (like a breeze), and *mild* or *gracious* when applied to a person. Barclay says the word "has a caress in it". It might aptly be used to describe a gentle giant like the English Shire horse which perfectly embodies the twin characteristics of strength and gentleness: it can pull a heavy plough or cart with little effort, and yet be docile enough to allow a youngster to enjoy a ride. It has strength under control. Believers with meekness have a strong character, not a weak one. They have great strength and power as children of God, and yet conduct themselves in a kindly, gracious manner. They have much to boast about, but they are restrained.

Some people are naturally timid. They are inherently shy and reticent. And you might think that such people have a head start on the rest of us when it comes to developing this aspect of the fruit. But that's not the case. The timid personality is a fearful personality, and fear has nothing to do with biblical meekness (unless it's a reverential fear of God. Timidity is a fear of man).

Even the unbelieving man of the world who has achieved much power and yet is still humble does not have the sort of meekness we're talking about here. Such characters may be *naturally* meek, or they may have learned meekness as a social ornament, but they are not *spiritually* meek. If they want to be *truly* meek, and to please God, they must become meek in the Biblical sense.

The same is true of believers. Natural meekness doesn't qualify as a fruit of the Spirit. The meekness we seek is not a natural timidity of character, which we might mistakenly pride ourselves is biblical meekness, but a product of the Spirit in our character. It grows within as a result of our continued delight and meditation in the Word of God.

God and meekness

The Almighty Himself is the greatest example of meekness. It may be difficult for you to attach a quality like meekness to the character of Almighty God, but it's self-evident that He must have it in superabundance. As soon as we appreciate that meekness is strength under control we can understand how great the meekness of God is. Try for a moment to imagine the omnipotence, omniscience, omnipresence and glory of God. It's an impossible task but try anyway! His presence is so unimaginably awesome that out of consideration for our welfare He has never allowed us to see Him face to face. Should the power and glory of God be allowed to fill this corner of the universe unchecked, we'd not survive the experience. All would be blinding, penetrating light and power against which nothing could stand.

Paul writing to Timothy described God as "dwelling in the light which no man can approach unto; whom no man hath seen, nor can see: to whom be honour and power everlasting. Amen" (1 Tim.6:16).

God's dealings with man have been carried out indirectly through His messengers the angels. But the presence of an angel could be terrifying when it reflected only a fraction of the Divine power. When the people of Israel waited at the foot of Mount Sinai while Moses received the ten commandments, they witnessed something of the awful majesty of God: "...and when the people saw it, they removed and stood afar off. And they said unto Moses, Speak thou with us, and we will hear: but let not God speak with us, lest we die" (Exod.20:19).

God is so far beyond us in power and glory that the gap is immeasurable. We might well ask with the Psalmist: "When I consider thy heavens, the work of thy fingers, the moon and the stars which thou hast ordained; what is man, that thou art mindful of him? and the son of man, that thou visitest him?" (Psalm 8:3,4). Why should God bother with us at all? And yet He does, as the astonished Psalmist goes on to say.

The fact that the great Creator and Sustainer of all things has *anything at all* to do with you and me, let alone *loves* us, and steers us towards a salvation in which we will ultimately be *with* Him—that is meekness unrivalled on His part. The control of His strength in dealing with us might be compared to the entire electrical energy output of the United States transformed down to a half volt output so as not to blow the bulb on a mini flashlight!

He speaks to us through His Word. He guides us by His unseen Hand of providence. He sent His own Son to die for us to open up a way to His presence. He hears our prayers. He asks us to cast all our cares on Him because He cares for us. All this is more than any of us could expect or deserve. Only a God who is love would ever be like this. And a prominent ingredient in the love God is, is meekness: **controlled strength**.

The meekness of Christ

When Christ was apprehended on the night of his betrayal, he had to stop Peter trying to defend him with a sword. Christ pointed out to Peter that God could send twelve legions of angels to his aid if it were necessary (Matt.26:52,53).

One of Christ's temptations in the wilderness was the appealing suggestion that he should demonstrate his great power to the people (and the religious leaders in particular) by throwing himself down from the highest pinnacle of the temple. According to a prophecy in Psalm 91 the angels would then catch Jesus and put him gently on the ground. "They shall bear thee up in their hands, lest thou dash thy foot against a stone" (Psalm 91:12). A spectacular demonstration of power was available to him.

Furthermore, on at least three occasions an angry mob threatened to kill Jesus (Luke 4:29,30, John 8:59 & 10:39), but he slipped away quietly and unseen instead of using his power to deal with them. Surely these were occasions when the angels did fulfil their prophesied role of Christ's protectors, ushering him to safety.

In all the above cases, Jesus resisted the temptation to show his power. It must have been severely tempting to show off in all these situations rather than be meek. Christ always had the great power that was available to him firmly under control. He never abused it by using it for selfish purposes. It's one of the things which mark him out as a very special person.

How many people given the power of the Spirit in such measure would have been able to handle it wisely and unselfishly? Christ is the only man in history who could ever have been trusted with so much power. Because Christ was *perfectly* meek.

The author H. G. Wells once wrote a story called *The Man Who Could Work Miracles*. It wasn't about Christ; it was about an ordinary man given extraordinary powers by the angels for a brief period to test how he would use them. The story concluded with the whole world in disarray and on the brink of destruction in the hands of this well-meaning though incapable man. I doubt if you or I would have fared any better. Wells' moral was that ordinary people like you and me can't handle extraordinary powers. It takes an extraordinary person.

Jesus never forgot that the power he had was not *his* power. He knew that of himself he could do nothing (John 5:30). In this knowledge lay the great secret of his meekness. And in this knowledge lies the secret of ours, too. Any power we have is derivative, and whatever we attempt to do in our own strength will cancel the quality of meekness in our character. Jesus always knew and acknowledged that the source of his power was his Father. At the miracle of the raising of Lazarus, Jesus said, "Father, I thank thee that thou hast heard me." He said it aloud on that occasion for the benefit of those who stood by. Usually he gave thanks quietly, mentally, to God. He always acknowledged the real power source. He was, and still is, a man of true Biblical meekness, of controlled strength.

The prophet Zechariah, who foretold Jesus' entry into Jerusalem, described him as "just, and having salvation; lowly, and riding upon an ass, and upon a colt the foal of an ass" (Zech.9:9). That event underscores the meekness of Jesus. It was a masterpiece of understated power. The heir to the whole world had his 'triumphal entry' not riding a dashing black charger, nor with a battalion of ceremonially dressed troops marching before and after, nor with fanfares or other orchestrated pomp. He merely rode alone and on an ass through the gates of Jerusalem to the cheers of many who would soon be calling for his blood.

Just think of the sort of show Christ *could* have put on—or the magnificence his Father in heaven *could* have lent to the occasion. It could have surpassed anything ever witnessed. Instead, this event, and indeed the whole life of Christ, from his birth in the stable to his crucifixion like a common criminal, was characterised by meekness. He was the lamb of God.

We should appreciate, in passing, though, that he will return soon as the *Lion of the Tribe of Judah*, to deal unflinchingly with all opposition to the Kingdom of God he comes to establish. His power may be under control, but that doesn't mean he'll never exercise it fully when the occasion demands. There is a time and a place for such use. The eviction of the unscrupulous traders from the Temple precincts was one: the eviction of the incorrigibly ungodly from the Kingdom of God will be another.

If you should ever wonder whether these seemingly uncharacteristic actions from the "gentle Jesus meek and mild" of the Christmas carol, or Christ's scathing denouncements of the Scribes and Pharisees, demonstrate a lack of meekness on his part, then you have misunderstood Biblical meekness and mistaken it for timidity. To be Biblically meek means you don't act in your own strength. It is to lean upon the power of God, and to be unselfish in the use of that power. Whenever Christ apparently stepped out of his characteristic meekness it was without exception not for himself, always as the perfect instrument of God's will. Even Christ's displays of strength were moments of submission.

The meekness of man

From the meekness of God and the meekness of Christ we now take a long, long drop down the scale to the meekness of man. Isn't it remarkable that the Almighty God and the perfect Christ exhibit meekness, while feeble and flawed mankind is so self-important! This is probably one of the reasons why *they* are Almighty and perfect and we are feeble and flawed!

We have nothing of ourselves to commend us. I'm reminded of something Winston Churchill once said when told that his political rival, Mr. Clement Attlee, was a modest man. Churchill responded typically, "He has much to be modest about." We all have 'much to be modest about.' Yet we flaunt and fancy ourselves, and are so proud of our puny achievements. We are so concerned and consumed with ourselves. Can we wonder that one of the things God hates most is "a proud look" (Prov.6:17), and that "Every one that is proud in heart is an abomination to the Lord" (Prov.16:5)? To which Jesus' words can be added: "For whosoever exalteth himself shall be abased; and he that humbleth himself shall be exalted" (Luke 14:11).

If only more people were strong enough to be meek! But we so want to *appear* strong. We admire self-reliance and assertiveness in others and we want it for ourselves. It's far more appealing than meekness, which although it embodies true strength of character might easily be mistaken for weakness. Even if we're not strong on the inside we like to appear it on the outside.

The greatest barrier to a believer's having Biblical meekness is the fear that it will appear to others as natural weakness. We don't like to be thought weak. We fear people will take advantage of us, that we'll get continually sidelined in life, we'll be the sort of people others take little notice of. Fears like these generate a need to assert ourselves, to make our mark with people.

So we worry and work for that promotion at the office, try and attract the boss's attention to our good work, instead of simply working "as unto the Lord" and being content with that. To be a Biblically meek believer is to be able to see beyond the boss you are *apparently* working for

to the God you are *actually* working for. You are not out to
please the apparent boss but God. You know that your
future as an employee depends not on what the boss thinks
or decides, but upon what God will allow. The boss, of
course, doesn't do too badly out of this arrangement.

When Jesus said before Pilate, "Thou couldest have no
power at all against me, except it were given thee from
above" (John 19:11), he wasn't boasting, he was meekly
stating the truth of the situation. Pilate had seriously
misjudged it. He had asked Jesus whether he realized that as
Governor of Judea he had the power of life and death over
Jesus. What foolishness that was! Jesus saw the truth of the
matter and where the real power lay.

In our own smaller way, what Jesus said to Pilate is true
of all believers, whatever the circumstances. Nothing and
no-one has any power over a believer apart from what God
will permit. The Governor of Judea had no real power over
Jesus, though he thought he had. Believers' governors in
their working environment have no real power over them,
only what is granted them.

God-reliance

A Biblically meek person realizes that the affairs of his
or her life are in no-one's hands but God's. Meekness is
God-reliance, not self reliance. It involves the rejection of
self-reliance—or indeed the rejection of reliance upon any
other human. Even the help we get from other people is
indirect help from God.

The result of God-reliance is not to make us weak,
isolated and dependent (which is how meekness might be
viewed), but strong, connected and, in a sense, *in*dependent.
God-reliance brings *independence* because through it we
are connected to the loving care of God. Insofar as we
practise God-reliance, we free ourselves from the cares of
this life. We no longer have to worry where the next meal is
coming from, the next pair of shoes, or whether we'll be
evicted from our house, whether another war will start,

whether people like you or not, or anything else that's bothering you at the moment.

"The Truth shall make you free," but....

"The truth shall make you free" (John 8:32) is a breathtakingly simple and direct statement about what happens for us when we follow Christ. The Jews who were present when Jesus said it misunderstood him entirely. They had a knack of doing that, and probably sometimes it was wilful. They complained *they* were free men already. As descendants of Abraham they were never in bondage to any man, they said. Which was blatant self-deception: the Jews at that time were under Roman governorship, and before that had been a captive nation in both Egypt and Babylon.

What Jesus meant when he said "the truth shall make you free" was that the Truth, once known and followed, will make a person free from sin and all its attendant anxieties. Not in the sense that we never sin again, but free from what might be called the 'system' of sin. When we serve (a meek thing to do, you'll notice) Christ and God we cease to serve sin and ourselves. By being baptised into Christ we give notice that we're under new management.

The Scriptures also speak of being baptised into Christ as shifting from being *in* Adam to being *in* Christ (1 Cor.15). Everybody is automatically born into the family of Adam; we have no choice in the matter, we're all his descendants. We all inherit Adam's sin-cursed and death-bound nature. But when we make the choice to become believers we become *in* Christ, related to an immortal being. If we remain on the spiritual path then immortality is our revised destination.

God takes a different view of us when we become in Christ. He becomes a loving Father. We begin trying to serve Him rather than ourselves. We move from being slaves to sin, to being sons and daughters of God: a shift from slavery to a harsh tyrant to adoption by a loving parent. So, "the truth *shall* make you free"—but only if you're meek. Only if you surrender your self-reliance and self-concern, and replace them with God-reliance and concern about Him. Only then will living the Truth be a truly liberating experience. It frees us from uncertainty, doubt and fear, and all other major and minor anxieties. It removes insecurity from our thinking. When we trust God as much as He wants us to, and invites us to; there is no place for fear and insecurity. **We are free.**

"This is all very easy to *say*," you may be thinking, "but I'm a believer and I still worry and feel insecure much of the time." Fine. I hear what you're saying. But what does that tell you? What you're saying is actually a comment about *yourself*; it's not a valid criticism of the Truth, which you are in effect complaining of as having 'let you down' in some way because you don't experience it as liberating. It tells you two things about yourself.

Firstly—it tells you that **you still have to develop more of this aspect of the fruit of the Spirit called meekness.** You're not relying on God enough. You can lean on Him a lot more than you do. (And always remember you won't have meekness fully until Christ returns to give believers complete freedom from the pull of sin. There will always be lapses while you're a spiritual being dragging round a mortal body. Though in a sense you *can* have perfect meekness even now. Paradoxically, if you're meek enough to recognise you'll never be meek enough, you'll be meek enough. Don't burn your brain out on that one.)

Secondly—it's a sad fact that some believers are set free of the problems of living in the world only to replace them with a whole new set of problems related to living in the Truth! These are usually problems related to being and doing which we discussed earlier. The problem is that if we're not careful we can build up a huge weight of anxiety about our standing and performance before God. We didn't have this when we were in the world, and we might begin to think that we were better off before we believed.

The people of Israel were like that after the exodus from Egypt. They ceased to trust in the care of God, and as a result wandered forty years in the wilderness. They even wished themselves *back* in Egypt. Mercifully most believers don't get so far as to wish themselves back in the world, but if trying to live the Truth is making them anxious they might from time to time hanker after some of the peace of mind they had then. They might almost be jealous of those who don't have the great responsibility (burden?) of being in the Truth.

The only reason we make ourselves anxious over life in the Truth (and it's the same reason Israel made themselves anxious over it) is this: **we think we've got to do it all ourselves**. Israel saw "giants in the land" of promise, and they couldn't cope with the idea of evicting them themselves. But they didn't have to do it themselves! God was going to do it *through* them. They should have had the faith to realize that. We often get anxious over the giants in our own landscape—problems we seem powerless to resolve, things we cannot cope with—when in reality we don't have to cope with them ourselves. God will deal with them through us, if we let Him. If, instead of bemoaning our lot, we become meek enough to trust in His power, He will do one of two things for us: He will either bring into our life whatever we need to resolve the problem, or He will give us the strength to live with it. One of these two will happen once we submit to God and cease imagining that we have to solve all of life's problems ourselves. Becoming a believer is more than being baptised, living by a set of rules, and hoping at last to be in the Kingdom of God: it's placing ourselves unreservedly in God's hands to the exclusion of all doubt, insecurity and fear. The psychologists' couches would all be empty, as would their wallets, if everyone discovered and lived real Christianity!

Perhaps we never thought of our anxieties and fears as being a result of self-reliance, but that's exactly what they are. We might even have thought of our *anxieties* as meekness, because being anxious make us somewhat timorous. And by being anxious we think we are not being self-assertive—we are dutifully worrying. Nothing could be further from the truth. Our anxieties are the product of trying to depend upon ourselves, they are self-reliance. They are the product of 'What-can-*I*-do?' thinking, or 'If-only-*I'd*-done...' thinking, or '*I*-can't-handle-it' thinking. It may not sound like self-reliance to you, but, believe me, if you started relying on God, you wouldn't feel like this any more!

Been there, seen that, done that....

Self-reliance causes anxiety and a spurious kind of meekness, but at the other end of the scale it also causes a brashness which could never be mistaken for meekness. How awful it is when almost every semblance of meekness is missing from a person's character! And how dreadful, too, that we don't notice ourselves slipping into pretentiousness!

We've all met people who need to tell us within two minutes of meeting them what a good job they have, what a nice house in such a good neighbourhood, and what an exotic holiday they've just had, or are about to have. Whatever you've done they've done that, been there, seen that—only *better*, of course!

The biblically meek person may also have 'been there, seen that, done that'—twice round—but you wouldn't know it, at least not from him or her. You might learn it from someone else about them, or in answer to a direct question, or if it's relevant to what you need to know about them. Otherwise you wouldn't know. Such people are not out to impress you. They don't feel the need, because they are free of insecurity.

Bragging, even in a minor way, is invariably a sign of insecurity. And something the biblically meek don't have is insecurity. The person who needs to impress you is not happy with who he is, or the way he thinks he appears to others. Deep down he believes he is not likeable or lovable for *himself* and he will only be liked for what he owns or does or knows. It's a sad reflection of his own distorted view of the people around him. He's envious of almost everybody, and evaluates them only by what *they* own or do. Hence he believes he is judged by the same criteria. As the saying goes: "Deep down he's really quite superficial."

To a degree we're all a little like this. We all worry to some extent what people think of us. We want to project a good image, a better one than the one we have of ourselves. We all like to be liked. To the extent, though, that we develop meekness we will eradicate the need to impress others. We must be independent of the good opinion of others. We care about our reputation, of course, and we try to keep it untarnished, but we should be aware that ultimately it's not in our hands. We have as many reputations as people who know us. We can agonise over that to no profit, or we can take the sensible approach: what you think of me is none of my business. The only One a believer really wants to impress is God—and paradoxically, if he knows God well enough, he will never despair that he knows he never will impress Him.

Virtual reality

Meekness embraces a deep trust in God. It's more than just a *belief* that He is looking after you in your humdrum daily round; it's a **knowing** that he is. If you don't see the difference, then consider that if you can ride a bike, you don't just *believe* you can, you **know** you can. You don't get into the saddle debating inwardly your belief that you can do this; you just *know* you can, it's a fact of your life. When you have a deep reliance upon God you don't honestly mind what other people think about you, or what you do or say, or even look like. Your only concern is what God thinks, and you can be happy in the knowledge that He never misunderstands or misinterprets you. When you have genuine meekness you see no point in inventing a false reality for yourself, hiding away from who you really are. Your first priority is what God thinks, and you know you can neither hoodwink nor impress Him.

We hear much of 'virtual reality' these days. Virtual reality is a computer-generated world in which games are played or skills learned. But the human brain has its own far superior capacity for virtual reality—and it got there a long time before the computer. So many people live in worlds of their own creation, self-centred and not God-centred. Those who understand the Truth should perhaps be incredulous that there are still people living today who believe the world revolves around people. It's like believing that the sun revolves around the earth. One day the spiritual Galileos will be seen to have been right all along.

In spite of all appearances, to be meek is not to make yourself less of a person than you might have been if you were self-assertive; it is to make yourself a person with a firm grasp on reality. The irony is, you don't have to tell yourself and other people lies about yourself, because the truth will serve you better. The truth will set you free. The Biblically meek personality is no less dynamic than it might otherwise have been. It has more real power then the brash personality: it has the power of God behind it. It may lack *self*-publicity and *self*-confidence, but all the while it radiates a quiet God-confidence it will never be bland. Self-generated confidence is shallow and limited; Bible-generated confidence runs deep and is lasting.

Anyone being told they will need to become meek to be a Christian will probably see it as a negative factor. But how wrong they'd be! After all, why choose to depend on yourself, on your own wisdom and strength, when you can depend upon God and His? It's hardly a difficult choice! As the Apostle Paul discovered, "For when I am weak, then am I strong" (2 Cor.12:10). When he was compelled to rely upon God he was at his strongest. Therefore he "took pleasure", he said, in "infirmities, in reproaches, in necessities, in persecutions, in distresses for Christ's sake." Seems perverse, but it's not really hard to understand. Like the Apostle Paul, we can so easily get caught up in what we're doing, what we have, etc. and forget God's hand in it all. When we are humbled by events, we are brought back to reality and discover the true strength of meekness. Life will continue to humble us all the while we are in the Truth because God is concerned that we should learn to live in His strength, not our own. He is concerned that we live in the real world and not as fully paid-up members of a spiritual flat-earth society.

What God and man can do together

A question that often troubles believers when it comes to this business of relying not on ourselves but upon God is, how much? How far should we go? The reason for the question is easy to see, because surely there has to be a practical limit to what we should leave to God. There is a difference between trusting God that everything will work out right and leaving absolutely everything to Him, expecting to do nothing for ourselves.

I heard a story on the radio some time ago that made me angry at first. It was about a man who bought a derelict plot of land. It was smothered in weeds and strewn with the rubbish that people had tipped on it over the years. The man worked long and hard to turn the plot into a beautiful garden. One day a friend called by and looked over the smart new fence to admire the lovely flowers and shrubs. He called out to the man in the garden, "Isn't it wonderful what God and man can do together!" To which the man replied, "You should have seen it when God had it on His own."

As I say, when I first heard that story it angered me. The story was intended, I thought, as an atheistic jibe at religion. I believed it was meant to illustrate that God really has no part in our affairs and that left to Him nothing would ever happen. But then I realized that what it actually illustrates is human short-sightedness. What the man of the story overlooked is that without God there would have been no plot of land, no raw materials for the man to work with, no food and drink to give him the energy for work. Without God there would have been no opportunity, and, oh yes... no man.

God does *not* need man's help, but men and women are blessed when they make themselves the willing tools for God's work.

We cannot be totally passive. There is some merit in the idea of "let go and let God", when for some reason we simply cannot handle what's going on in our life. There is a right time for that attitude. It's a healthy recognition that we are powerless and must trust to God for an answer. **But it's no good as a way of life!** Our trust in God doesn't mean we leave it all to Him, always; it means we live and work in a faithful manner and leave the *outcome* to Him. Ours is not to worry but to trust. The outcome of what we do doesn't ultimately depend on our own skill and performance. "A man's heart deviseth his way: but the Lord directeth his steps" (Prov.16:9).

We have free will over what we do and how we go about it, how great or little effort we put into it, but thankfully the results and effects (assuming we pray about such things) are not left to chance. In a sense there are no such things as failure or success for a believer. He or she must know that all the outcomes of life are simply either lessons of encouragement or chastening from a loving God. If only we could always recognise them as such and remember that this is how life works.

Above the entrance to the Centre Court at the Wimbledon All England Tennis Club are two lines from Rudyard Kipling's famous poem *If*: "If you can meet with triumph and disaster and treat those two impostors both the same...." Kipling had insight enough to recognise what many believers sometimes miss: that triumph and disaster are impostors, they are imaginary—if only we are sufficiently meek and God-reliant to know it!

We work, we plan, we scheme, but we don't trust to ourselves for the outcome. We do what we can, we live in a conscientious manner, and *leave the results to God*. That's the way of meekness. As the wise man of Ecclesiastes found: "The race is not to the swift, nor the battle to the strong, neither yet bread to the wise, nor yet riches to men of understanding, nor yet favour to men of skill; but time [God's time] and chance [happenings at God's disposal—check the use of the word in a concordance] happeneth to them all" (Ecc.9:11). Life doesn't always proceed in an orderly fashion with everything working out exactly as it should. And if you don't know that, you can't be more than a few months old! Logically the swift will win the race, *but not always*; the strong will win the battle, *but not always*; skilful men will be rewarded, *but not always*. The outcome of everything is in God's hands and He may decide the *best* result is not what we expect. The Biblically meek person recognises this and always leaves the result to God, knowing that, for him, it will be good, no matter how it might appear to him or anybody else. Nothing in the life of a believer is left to chance. Events are not random for him or her.

God willing

The practice of saying and writing "God willing" is common among believers, and even sometimes among unbelievers. Saying it is almost superfluous if you live with the understanding that everything in life *is* God willing. But the practice has Scriptural backing. It serves to remove presumption from our day-to-day planning. The problem with such an oft-repeated phrase is that it can lose its force for those who use it. It can be trotted out habitually without conviction—even superstitiously, as if to ward off evil.

It's rather like the phrase "God bless". In business I once spoke on the telephone regularly with a man who had the habit of signing off with "God bless". When I asked him if he was religious he was amazed. "Whatever gave you that impression?" he said. I can't think. Whatever did? Saying "God bless" was just a habit to which he never gave any thought.

The use of "God willing" can be equally without thought, even among believers. But *never* if meekness is sufficiently developed.

Non-believers and believers alike have taken to using the insupportable alternative "all being well". They'll say something like, "I'm going to the market on Tuesday, all being well." It doesn't mean "God willing"—at least I can't convince myself it does. It's just a way of saying it without the possible embarrassment of saying the word 'God' in this Godless society. And what it actually means, if you pause to think about it, is "if nothing untoward happens". "All being well" actually casts Divine providence in a rather sinister role. It's like saying, "Things will all be well if they work out according to my plans, but if God intervenes things won't all be well!"

When a believer uses "God willing" in a conscious, not purely habitual, way he gladly acknowledges God's benevolent hand in his life. In meekness he submits to that hand, knowing that his plans will prosper or be cancelled by a caring higher power who has far more idea of what is good for him than he does. But if he uses "all being well" he gives the impression that if his plans don't work out as he'd hoped then all is not well. God's hand is portrayed as an unwelcome intrusion in his life.

When James exhorted us to say "If the Lord wills" he was thinking primarily of the believers of his day who were business people.

> "Come now, you who say, 'Today or tomorrow we will go to such and such a city, spend a year there, buy and sell, and make a profit,' whereas you do not know what will happen tomorrow. For what is your life? It is even a vapour that appears for a little time and then vanishes away. Instead you ought to say, 'If the Lord wills, we shall live and do this or that.' But now you boast in your arrogance. All such boasting is evil." (Jas.4:13-16 NKJV).

It is in our business lives that we are most likely to leave God out of account. Ironically this is where we most need Him. It's generally through our work that God provides what we need. It is an obvious channel of His goodness and care.

Yet it's in our work that we are more likely to forget that *outcome* depends on God. We may think that we have our job and get our salary because *we* are so good at what we do, so clever, so qualified, so useful to others. And our business planning, as in James's day, probably doesn't take God into account. Okay, we don't expect to hear a "God willing" at a business meeting (though it's not unknown!), or around the boardroom table if we're in company management, but the *thought* can at least be in our heart, and expressed if appropriate.

Whatever line of work you're in, white collar, blue collar, or donkey jacket, employed or self-employed, you must know that you are working "as to the Lord". And even if you don't work in the accepted sense of having salaried employment, if you're a home-maker, or retired or unemployed, you can still work "as to the Lord" in whatever you do. James doesn't confine the use of "if the Lord wills" to our business life; he extends it to all life: "if the Lord wills **we shall live** and do this or that."

Even in the making of simple daily appointments and arrangements, whether it be for the dentist, a cup of coffee with a friend, or a business meeting, the thought "God willing" should be implicit. And it *will* be if you have cultivated the quality of meekness in your character. You don't need to keep obsessively repeating the phrase at every turn like a mantra; you need only to live with a spirit of meekness. When you have meekness you *know* that God is in control, and all the outcomes of your life are in His good hands. You are God-reliant.

A life of meekness

Biblical meekness is a valuable asset in every facet of life. Without this special aspect, love is certainly incomplete. Just a glance at some of the sixteen occasions where *praotes* and its variants occur in Scripture should be enough to convince you of its value.

It is linked with **love**, with **glorying in the Lord** (not ourselves), with **walking worthily**, with **being one of the elect of God**, with **fleeing the love of money and covetousness**, with **Christ** himself, with **inheriting the Kingdom of God**, and with **beauty** and **wisdom**.

In addition to these, three times meekness is related to an absence of striving. The Biblically meek have no desire for strife, and will not cause it. They do not strive in the sense of being 'pushy': they are not ' brawlers' in either their actions or words.

Also the preaching of the meek is done with gentleness. They don't ride rough-shod over the opinions of others. Moreover their attempts to instruct believers they consider to be in error, in either doctrine or practice, are carried out in gentleness. How easy it is to lose meekness when dealing with what we perceive to be error among our fellows! We might protest that our direct, no-nonsense approach is motivated by love, but if love lacks the vital element of meekness it ceases to be love. In such situations we have to make sure we're not acting from our own strength (championing our own cause) and being *self*-assertive, rather than proceeding gently and in God's strength. Don't make a similar mistake to the man who bought the plot of land: don't imagine that, but for you, the brotherhood would be in an awful state!

The meek shall inherit the earth

We cannot leave the subject of meekness without reference to the most famous passage of all on the subject: "Blessed are the meek: for they shall inherit the earth." Instantly recognizable, I would say, even in these days of unread Bibles, as one of the Beatitudes. They are the opening words of Jesus' sermon on the mount (Matt.5:1-12).

Interestingly, there are nine Beatitudes, as there are nine items listed as the fruit of the Spirit. I'm sure that here we have another appearance of the fruit of the Spirit, dressed in different clothes. The nine Beatitudes don't describe nine *different* types of people—the poor in spirit, the meek, those that hunger and thirst after righteousness, etc.—as if there are nine distinct groups of believers who are acceptable to God! The Beatitudes describe the different qualities of character that together make the whole character of a saint (the eight aspects that equal love). This is how I suggest the two lists line up:

Blessed are-	**The fruit of the Spirit is-**
1 the poor in spirit	longsuffering
2 they that mourn	faith
3 the meek	meekness
4 they which hunger and thirst after righteousness	temperance
5 the merciful	love
6 the pure in heart	goodness
7 the peacemakers	peace
8 the persecuted for righteousness	gentleness
9 the reviled, falsely accused, for Christ—rejoice, be glad.	joy

Some of the connections are less obvious than others (linking the mourners with faith, for instance, but the believer who mourns must do so with faith, seeing the unseen hand of God in whatever occurs: faith must be a quality that arises from mourning, or the believer may become an unbeliever!) It might be argued that some could be better assigned. But I believe the comparison does show a general correspondence between the two lists.

As I mentioned back in Chapter Six, there are a number of appearances in the Scriptures of lists that equate with the fruit of the Spirit. The Beatitudes is one that could easily go unnoticed. I'm sure many do. So far I've not noticed one in the Old Testament, and it would give me great delight to find one. I'm sure they're there.

What the merging of the Beatitudes with the fruit of the Spirit adds up to is this:

> *Blessed is the man or woman who has love in all its aspects: theirs is the kingdom of heaven; they shall be comforted; they shall inherit the earth; they shall be filled with righteousness; they shall obtain mercy; they shall see God; they shall be called the children of God; and great is their reward in heaven.*

The proud, ungodly, unruly, self-reliant of this present world scoff at the idea of the meek ever inheriting the earth. Nothing could be more ridiculous to them. They fail to see where true strength lies. It lies in submission to God. Ultimately all those who won't submit to Him will simply be removed from the earth. Psalm 37 makes that abundantly plain. The meek shall then inherit the earth, "and delight themselves in the abundance of peace"—to complete the quotation Christ used from Psalm 37 (v11).

Christ will be more than pleased to welcome those who are meek (and who have, of course, the other aspects of love), into his kingdom. They will **be** the right people to inhabit the paradise of God. You'll recall that the fruit of the Spirit is about *being* and not *doing*: it's about who we *are* before what we *do*. The elements of the fruit are all aspects of the character that we need to please Christ—they are things we must **be**. And they are, as I've said, healthy and correct **attitudes** to life.

In fact, if I may be so bold as to finish this chapter on the worst pun you may hear for some time—they are all **be-attitudes**! I'll now escape quickly to the next chapter.

CHAPTER FOURTEEN

TEMPERANCE: *(egkrateia)*

SINCE the early 1900s when the Temperance Movement began in America, temperance has been commonly associated with abstinence from alcohol. The demon drink was ruining the lives of ordinary folk in increasing numbers. As a reaction many 'signed the pledge' committing themselves never to touch another drop. American wives and mothers discovered then, as many governments forced to introduce legislation have since discovered—alcohol is a killer.

Nothing exceeds like excess

Alcohol is a killer. But so is anything we might crave and let get the better of us. So many of our bodily needs and pleasures are potential killers if we let them get control of us. Things which are good and healthy in moderation, within God's guidelines, can be lethal when taken to excess: eating, drinking, exercise, sex, even sleep and cleanliness, and anything else to which we might become addicted like drugs, gambling, money, television—any pleasure or excitement over which we lose control.

I don't mean that you will necessarily be killed *directly* by lack of temperance in any of these areas: sleep and television, for instance. What I'm talking about here is the ultimately more serious harm to our *spiritual* prospects that intemperance and addiction cause. Our spiritual will and commitment is sapped when we surrender control of our life to any bodily or psychological need or pleasure. And that can be fatal.

Control

To be temperate is to have control. Most people would think of it as self-control. But the temperance that is a part of the fruit of the Spirit is not gained through *self*-control but through *God*-control. Just as the reliance we get from Biblical meekness is not self-reliance but God-reliance, so the control we get from temperance is obtained from God and not through our own efforts. Our own wills are weak things at best and need to be aligned to some higher force if we are ever going to achieve anything. Temperance comes through delight and meditation in the Word of God. Take the Word to heart and it has a transforming power beyond anything else in this world.

As I've already mentioned, a number of the aspects of the fruit of the Spirit give the impression of being undesirable, wishy-washy characteristics. Gentleness, kindness and meekness fall into this category. But when we delved behind the words to the true spiritual meaning, we found they were not weaknesses but strengths. This is very much the case with temperance. Temperance is holding back our natural inclinations, not running to the same excesses that may be perfectly acceptable to unbelievers. Ironically they will probably see temperance not as a fruit of the Spirit but as a *lack* of spirit! Temperance to many people means being over-conservative, unadventurous.

A typical reaction of non-Christians to the changed lifestyle of newly-baptised believers is to think they've *lost* so much of what makes life interesting and exciting. The new Christian's old friends, family and acquaintances often can't understand the changes that have come about in the person they thought they knew. The Apostle Peter summed up the situation well for us in his first letter: "For we have spent enough of our past lifetime in doing the will of the Gentiles—when we walked in licentiousness, lusts, drunkenness, revelries, drinking parties, and abominable idolatries. In regard to these, they think it strange that you do not run with them in the same flood of dissipation, speaking evil of you" (1 Pet.4:3.4 NKJV). Isn't it marvellous!—as soon as you stop your evil ways, your running to excess, evil is spoken of you!

Well, it's not really so surprising. All the while you were as godless as most other people nobody really noticed how you behaved: you blended in with everybody else. As soon as you change your lifestyle you become a target for criticism. "Who does he think he is? What's wrong with a good drinking party anyway? What's the matter with whooping it up a bit? How deadly dull he's become since he got religion. If that's what Christianity does to you, then no thank you! He takes himself far too seriously. Surely you can be a believer and still have a good time?"

Actually the answer to that last question is a resounding **YES!** You can believe the Gospel and still have a good time—**but not always the same good time.** And if you think you can you're seriously kidding yourself. What commonly passes for a good time is often a bad time. It's usually running to excess. If you want to run to the same excesses as unbelievers, enjoying almost everything that takes your fancy to whatever degree you like, then you can kiss good-bye to any serious notions you have about being a believer. I might just as easily call myself a fisherman, though I don't own a rod and line and never go fishing! I could talk about it a lot, read about it, even meet up with real fishermen, but I still wouldn't qualify, however much I insisted.

If you want to be a believer you must learn a measure of temperance. It sounds painfully inhibiting. In fact it sounds so off-putting that it's a major block to people becoming believers. The fact that it's for their own immediate *and eternal* good doesn't influence people much either.

A caring Heavenly Father wants to lead us in the right direction, away from all the things which will ruin our lives now, and which will cause Him, in the long run, to disown us. From God's fatherly point of view the human race must seem eternally stuck in adolescence—and that goes for some believers too. Where He is concerned we may be spending our whole lives as difficult teenagers, never reaching maturity. Most of the world does. It's a rare teenager who quickly grasps the fact that what his or her parents suggest might actually be a good thing. After all, why shouldn't they do anything they want and not consider the consequences? It has been said that teenagers want all the benefits of adulthood with none of the responsibilities. I fear the same is sometimes true of believers who expect all the benefits from their Heavenly Father of Christian maturity, but will take on few, if any, of the responsibilities. Mostly it's a temperance problem.

Temperance is hard for teenagers. And it's hard for spiritual adolescents of all ages. The problem, as every believer knows, is that we don't trade our body for a new one with different desires at the moment of baptism. We might imagine it's going to be like that, but we soon learn differently. We still have the same old rebellious nature—but now we have the problem of trying to control it far more than we did! And to do this we need the knowledge, wisdom and understanding that can come only from personal delight and meditation in the Word of a Father who really *does* know best. Our lives are the richer for it, and our future prospects improved beyond measure.

Felix

The Greek word for temperance is *egkrateia* (pronounced *en*-krateia). It is a compound of two words *en* and *kratos*, and taken literally means *in strength*. It means to have power over oneself. And, let's face it, that takes a lot of strength! We tend to give in to our inborn desires because the lure from within is so strong. We have to be even stronger, and perhaps even a little devious with ourselves, if we are to overcome it. "He who rules his spirit [is better] than he who takes a city" (Prov.16:32). A man may conquer many things and achieve much in his life without ever succeeding in his greatest challenge—himself.

In the Acts of the Apostles we meet a man who had done well for himself. He'd risen from being a slave to become Procurator of Judea. But "The most excellent

Governor Felix", for such was his title and name according to the protocol of the times, failed abysmally as a person. While Felix was in his exalted office as Procurator, the Apostle Paul was sent to him by a Roman officer, Claudius Lysias, for the benefit of his judgement. Felix was to help decide what to do with this Jewish academic turned Christian whom the Jews so passionately wanted out of the way.

Paul was taken before Felix to plead his cause. Initially Paul's defence made no impression on the man. Felix kept him a prisoner, though, in the hope of receiving a bribe to free him. What a nice man! But at one of their meetings, "Paul reasoned of righteousness, temperance, and judgment to come" and "Felix trembled, and answered, Go thy way for this time; when I have a convenient season, I will call for thee" (Acts 24:25). As well as *having* some nerve, Paul must have *hit* a nerve! Felix said, in effect, "I've had enough of this! Don't call me, I'll call you!" The last things he wanted to hear about were temperance and judgement— judgement being the consequence of not being temperate.

Tacitus, the Roman historian, records that Felix indulged in all kinds of cruelty and lust, exercising his royal powers with the disposition of the slave he once was. Adultery and murder were but two of the excesses of his character. He was known for extreme ruthlessness. No doubt he obtained his position of power through his vicious nature. Such people don't mind who they tread on along the road to power. Sadly such people can be useful to those with greater power. A 'hatchet man' is often useful to those who want to distance themselves from unsavoury deeds. A Felix would certainly have his uses in the Roman political world.

What is odd is that the Roman captain, Claudius Lysias, who appears in the record of the Acts to be such a decent sort, should send Paul to such a monster as Felix. For the benefit of his judgement, no less! One is left to think that either there was, after all, some mischief in the man, or, and perhaps worse, he was simply following standard procedures—just doing his job. How much mischief is sometimes perpetrated under the slogan of "Just doing my job"!

But Paul survived his meetings with Felix. What a testimony that is to the extraordinary nature of the Apostle Paul, that he could deliver a sermon on righteousness, temperance and judgement to such a monster and get away with it! Felix's name means 'happy', but he wasn't very happy when Paul left him that day. Paul unsettled his arrogant self-confidence, found an unexpected soft spot in a granite heart.

Ultimately, at least as far as we can tell from the history books, there was no change in Felix, even though he saw Paul a number of times over the next two years. I would think it likely that Paul was forbidden to speak on certain subjects when they met. Felix's interest remained not in his own reformation but in how much money he might extort for his release from Paul's friends or supposedly wealthy family. Knowing that Paul was a scholar from Tarsus ("no mean city"—Acts 21:39), Felix doubtless conjectured a well-to-do family.

An adulterous generation

The tragedy with regard to temperance, as demonstrated by Felix, is that those who most need to hear about it are those least likely to listen—the eternal teenagers who don't need to be told how to run their lives, thank you very much! But just because we're not as bad as Felix doesn't mean we don't have a problem with temperance. Even though we may not be guilty of adultery and murder, we can still be guilty of the spiritual equivalents. According to Jesus: "Whosoever looketh upon a woman to lust after her hath committed adultery with her already in his heart" (Matt.5:28), and "Whosoever is angry with his brother without a cause" is in danger of the same judgement as a murderer (Matt.5:21,22). Intemperate thinking puts us in as much danger as intemperate action. Because what we *are* governs what we do. Often the only difference between the mental and physical adulterer is lack of opportunity, or lack of courage.

Where Felix was concerned, Paul's chief criticism must have been levelled at the governor's adulterous lifestyle. It can be no accident that on the occasion Paul exhorted Felix about temperance and judgement we are particularly told that Felix's wife Drusilla was present (Acts 24:24,25). This Drusilla, a Jewess, had been wife to Aziz, king of Amesa, and had been persuaded away from him by Felix. The implications are strong that Paul's remonstrations about temperance and judgement were aimed directly at Felix and Drusilla's adulterous relationship. A temperate man or woman would have enough control over themselves to leave another's spouse alone, however attractive the spouse might be.

Biblical temperance is very much about control of the sexual drive. On every occasion when temperance (*egkrateia*) and intemperance (*akrasia*) are used in Scripture in a context which clearly identifies what we are to be temperate about, it is unmistakably the sexual appetite that is meant.

This makes the subject a little delicate. Believers generally don't like to talk about the sexual drive too openly or too often. And I can understand people not wanting to dwell on it or go into specifics. As Paul said, regarding some forms of immoral behaviour, "It is a shame even to speak of those things" (Eph.5:12). Discussion itself can be intemperate!

But that's no reason to duck the issue entirely. The Scriptures certainly don't. They have a lot to say about sexual matters. And we cannot properly discuss Biblical temperance without reference to the subject.

Temperance is all about being strong in the control of our natural tendencies, and the sexual drive is sometimes the strongest natural tendency we have to deal with. We can't be head in the sand about it. And I'm not talking only about the young, or about men only. This applies to men and women across the age range. The sexual urge can be strong and persistent and sometimes chronic, even addictive, for anyone.

To love, honour and... betray

What was once sniggered at in school sex education classes is hardly enough to set us on the straight and narrow for life. Our western society has dropped many of the sexual barriers since the 'swinging sixties' and things which are Biblically sin are no longer socially sin. The exercise of temperance is now rated prudish and old-hat. And you don't have to be a prophet to see that it will get worse. The trend is towards more 'open' marriages. I don't have to bore you with statistics. You must know from your own experience of society how far it has gone down the road of immorality—a road which now has a new sign up, saying 'sexual freedom'. I have children at school and I can't help noticing how many of their classmates lack both parents at home, or no longer have their original parents.

Okay, one has to accept that awful and insurmountable problems sometimes devastate a relationship, and one must feel truly sorry for all concerned. They need our understanding, not censure. But the sheer numbers involved nowadays indicate a lack of commitment more than an increase in truly serious problems. "If it isn't working, don't hang around and work at it—get out." Or if someone is strongly attracted to someone outside their rather ordinary marriage (or their "common law" marriage) then, "How can it be wrong when it feels so right?" It's a protest worthy of Felix. How, indeed, can it be wrong? Do they really want to know? Do they really want to be spoken to of righteousness, temperance and judgement to come? I doubt it.

Society may 'progress' as far as it likes (and doubtless will) away from the Biblical guidelines of a caring God, but those guidelines will never change to accommodate society. We must be highly suspicious of all attempts to re-interpret the guidelines. God cares too much to encourage us in destructive behaviour. I don't know who gave the 'permissive society' its permission, but it certainly wasn't God!

Striking at the root

But, as I said earlier, we don't have to be living a *visibly* immoral life to be censured as adulterers by Biblical standards. Christ said that to look lustfully at a woman was adultery too. The same applies to women looking at men. To entertain the *idea* of adultery is also a defilement. And it can lead to the act. It's difficult to believe that anybody who commits adultery or fornication does it right out of the blue, having never entertained or savoured the idea beforehand. What appears to be a sudden lapse cannot be really, except in the rarest of cases (David and Bathsheba). This is why Christ strikes at the root of the problem. The heart/mind is where it all begins. Christ isn't going over the top when he draws a parallel between the seriousness of the thought and the deed. He was in earnest; he always is.

So how do believers deal with the problem in themselves? How many can put up their hands and say they've *never* turned their head to glance at a pretty girl or handsome male? Even among the married? To be honest, I think you'd be unusual if you never did. There's no harm in an admiring glance at someone who catches your eye— Christ wasn't concerned with that. It's looking lustfully that he warned against: dwelling persistently upon, entertaining and savouring immoral thoughts. Perhaps many believers have learned to control it after their years in the Truth. But how many are entirely free? And, it must be asked, how many go through continual horrors of recrimination and self-hatred because of giving in to the weakness of intemperance?

Helpful words

The Truth's literature is mostly either silent or indirect on the subject. Which must leave the afflicted feeling isolated. It isn't *done* to talk about such problems. Who can you turn to, anyway? Who would you trust? That's an indictment of a lot of us, I suppose, but I am only guessing. I'd like to believe that so little is known about such problems among believers because we are sufficiently discreet, rather than that we are afraid to confide. But I wonder. In almost thirty years in the Truth only three people have ever mentioned the problem to me. It's a fair guess there are more, knowing human nature.

Letters to George and Jenny (H.A.Whittaker) approaches the problem fairly straightforwardly. But it's aimed particularly at the young. We have to look further afield for a reasonable general appraisal of the subject. Merlin Carothers is an American author who writes mostly on the subject of praise, but he also produced an interesting little book called *What's on Your Mind?* In it he cites his own battle with the problem, and refers to it as "our most consuming temptation". His theology is occasionally adrift, but his observations and experiences of human nature are worthy of attention. It may surprise some to learn how almost universal he discovered intemperance to be.

Working as a U.S. army chaplain at one time in his life, Carothers was at the side of many men who believed they were dying. When asked what sins they wanted to confess, "their first thoughts were frequently about men they had been forced to kill in their roles as soldiers. Their next requests were usually about immoral acts or thoughts." In dealing with his fellow Christians he says that "thousands of men have told me that their most consuming and overpowering temptation is immoral thinking."

Carothers speaks of Satan's involvement at times, but he does occasionally concede that Satan appears to be working from *within* us. And though he mentions the power of the Holy Spirit as a force to lead us out of temptation, his ultimate solution is not that. At least not directly.

Interestingly, the only workable solution to the problem of indulging immoral thoughts and behaviour that Carothers could find is to focus on a collection of appropriate Bible statements. He produces a list of them at the back of his book. The conclusion he reached was that the only personally attested answer to the problem was, in effect, delight and meditation in the Word of God. The verses he picked are culled from Genesis to Revelation. **"The ultimate solution:"** he says, **"God's written word."**

Triggers

Merlin Carothers' answer is to use tempting circumstances as triggers for instant Bible help. It's a kind of spiritual Judo in which you use your opponent's strength against him. His solution, in fact, brings together two ideas we've covered already in this book.

1 When dealing with *goodness* we explored the concept of using to our advantage the self-talk that goes on in our heads all the while. When we delight and meditate in the Word our inner dialogue is considerably affected for the better. It becomes more of a dialogue with God. His thoughts lodge in our mind to be touched off by our own thoughts.

2 In another chapter, I introduced the idea of allowing so-called bad happenings to work for our good. They can be *triggers* to remind us of God's presence and help. So, when you knock over your cup of coffee, say, or somebody knocks it over you, instead of bemoaning your lot and acting foolishly, you are instantly reminded of God's providence. It may seem like a trivial prompt, but, let's face it, most of our days are spent in fairly ordinary, low-key activities. If you don't find God in those ordinary moments, when *are* you going to find Him! If you wait for earth-shattering events you might wait an earth-shatteringly long time—and forget God in the meantime.

Bring triggers **1** and **2** together and you have the perfect double-handed device for promoting temperance in yourself. Keep in mind some appropriate pieces from your delight and meditation in the Word and consciously associate them with tempting thoughts and situations. This way the right Biblical counsel is always triggered at the right moment.

Whether you act on it is up to you. But at least you will have given yourself a fighting chance: a strong pull from the right direction to counter the pull you experience from your basic drives. It's a method that can help in all situations where temptation is strong. It may seem like a trivial way to deal with a big problem, but it has been *shown* to be successful. Because our problems appear complex we may be inclined to search for, and expect a complex solution, when all the while the answer is simple. We may even reject a simple answer because it doesn't seem worthy of our problem! The smart approach is quite simply, **if it works, use it.**

Another trigger

While we're on the subject of triggers, here's another one that will help. If you believe that you're stuck with a certain pattern of thought or behaviour, try this little test. Answer the following question seriously. Someone is holding a gun to your head saying, "If you carry on thinking like that, or doing that, I'll pull this trigger." If that was a *real* situation for you, would you be able to stop? If you believe you would still continue then you really do have a problem! Ninety-nine point nine nine per cent of people would find sufficient motivation to stop faced with a trigger like that. Which surely proves that, in the final analysis, you *are* making a choice. You may not think you have a choice, that your impulses are too strong, but, in reality, you are doing what most appeals to you, not what you cannot help doing. What you lack is sufficient motivation to be temperate. That level of motivation is thankfully available from the Word of God rather than the barrel of a gun.

But even when presented with clear-cut solutions, our problems can still appear insurmountable. And when some Smart Alec tells you the answer is straightforward and you still fail, it can make you all the more miserable. **It helps to**

talk about problems with temperance if you can, especially if the problem is shaming you into a poor spiritual life and low expectations of a future reward. As with most difficulties in spiritual life, we all need help and understanding, not censure and rejection.

It's not the end of the world

I wonder how many believers secretly suspect they won't be in the Kingdom of God because they are short on temperance. Would those same people consider a shortage of joy a bar to the Kingdom? Or longsuffering? I'm not saying we necessarily downgrade lust on the league table of sins, but that we keep it in perspective.

There may be a case for saying that the *consequences* of lust can be more serious than other sins. Paul makes the case when he says, "Flee fornication. Every sin that a man doeth is without the body; but he that committeth fornication sinneth against his own body" (1 Cor.6:18). Paul does *appear* to be elevating sexual sin above other sins. The reason for this is surely because fornication in those days often involved a harlot who worked in one of the pagan temples. Idol worship involved certain sexual rites. A believer is joined to God; his body is a "temple of the holy Spirit"—the Spirit Word resides in him. He should not defile that temple by joining it to the harlot servant of a pagan god.

Such idol worship, complete with sexual rituals, is not a problem these days, certainly not in my part of the world. But the principle Paul laid down still applies: that sexual sin is viewed by God as *more* of a defilement than other sin.

But, even so, *neither lust nor its consequences qualify as an unforgivable sin.* There is nothing in Galatians 5 to suggest that temperance is any more important and more to be sought than any other aspect of the fruit of the Spirit. Can the lack of it therefore be any more serious than the lack of any other?

A believer who lacks temperance is in no greater danger of losing his or her reward than one who lacks any other aspect of the fruit. This doesn't make their position any happier, of course, but it does put things in perspective—especially for those who might fail in meekness when dealing with one who has failed in temperance. Anyone who is failing in temperance must remember that every believer who goes before Christ at his return will lack the fruit of the Spirit in some way, in both quality and quantity. This isn't an excuse for you to give up trying, but a reminder that you'll never have all eight aspects of love in full—not in this life. **But if you 'hunger and thirst' after them you 'shall be filled' in the next.** *Nil desperandum* should be inscribed upon your shield of faith.

Temperance and *Super*-temperance

Of all the verses in which *egkrateia* appears, the most useful from the point of view of establishing the meaning of the word are 1 Corinthians 7:9 and 1 Corinthians 9:25. These verses show the word in a helpful context and not simply as part of a list of qualities, such as "a bishop must be... sober, just, holy, temperate" (Titus 1:7,8). Lists are not helpful when it comes to working out what individual words mean; we have to find a better context. Those two verses in 1 Corinthians provide exactly what we need. And being so close together in the same epistle, we have the added help of a link between them.

In the verses just prior to 1 Corinthians 7:9, Paul writes about how much easier he believes it is to serve God if one remains unmarried. He cites his own example. It left him free to dedicate himself wholly to the work of the Truth, getting the first century churches established. Then he continues, "I say therefore to the unmarried and widows, It is good for them if they abide even as I. But if they cannot contain, let them marry: for it is better to marry than to burn" (1 Cor 7:8,9).

"Where is the word temperate in that?" you might well ask. It isn't. But the word *egkratiea* (the *temperance* of the fruit of the Spirit) *is* there. On this occasion, though, the word has been translated *contain*. "If they cannot contain..." If they cannot practise temperance, let them marry. Or as Moffatt's more racy version has it, "Better marry than be aflame with passion." So we are back with temperance as a restraining of the sexual drive. Paul says that the unmarried and widows, *if* they have a suitable partner in the offing (otherwise the advice doesn't apply), are better off marrying than suffering the distractions of a consuming passion.

Paul had no mandate to say that because *he* could cope with the single life therefore every other believer should do the same. In fact experience tells us that Paul is the exception rather than the rule. A bishop has to be temperate (Titus 1:8) but he can still be "the husband of one wife" (Titus 1:6). Paul was extraordinarily temperate—super-temperate!—but he could not, and would not, make his celibacy the rule for everyone. It's not for everyone. In fact, it's not for most.

Temporary celibacy

While we're on the subject of celibacy, if we go back a few verses from "if they cannot contain..." to verse five of 1 Corinthians 7, we find Paul writing about periods of temporary celibacy. The verse is relevant to our train of thought because it contains the Greek word *akrasia* (intemperance) which is the direct opposite of *egkrateia*. "Defraud ye not one another, except it be with consent for a time, that ye may give yourselves to fasting and prayer; and come together again, that Satan tempt you not for your incontinency." That last word is the one. The sense is more clear in the NKJV: "and come together again so that Satan does not tempt you because of your lack of self-control."

What Paul is getting at is that these times of temporary celibacy have to be worked out and agreed upon by *both* partners, not by one partner imposing his or her requirements on the other, and they should not be for too long either. It's dangerous if one partner enforces a longer time apart than the other can cope with. Self-control (*egkrateia*) can easily degenerate to lack of self-control (*akrasia*) when one or both partners tries to play the hero against a strong basic drive. It's okay for some, but it isn't okay for everyone.

Now let's have a look at another helpful verse containing *egkrateia*: 1 Cor 9:25. The verse contains one of Paul's sporting analogies: "Know ye not that they which run in a race run all, but one receiveth the prize? So run, that ye may obtain. And every man that striveth for the mastery is temperate in all things. Now they do it to obtain a corruptible crown; but we an incorruptible."

Top class athletes of Paul's day (and our own) had to be temperate in all things to keep themselves in tip-top condition for races and other events. They had to practise self-control over diet, the amount of training they did, and the sort of amusements they allowed themselves. Paul felt the same way about the race for eternal life. If he did not keep himself temperate in all things, if he did not keep his "body in subjection" (a telling phrase in the light of what we've learned about temperance), he felt sure he would end up a castaway regarding the faith. Actually 'castaway' is rather a soft word; it hardly conveys Paul's thought. The Greek word he used is better translated *reprobate*. Every other use of that word reprobate in the New Testament is connected with immoral behaviour. Obviously what Paul feared for himself and for all his fellow believers was a lapse into immoral ways from failing to treat the race for eternal life with as much seriousness and dedication as the athletes treated their races. Corinth in Paul's day was a degenerate place, and so is the world we live in now. If we don't practise temperance, keep our bodies in subjection, we will fall into immoral ways.

An excess of moderation

Perhaps you think I'm being too specific about temperance, relating it exclusively to our need to overcome a tendency to think and act immorally? But I believe, and hopefully have demonstrated, that this is what it is *mostly* about. Although, as I said at the outset of this chapter, temperance is a quality we can apply profitably to many areas of life. Drinking alcohol, amassing money, or spending it, eating—these are all activities over which for a better physical and spiritual lifestyle we are better off exercising some self-control. The Scriptures tell us God's will for us in these and other things. Temperance, or sometimes abstinence, is either recommended or commanded. It's necessary to keep these things in mind, and not be excessive in our habits. But where the fruit of the Spirit in concerned I believe it can be demonstrated that temperance is not general in its application but specific. It relates to the sexual drive.

The fact that Paul said "temperate in *all* things" doesn't change my view of the specific nature of temperance as a fruit of the Spirit—for reasons I'll give in a moment.

A phrase that is often heard, and which is *not* found in Scripture, is "moderation in all things". It's thought, I'm sure, to be the equivalent of saying 'temperate in all things', though Scripturally moderation and temperance are very different.

I'm very careful these days about using the phrase "moderation in all things"—ever since some Smart Alec told me that this was an *excess of moderation!* In a sense he was right. And the Scriptures never tell us to be either moderate or temperate in *all* things. Think about it: it would be unworkable.

So what are we to make of Paul's advice that we be 'temperate in all things' like the Corinthian athletes? If you look at the context you'll see that the word *all* is not the universal *all*. We've looked at this problem with *all* before. Scripturally it doesn't always mean absolutely everything. As always, the context must be taken into account.

In Paul's words in 1 Corinthians 9 the context is clearly confined to bodily excesses. Being temperate in all things equates to "keeping under [subduing] my body." The Corinthian athletes limited their diets and social lives to keep in peak fitness. They were temperate in all things related to their bodies, but they weren't temperate in other things. Neither should we be. In their desire to be the first over the finishing line, and in their love of their sport they were anything but temperate!

We are to be self-controlled when it comes to our bodily needs and inclinations, but in other concerns there's no restriction. We can soar as high as our heart will take us. "Love the Lord with **all** thy heart, and with **all** thy soul, and with **all** thy mind..." (Matt. 22:37). No restrictions there. There's no limit to how much we can try to love God and serve Him. *All* means *all* in that verse. There are many good things about which we should not be temperate. The phrase 'temperate in all things' cannot be taken at face value—it has to be qualified. It concerns bodily needs and urges—and where these things are concerned, temperance is required.

Temperance and moderation

Let's go back to the point I made about temperance and moderation being different. In English there's hardly any difference. They are close synonyms. But in the Greek from which the New Testament was translated *temperance* means the sort of self-control we are to exercise over our bodies, and *moderation* means flexibility in our dealings with other people.

Paul's advice to "Let your moderation be known unto all men" (Phil.4:5) is not a recommendation to be temperate, self-controlled, but to be tolerant and flexible towards others. And by that he didn't mean, of course, flexible in *doctrine*, or in ways which would make you appear to condone outrageous behaviour. There *are* times when we need to moderate our approach. We can sometimes be too rigid in our treatment and expectations of one another in matters of no great consequence. We do better to let our moderation be known to all. Which, to make the point one last time, has nothing to do with the temperance we must exercise over our bodies.

God and temperance

Every man and woman who strives for spiritual mastery must work at having self-control in this area of bodily needs and desires. This is temperance, the final aspect of the fruit of the Spirit. Last and definitely not least of the parts of love. The order of the aspects is probably irrelevant. That the aspects of the fruit appear in a sequence suggesting order is just one of the inadequacies of living within the constraints of time. We see things consecutively, experience things one after another, so a list always appears as a series of items, when in fact, in the case of the fruit of the Spirit, the items should all appear at the same moment on the page to avoid the misleading appearance of an order of merit. Now *there's* an interesting challenge for the printer.

All the parts of love have equal merit. They are all equally desirable if we truly want to be like Christ and have *agape* for ourselves. Christ self-evidently had this quality of temperance along with all the other parts of the fruit of the Spirit. He had it to the point of remaining unmarried like Paul in order to give himself wholly to the things of God.

What I find a little perplexing, though, is the question of God and temperance. How could God have temperance? God is love, therefore He possesses all the qualities of *agape*. But it's difficult to comprehend how God has temperance when He does not have a physical body, and could not be prompted to do wrong. What are we to make of it?

When we looked at the *meekness* of God in the previous chapter, we considered how God contained His mighty strength. How little of His awesome power is actually manifested in the universe. He exhibits the controlled strength of meekness to perfection, as one would expect.

It seems to me that the temperance of God must work alongside His meekness. The two are complementary aspects of His character. Because He is meek He is not given to showy demonstrations of power just to let everyone know what He can do. Because He is temperate He is not given to the *uncontrolled* use of His power. In fact God is extremely sparing in the use of His phenomenal abilities. The Bible tells us—even as our own *lives* tell us—that God is far more likely to use seemingly natural means to bring about His purpose than supernatural means. Considering His abilities He does have an astonishing level of self-control.

The lessons for us? To encourage meekness in ourselves and thereby prevent unseemly showiness. To encourage temperance in ourselves and thereby conserve our bodily energies for less sensational (at present), though ultimately *more* pleasing experiences.

CHAPTER FIFTEEN

THE WORKS OF THE FLESH

STANDING right in front of the list of all the fine qualities of the fruit of the Spirit in Galatians 5 is another list which summarises all the very worst that the human character is capable of producing. The list is titled "the works of the flesh". It's a real nasty crop of evil traits, and if one were looking for a suitable collective noun for them, then perhaps 'foulness' might be a good choice: a foulness of works of the flesh!

I'd not intended this originally, but I think we should give some thought to this ghastly list because it so closely relates to the fruit of the Spirit. An understanding of the relationship between the two lists will help us to put the fruit of the Spirit to work in our lives.

The law of mutual exclusion

The two lists are mutually exclusive. When you manifest the works of the flesh, you exclude the fruit of the Spirit. If you produce the fruit, you obliterate the works of the flesh. It's as simple (and as *difficult!*) as that. In reality it's not quite so black and white, and we are all somewhere in the middle, having produced only a certain amount of the fruit and obliterated only a certain amount of the works.

And there would appear to be a fairly precise ratio here —a law, in fact—that **to whatever degree you produce the fruit of the Spirit, to that same degree you will eliminate the works of the flesh.** And vice versa: you will have pretty well the same level of works of the flesh in your life as you lack fruit of the Spirit in your character.

An important part of the life's work of a believer is to produce as much fruit as possible and thereby eliminate as much of the works as possible. And we can be helped in doing this by knowing how the fruit and the works interact.

The two lists are not mutually exclusive in a *general* way. It's not hit and miss, that when you produce a certain aspect of the fruit in your character some totally unrelated work of the flesh is overcome. There is a distinct logical correlation between individual aspects of the fruit and works. For example, when you become more longsuffering you reduce anger, you don't reduce a tendency to lust.

The purpose of adding these chapters on the works of the flesh is to see which aspect of the fruit of the Spirit cancels which work of the flesh. It's useful to know this because it can help us in dealing with our failings—which, let's be honest, sometimes we are at a loss to know how to deal with. Especially when it comes to a besetting sin that we've all but given up on, it would be useful to know which aspect of the fruit we are lacking and need to cultivate to eliminate it.

The spiritual is like the physical: once you identify the right treatment for what's ailing you, you stand a better chance of getting well! I can testify from experience that by using this approach it *is* possible to overcome specific areas of failure. Though, as I've said many times in these pages, none of us will ever eliminate *all* sin from our character. All the while we inhabit these mortal bodies perfection will elude us. But almost all of us can be better than we are. A higher spirituality is possible for ninety-nine per cent of believers, maybe more. A number of men and women, made of the same stuff as you and I, have reached uncommon heights of spirituality. There's no reason why you or I can't do the same—except lack of intention, or the misbelief that a higher level is beyond reach. Let's not settle for who we are. Let's always be aiming for our personal **M**aximum **A**chievable **S**pirituality (more about **M.A.S.** in the final chapter). Let's always be trying, through our devotion to the Word, to eliminate the works of the flesh a little more, and grow the fruit of the Spirit a little more.

As I say, we can help ourselves do this by understanding the relationship between the fruit and the works. This, then, is what a 'foulness' of works of the flesh looks like.

"Now the works of the flesh are manifest, which are these;

adultery
fornication
uncleanness
lasciviousness
idolatry
witchcraft
hatred
variance
emulations
wrath
strife
seditions
heresies
envyings
murders
drunkenness
revellings,

and such like: of the which I tell you before, as I have also told you in time past, that they which do such things shall not inherit the kingdom of God" (Gal.5:19-21).

What an ugly brood. When I look at that list in conjunction with the list of the aspects of the fruit of the Spirit I'm reminded of the chapter headings that the translators of the Authorised Version put above many of the chapters of the Proverbs: *"Moral virtues and their contrary vices."* The fruit has the moral virtues and the works the contrary vices. And there is inescapably a relationship between the two.

The power of love

The first thing one notices about the two lists is, of course, the glaring difference in the sort of things they contain. The next thing one notices is the differing length of the lists. There are twice as many items on the list of vices as there are on the list of virtues! Whatever could that be telling us, I wonder? It suggests a number of things. Maybe it's telling us that we're twice as prone to vice as virtue—a conservative estimate, I should think. Or perhaps it's telling us that vice is more varied than virtue—which rings true; as Ecclesiastes says: "God made man straightforward, but man invents endless subtleties of his own" (Ecc.7:29 NEB). Then again, maybe the Spirit through Paul simply wanted to hammer home the point about how naturally wayward we are by including so many aspects of the works of the flesh. The reason is probably a combination of the three—they're all valid.

But what I see as the *overriding* reason for there being twice as many works as fruit is something good and positive. It's a reason that should give heart to every believer struggling with the works of the flesh (and who does that leave out?) and it's this: **that the fruit of the Spirit is *twice* as powerful as the works of the flesh.** It must be, because our list of *nine* virtues cancels out the list of *seventeen* vices! Love's eight aspects will defeat all the many and varied manifestations of the flesh. It will do that for us perfectly when the kingdom of God is here, and it will do it for us to a great extent even *now* if we apply ourselves seriously to it, delighting and meditating in the Word of God.

Omit adultery and murder?!

While we're on the subject of the number of items on the lists, this is a good place to mention a little problem over how many works of the flesh there are. The list I've chosen is from the Authorised Version and it shows seventeen. Moffat gives sixteen in his version. But the majority of translators go for fifteen. Most of them omit adultery and murder!

The reason they do this is found in a footnote in the Revised Authorised Version. This version gives all seventeen, but against adultery and murder gives the note: *"NU-Text omits"*. The highly regarded *Nestle-Aland and United Bible Society Text* omits these two items. And as that text is founded upon older and supposedly more reliable manuscripts, most translators now opt for the shorter list. But how remarkable it is to leave out adultery and murder from a list of works of the flesh!

What are we to make of it? Do we keep to the old Authorised or go with the newer versions? Seventeen or fifteen?

It's a conundrum quite in keeping, I believe, with Paul's original intention when he wrote the letter to the Galatians. He prefaced the list like this: "Now the works of the flesh are manifest, which are these...." That phrase *which are these* could equally be translated *'such as'* or *'of which kind are'*. And Paul concludes the list with a similar thought: "...and such like." He seems to be going out of his way to make it clear that he is not giving a *fixed* list. There are dangers inherent in a fixed list: people, being what people are, might assume that anything not on the list is okay. He doesn't mention wife-beating and swearing specifically so they must be all right!

What Paul does is describe some of the more obvious ('manifest') works of the flesh. He disowns the idea that it is an exhaustive list.

So the problem the translators give us of not being able to pin down precisely the number of the works of the flesh is entirely in keeping with Paul's intentions. It's not a fixed list; it's a list representative of the sorts of actions that come under the heading of works of the flesh. And, as it happens, whether we choose seventeen or fifteen makes no difference to the *types* of works covered on the list.

I'm going to be so bold as to ignore the NU-Text on this occasion and keep with the seventeen of the Authorised Version. Not that I'm an incurable traditionalist, but I have to make a choice, and there's no denying that adultery and murder *are* works of the flesh. So it's not that difficult a decision. I'm also led to this decision by the thought that the Authorised and Revised Authorised Versions were translated from more full and more closely related manuscripts, whereas the modern translations are 'pick-and-mix' translations, meaning that the translators have picked the bits they preferred from a number of source manuscripts, making their translations more open to the bias of the translators than the older Authorised and its Revised modern counterpart.

There is a problem, though, for Bible numerologists if we can't be sure whether the works of the flesh are fifteen or seventeen. Back in chapter six I said a few words about the eight parts of love signifying the new man in Christ, eight being the number of new beginning. But what about the numbers fifteen or seventeen? If one or the other had particular associations with evil it would help us decide which is correct. But (according to Bullinger at least) both numbers have good connotations.

The number six being the number of man and sin, I was expecting six, or multiples of six to figure in the works of the flesh. But no, all you can say of fifteen is that its components five and one add together to equal six. Which doesn't seem enough proof for fifteen being right. I'm guessing, of course, but perhaps the full and precise number of works is 666, and it wouldn't have been appropriate or convenient for Paul to list them all. Maybe they can be found throughout the Scriptures—and I have to say it isn't convenient for me to look for them all right now either!

Aspects of adultery

An intriguing thought occurs regarding the list of fleshly works. If the fruit of the Spirit is love with eight aspects, then might not the works of the flesh somehow be adultery in sixteen parts? Love and adultery head the two lists, and are direct opposites, the one founded on selfless giving, the other on selfish taking. And adultery is used in the broader figurative sense in the Scriptures. In this sense it describes a desertion from the *agape* of God to the godless and fleshly ways of the world. The more I think about it, the more possibilities I see in the idea, but to keep this book to an acceptable length I feel I should resist the temptation to explore.

The four categories

Something we can do with the list of the works of the flesh, and which helps us deal with it in a systematic way, is break it down into four easily identifiable categories: **1** sexual sins, **2** idolatry, **3** strife, **4** excess. The following boxes show how the works can be grouped under these headings.

SEXUAL SINS

adultery, fornication

uncleanness,
lasciviousness

IDOLATRY

idolatry, witchcraft

STRIFE

hatred, variance,
emulations,
wrath, strife, seditions,
heresies, envyings,
murder

EXCESS

drunkenness, revellings

Remember, Paul uses the phrase 'and such like'. The list is **representative** of all the works of the flesh. So all the works not specifically mentioned will fit into one of these four categories. Wife-beating and swearing, for instance, will come under strife and excess respectively

Now that we have *four* categories of works we see that numerically the position has reversed. It's no longer eight aspects of love against a giant seventeen works of the flesh, but *eight* aspects of love against *four* categories of works. That's cutting them down to size!

Over the next four chapters, I want to take each of the categories in turn, have a brief look at how each one of them affects us, and then pinpoint which of the fruits are used to defeat it.

Just one thing before we start. It's about our old friends *being* and *doing*. You may have noticed that the Spirit produces *fruit* and the flesh produces *works*. Though, of course, when we have the fruit we also produce works— *good* works—but the works are not the goal, as I've said before; they are **the by-product of who we have become because of the fruit**

The flesh (a term which describes our natural selves without the influence of the Spirit Word) simply produces works. And because these works have not been processed by a truly spiritual heart, they are just works of (or from) the flesh. We must transform our *being* by generating the fruit of the Spirit, or we will be merely *doers*: unwilling and unwitting slaves of our natures, instead of free men and women in Christ.

And if life in Christ doesn't seem too much like freedom to you, then remember that even freedom has its obligations. A man released from prison is free but he is not without obligations towards the society he enters. Entering the society of Christ is liberating, but it brings responsibilities. Freedom without responsibility is anarchy, not emancipation.

CHAPTER SIXTEEN

SEXUAL SINS AND THE ANTIDOTES

(Adultery, fornication, uncleanness, lasciviousness)

Adultery and fornication

There is sometimes a blurring of the meaning of adultery and fornication in Scripture, but when the words appear together in the same sentence I think it's safe to assume they mean different things. Adultery occurs when a married person indulges in sexual activity with someone other than their spouse. Fornication occurs when *un*married people indulge in sex. All very straightforward.

I'm probably being too simplistic here for those who would debate shades of meaning, and argue about the role of context, and complain I'm not taking sufficient account of ancient Hebrew marital mores. So be it. The definitions I've opted for are not a million miles from the truth, even if they are not accurate in *every possible* circumstance. But it is certain that adultery and fornication as I've defined them—and which is how they are often intended in Scripture and how we understand the terms today—are sexual sins under the general heading of works of the flesh. So there will be no grievous harm done if I have *ever so slightly* misrepresented them!

Uncleanness

Adultery and fornication are among the most common abuses of sexuality. There are abuses which fall outside these two categories. But as we spent most of chapter fourteen discussing lustful thoughts and behaviour, there's no need to go into all that again here. Certainly what we dealt with in that chapter comes under the heading of *uncleanness*.

The word for *uncleanness* is *akatharsia*, and interestingly it's the word that occurs when unclean spirits are mentioned in the New Testament. Jesus met people with unclean spirits and he cured them. How curious it seems to us that someone mentally ill should be described as having an unclean spirit. But it's worth remembering that the word spirit in the New Testament, even as in our own day, can refer to an attitude of mind. We can speak of a spirit of optimism and we know it's an optimistic state of mind, not an optimistic demon of some kind. And when John tells us that Jesus "was troubled in spirit" (John 13:21) we know Jesus' mind was troubled. He was simply in a troubled state of mind.

So an unclean spirit need be nothing more sinister than an unclean or impure state of mind. As many a psychologist since Sigmund Freud has found, people with impure states of mind can become psychologically disturbed. If we allow the natural sensual side of our natures to get the upper hand, the result will be an impure state of mind. It's common knowledge to those who study the mind that sexual confusion, with its resultant anxiety and guilt, can lead to mental disorders. It is just possible that this is what lies behind the phrase 'unclean spirit': it may be an impure mind that has led to psychosis. Such danger is always present for those who lack temperance, who allow uncleanness to take over their thinking.

Lasciviousness

Lasciviousness is thankfully the last of this unwhole-some foursome. Although there is a certain amount of overlap with all of them, lasciviousness differs from the other three in that it relates to homosexuality.

It's the Apostle Peter who makes the connection for us in his second letter (2 Pet.2:7). He writes of "the filthy conversation of the wicked" people of Sodom and Gomorrah. The word 'filthy' in that verse is *aselgeia*, the same word translated lasciviousness in the works of the flesh. And the term 'conversation' is used there in its old English sense of 'way of life'. So Peter actually wrote of "the lascivious way of life of the wicked" people of Sodom and Gomorrah. Jude also mentions lasciviousness and then proceeds to talk of Sodom and Gomorrah. We know that the nature of the sin of those cities of the plain was homosexuality. They were so shameless about it that God destroyed them.

These days homosexuality is becoming increasingly acceptable. Even the established church is ambivalent about it. Celebrities who die of AIDS are lauded as heroes rather than deplored or pitied as incorrigibly immoral.

The liberal Christian argument runs that it's no worse than any other sin and therefore shouldn't be treated as especially bad. There is some truth in that, but that doesn't mean we have to go soft on it—or any other sin. *All* sin, sexual or otherwise, needs to be regarded as wrong.

But it's not just that homosexuality is wrong; the reason why many homosexuals meet with particular censure from God is because they refuse to *see* it as wrong. One can (and *should*) be understanding towards those who feel trapped in this particular work of the flesh, as with any other besetting sin, but not towards the notion that there's really nothing wrong with it and no steps need be taken to overcome or resist the practice of it. That attitude of acceptance was the grosser sin of Sodom. In Isaiah 3:9 the Prophet relays God's anger towards some flesh-pleasers of his own day by comparing them to those of Sodom: "They parade their sin like Sodom; they do not hide it. Woe to them" (NIV). They had no shame, and *that* was their destruction. If you're doing wrong, at least accept it and in your shame agree with God that it is wrong. That way there is hope. Even if you absolutely can't overcome it, you can be honest with God about it, and trust to grace. But to parade your sin as if it were excusable and normal behaviour is to invite the anger of God.

If our present generation wants to parade its lasciviousness as Sodom, then it cannot expect the approval of God, or of the people who truly follow God.

However, there is a point made in Scripture *in favour* of the people of Sodom. And it was Christ himself who made it. While castigating the people of Capernaum for not listening to him, and for not being convinced of who he was by his miracles, Christ said, "For if the mighty works, which have been done in thee, had been done in Sodom, it would have remained until this day" (Matt.11:23). So there was something to be said *for* the people of Sodom. They weren't as bad as some. And what Christ said about them raises a significant issue. If a prophet of the stature of Christ had been around in their day and had gone to Sodom, the city and its people would not have been destroyed. They would have listened. They would have taken note of the miracles and realised that here was somebody very special. The people of Sodom wouldn't have been so spiritually inept as Capernaum. They would, in fact, have repented!

The point being made is: what does that tell us about the supposed inability of homosexuals to be and do anything other than homosexuals? Christ considers homosexuality a sin for which repentance (meaning change) is possible. Are we so wrong—are we really expecting the impossible—to expect those with such tendencies to resist and overcome them (or at least *try*) if they would follow Christ?

The antidotes to sexual sins

The way to overcome all works of the flesh is through the fruit of the Spirit. Overcoming by force of will may work for a time, but it leaves a vacuum. You have pushed something out of your life and left a gap as a consequence.

You need to do *two* things if you really want to overcome effectively. And sometimes we have to admit that we are so attached to our sins that deep down we don't want to overcome them effectively, so we sabotage our own efforts. What is it that the Scriptures say about the heart of man?—"deceitful", "who can know it?" So perhaps I should say you have to do *three* things if you want to overcome effectively. First, you must *really want* to overcome your problem. Second and Third, you must resist the devil AND draw near to God (James 4:7,8).

When you banish something bad from your life you must replace it with something good. This is known not surprisingly as The Replacement Principle. Psychologists have discovered that it works—the Bible got there a few thousand years before them. If you force something bad out of your life and leave a vacuum, you are simply leaving yourself open for something bad to come back and fill the gap—probably something worse than you had before. (Which is what your deceitful heart might have wanted all along!) Christ illustrates it in a parable:

> "When an unclean spirit goes out of a man, he goes through dry places, seeking rest, and finds none. Then he says, I will return to my house from which I came. And when he comes, he finds it empty, swept, and put in order. Then he goes and takes with him seven other spirits more wicked than himself, and they enter and dwell there; and the last state of that man is worst than the first. So shall it be with this wicked generation" (Matt.12:43-45 RAV).

Christ said that "this wicked generation"—the people of Israel of his day, especially the religious leaders—had made the mistake of casting out one unclean spirit and letting in seven. As he said elsewhere of them, they "strain at a gnat, and swallow a camel" (Matt.23:24). They were so fastidious about the minor elements of the Law of Moses, even adding more minor ones of their own, that they missed the BIG point about loving one's neighbour as oneself. That's what it means to cast out one bad attitude (carelessness over details) and introduce an even greater one, seven times worse (carelessness over *agape*).

The parable also highlights the general truth that if you don't fill a gap with something good, sooner or later something bad, and in all probability something worse than you originally threw out, will crawl in to take up residence.

So if you're trying to overcome a particular sin, don't try just banishing it, use **The Replacement Principle.** Replace it with a good habit. Replace your negatives with positives, before the negatives bring home a few friends!

When trying to evict the works of the flesh, throwing them out is never enough on its own; you must also invite round the appropriate fruit of the Spirit to fill the vacancy and actively discourage the return of the old habit. When you replace a work of the flesh with an element of the fruit of the Spirit, you are applying the Scripturally effective psychology of not merely changing what you *do*, but changing what you *are*. If you change only what you *do*, you deal with the symptom, not the problem. When you introduce the fruit of the Spirit by delight and meditation in the Word of God, you change what you *are*—and that will change what you *do* far more effectively.

When it comes to combating the sexual works of the flesh with something good from the fruit of the Spirit, the obvious choice is **temperance**. This is the one to cultivate. It is specifically programmed to cancel out the lustful side of our nature, as we saw in chapter fourteen.

But as we have eight aspects of fruit of the Spirit and only four categories of works of the flesh, we can apply *two* aspects of fruit to each category. And it works out so well that I feel it must be more than a coincidence.

Works of the flesh	Antidotes
sexual	temperance
	goodness
idolatry	joy
	faith
strife	longsuffering
	gentleness
excess	peace
	meekness

With temperance you'll see I've paired goodness. Goodness you may recall is that quality of character through which we talk to ourselves—or rather we allow the wisdom of God to talk to us. The voice is implanted not by super-natural means but by familiarity with the Word of God through reading and thinking on it. More than anything else (except temperance) we need a strong voice within us to argue us out of following what for many people is the strongest pull of the flesh: lustful thoughts and behaviour.

Lust *is* a voice. In the book of Proverbs the path of evil, as opposed to the spiritual path, is likened to a "strange woman which flattereth with her words" (Prov.2:16), "her mouth is smoother than oil" (Prov.5:3). And Proverbs 7:11 describes her well when it says "she is loud and stubborn"!

The lustful side of our nature *is* loud and stubborn. It needs the two-pronged attack of temperance and goodness to silence it. It's easy to see how the two work together. Temperance might even be said to be achieved *through* goodness. Self-control is achieved by listening to the voice of a louder and even more stubborn Spirit Word. But it will only *be* louder and more stubborn through continual delight and meditation in the Word. If the Spirit voice is weak, through inattention to the Word, you can be sure the voice of the flesh will be loud. So drown it out!

CHAPTER SEVENTEEN

IDOLATRY AND THE ANTIDOTES
(Idolatry and witchcraft)

IDOLATRY and witchcraft are not a problem these days, you might think, so no point lingering long here. But you'd be wrong. Okay, we no longer fall down before carved statues of imagined deities, or offer our children as sacrifices to them—at least not in my part of Surrey—but you'd be wrong to believe that we are no longer troubled by the ugly sisters of idolatry and witchcraft.

Another mistake that believers are apt to make is to suppose that idolatry comes in a different form today. The usual view is that idolatry is anything that takes the place of God in a person's life. But that's not the whole truth. Something that takes the place of God in someone's life is not necessarily their idol. The point I'm trying to make is that not everything that takes God's place is *worshipped*. Often, what it amounts to is ignoring God, not worshipping something else. It only becomes idolatry when the thing which has replaced God is assumed to have a controlling influence in a person's life, when it's seen as somehow guiding and protecting and giving meaning to life for them. **To be idol worship the attachment has not only to supplant God but also to take on the role of God.**

The man who collects match-box labels for a hobby, however fanatical he may be, is not indulging in a twentieth century version of idol worship! If, because of his hobby, he neglects his spiritual welfare, then he'd be well advised to spend time on that rather than on cutting and sticking his trophies, on admiring them, swapping them, going to auctions and clubs, and reading the monthly journal of the match-box label collectors. But that's not idol worship. Unless he is very strange indeed, and relies on his collection of labels to provide the meaning of life, and to guide and protect him through life. That's not idolatry, that's insanity!

An idol is not simply what we substitute for God; it's what we substitute for Him as a creative force in the universe and a guiding light in our lives. Which is precisely why idolatry and witchcraft are linked. Although different, they go hand in hand.

Galatians 5 is not the only place idolatry and witchcraft are brought together. It happens in Deuteronomy 18:10-11, 2 Chronicles 33:6-7, and Micah 5:12-14. But the verse that throws most light on the connection between the two is 1 Samuel 15:23:

> "For rebellion is as the sin of witchcraft, and stubbornness is as iniquity and idolatry. Because thou hast rejected the word of the Lord, he hath also rejected thee from being king."

To understand this verse it helps to re-interpret some of the key words:

rebellion (*meri*) equals **bitterness;**

witchcraft (*gerer*) is more particularly **divination** in this case;

stubbornness (*patser*) means **to press** or **urge**, **be insistent**, and

idolatry is the Hebrew *teraphim*, meaning **household gods** (probably small carvings or castings in human form).

In the light of the above information we can re-cast the verse like this: "For your bitterness is as the sin of divination, and your insistence on your own way is as if you were using household gods."

To put the words into their context, this was the prophet Samuel speaking to Saul, king of Israel. Saul's failure to carry out a command of God was likened to witchcraft and idolatry. God had told Saul to destroy all the livestock of the Amalekites once he had defeated them in battle. But Saul couldn't resist the best of the sheep and cattle. He was happy to have God's help to defeat the

Amalekites, but he didn't want to follow through with his part of the agreement. He kept the best livestock. At the back of his mind were thoughts something like this, "I could do with all these excellent animals. I'll be better provided for if I keep them. It's a shame to waste them. And my soldiers and their families will be pleased with me if I share with them "

Saul rejected God in two ways: he rebelled (was bitter), and he was stubborn. Saul was bitter at being challenged by God's prophet over keeping the best of the sheep and oxen. He blamed his soldiers for taking and keeping them, though he definitely played a key part in it, and then he argued that they had taken the good livestock in order to offer some of it to God as sacrifices. Saul reasoned it was okay to disobey God so long as you appeased Him with sacrifices. It was a cynical attitude, and it showed that Saul's approach to God was no different, in essence, from the approach of the heathen to an idol. He had superstition, not faith in God.

Saul's stubbornness was his headstrong attitude, insisting he was right even in the face of what God had said. This was an iniquity akin to idolatry. God was saying, in effect, through his prophet, "If you're going to decide for yourself what to do, disregarding my Word, you might as well have gone to some teraphim and enquired of them."

One seriously wonders if Saul had *actually* consulted teraphim on this and possibly other matters. It would be in keeping with his superstitious nature. It's worth noting that in 1 Sam.15:23 the phrase "...*is as*..." occurs both times in italics signifying that it's not in the original Hebrew text. So perhaps his sin was not "as" divination and using teraphim, but *actually* these things!

Saul denied the power of God in his life and looked elsewhere for guidance: to teraphim, or to his own counsel.

You don't have to set up an idol in your back garden or buy yourself a broomstick to practise idolatry and witchcraft. All you need to do is rely on something other than

God for your prosperity and your physical and emotional needs.

"Covetousness, which is idolatry"

When Paul wrote to the Colossian believers, he linked idolatry with covetousness. This is a little misleading. It's easy to get the impression from what he says that covetousness is a form of idolatry. It is, but only in a limited sense. Simply wanting something very badly—covetousness—is not necessarily to make an idol of it. We don't generally worship the things we want, or rely on them to guide our destiny.

Context, context, context!—to rework a well-known estate agents' dictum. If you look at the whole verse you'll see that it all relates to sexual sin with the *apparent* exception of "covetousness, which is idolatry".

> "Mortify your members which are upon the earth; fornication, uncleanness, inordinate affection, evil concupiscence, and covetousness, which is idolatry" (Col.3:5).

The fact that five out of six of the sins mentioned are sexual in nature is a powerful hint that the sixth one is also. It's unlikely that it would be totally unrelated to the rest of the list. Sure enough, when you check out that word covetousness (*pleonexia*) you find that Paul does use it in other places for coveting a woman you have no right to. Linking this covetousness to idolatry, Paul must have had in mind the practice common in his day of consorting with temple prostitutes. (See *7 Short Epistles* p.35 by H. A. Whittaker.) The sexual act was a part of the idol worship of the day. Therefore a strong desire for, and the likely subsequent association with the temple girls *was* idolatry.

Therefore Paul could say, "covetousness, which is idolatry." This doesn't mean that covetousness is always idolatry, or that idolatry is always covetousness; it means only that one particular form of covetousness is idolatry.

And it's clear enough from the context that's what Paul had in mind.

The New Age

The word for witchcraft in the New Testament is *pharmakeia*, and it relates to charms and medicines. As you might guess, our word *pharmacy* comes from this word, but don't let that stop you going to the chemist. *Pharmakeia* apparently refers to the chants and incantations which were said *over* the medicines rather than the potions themselves. There was much superstition surrounding medicine in the past, even as there is today in some parts of the world where *witch-doctors* and *medicine* men still ply their trade. Where people are gullible and desperate enough—or, sad to say, poor enough—such men will generally be around to assume power over them.

In England the practice of witchcraft was forbidden by law for centuries—until quite recently, in fact. The Witchcraft Act was repealed in 1951. Nowadays you can practise as a witch, and even advertise your enchantments in the columns of the daily newspapers. No-one will burn you at the stake.

But it's not blatant witchcraft with its covens and pentangles that has flourished since the 1950s (though that certainly is on the increase); it's the more subtle forms that have become popular. The so-called New Age movement is little more than a thinly disguised promotion of idolatry and witchcraft. Which may sound like the over-the-top rantings of a red-eyed Christian fundamentalist, but you can't escape the fact that the New Age movement promotes a replacement of the God of the Bible with a depersonalised 'Universal Force'—an occult force—and encourages us to find the 'god within ourselves'. If that's not idolatry and witchcraft then I don't know what is. Many New Age followers are quite happy to call themselves pagans.

A lot of different beliefs and phenomena come under the umbrella of the term New Age. The movement is supposed to be a symptom of a new age of enlightenment, of personal and planetary transformation. It's a nice idea, and I'd be the last to pour cold water on such high-flying aspirations, but the New Age is nothing other than *old age* superstition in a new dress, and the so-called age of enlightenment is a return to the dark ages. It's just the bad old works of the flesh that have been around since Adam.

It's so easy for *anyone* these days to get caught up in New Age practices unwittingly. New Age covers a whole smorgasbord of one-time fringe activities which are becoming ever more popular and acceptable. Here are a few you may have come across: nature worship ("hug a tree" say some New Agers, "and get in tune with the vibrations of the life force"); spirit channelling (supposed messages from the dead to guide the living); past life regression (the idea that we can go back to supposed former lives); U.F.O.s (the belief that aliens will rescue a suicidal earth); astrology (guidance from the stars); tarot cards and the I-Ching, pendulum dowsing, and other such popular methods of divination; crystal healing and many other alternative health treatments (some of these treatments are good and work, but you have to beware the philosophy that sometimes goes with them as part of the package); graphology (character analysis from handwriting).... The list goes on. It also covers aspects of the paranormal—things which in general any stage magician worth his salt can duplicate.

Maybe you think *you'd* never get caught up in anything like that. Not for a moment! A prominent believer once dallied briefly with the pseudo-science of phrenology, the reading of your character from the bumps on your head. And if Robert Roberts could take even a passing interest in such things, then who could boast that they never have, and *never* would?

Am I right in saying that you know your star sign? Are you Capricorn or Leo? Sagittarius or Virgo? So, why do you know? And what use is it to you? Do you believe at some level that this star sign fixes or determines your character? Or that the stars have some influence on your future? A look at the daily horoscope in a newspaper isn't really a harmless bit of fun. Not for someone who thinks of himself as a believer it isn't. Have you noticed how many people who treat it as harmless fun also seem to be hooked on it?

I've asked daily horoscope readers to keep a record of how often it's right. They prefer not to. They turn a blind eye to the fact that it's wrong most days, or so general as to be worthless. For an example, I looked at my stars in a newspaper (I'm a Cancerian, by the way!), and I was given this gem, that I should "make plans like there's no tomorrow"! If there's no tomorrow—what plans can I make?!

Some years ago I worked with a girl who regularly popped into my office at lunch-time to borrow my midday edition of a London newspaper to check her stars for that day. She often said how accurate they were and what a good astrologer the writer was. One day I happened to notice in the small print at the head of the astrology column the words "*your star forecast for tomorrow*." When I told her she'd been reading it for the wrong day all this time she didn't seem at all put out.

People will believe what they want regardless of the facts. In fact, since the star signs were first allocated to their particular times of the year, owing to an astronomical phenomenon called the 'precession of the equinoxes', the star signs have all moved up a month. Nobody seems to notice that we all now have the *wrong* star sign! (Isaac Asimov: Introduction to *The Stars in Their Courses*).

A selective memory is a great asset when it comes to New Age phenomena. With things like astrology you have to remember the few *amazing!* moments when it's correct and shut out all the boring moments when it isn't. It's very subjective. I recall being told by a work colleague that I had a remarkable resemblance to his son, not so much in looks but in general build, mannerisms and the things I liked and disliked. When we discovered that his son and I were born only one day apart in the same year—wow! It's so easy to build something on that, and forget all the people you could muster born at the same time who are very different.

Have you ever noticed how subjective Ufology is? In case you haven't heard it, that's the term for the study of flying saucers. I speak with authority here, having witnessed *four* U.F.O.s in my life so far. They were definitely *un*identified flying objects, because I couldn't identify them. But it's rather "a giant step for mankind" to say these things are piloted by alien beings. What I find most curious is that when you look at early drawings and photographs from the 1950s, the flying saucers look like antiques, whereas the ones pictured now are far more modern and sophisticated. This is what I mean by subjective. I don't believe that real aliens would have fashions in spacecraft that move with *our* times!

Having said all that, I do, however, believe that someone not from our world will one day arrive to rescue this doomed planet. But he will be no alien. He was born here, grew up here, and he won't need a flying machine of any description to bring him back here. I'm talking of Jesus, of course. The Truth is actually more breathtaking than any of the fables men dream up. We *have* already had a communication from a higher intelligence beyond the stars. It's called the Bible.

Society is riddled with subtle forms of witchcraft and idolatry. There are hundreds of little, seemingly innocuous ways of leaving God out of the picture and relying on superstitious beliefs and charms to guide and help through life. Believers need to stay awake to what these things are.

The Antidotes

The antidotes from the fruit of the Spirit that will counteract idolatry and witchcraft are without hesitation joy and faith.

Joy—because, as we found when dealing with that aspect of the fruit, the joy of the fruit is the joy of knowing you're on the right road and that your expectations will soon be fulfilled. When you have this kind of joy, you have no desire to look down other roads, or to put your trust in anyone or anything other than God to fulfil your expectations. **When you're truly happy about what you *have*, you don't want or need anything else.** In the face of day-to-day problems and decisions, you don't cross your fingers and trust to luck, or clutch a rabbit's severed foot, or consult the daily horoscope column, or whatever; you turn to God. You pray, and you know that the providence of God is working for you.

Faith—because faith underpins that joy. By faith we *see* providence in our lives. We see the kingdom of God here on earth in our mind's eye, and we know that we have a part in it, in God's mercy. We believe firmly in God and in our salvation. We *know* these things are so. And from this rock-like standpoint, all superstition, idolatry and witchcraft is absolutely out of the question. It's twaddle, but it's dangerous twaddle. And to make sure we don't inadvertently get sucked into it, we need to do what we can to promote joy and faith through delight and meditation in the Word.

CHAPTER EIGHTEEN

STRIFE AND THE ANTIDOTES

(Hatred, variance, emulations, wrath, strife,
seditions, heresies, envyings, murder)

MORE vices fall into this category than any other category of the works of the flesh. Over half the works relate to strife. Is that trying to tell us something? That we're more prone to this kind of failing than any other? Who can doubt it? The history of the human race is one long, sorry tale of strife, from Cain and Abel onwards. Man against man, faction against faction, religion against religion, party against party, community against community, nation against nation. Every generation, every society, has been plagued by animosity.

Strife seems always to have been mankind's preoccupation, as if we've never had anything better to do. Without something to struggle against we often lose our sense of purpose. It's as if people can't cope with the quiet life! Even our entertainments are mostly strife-centred. Ask yourself how many books, films and plays would vanish if all those which depended on some kind of conflict were removed. Ninety-nine per cent of the fiction would disappear. Though, to our credit, most people enjoy such entertainments because through them they can fantasise about good triumphing over evil, the good guy over the bad—which is so often missing from real life.

Do you realise that a stable world of permanent peace would be totally lacking in material for novelists, screenwriters and playwrights? Such entertainments are certain to be missing from the future age, when God "shall wipe away all tears from their eyes; and there shall be no more death, neither sorrow, nor crying, neither shall there be any more pain: for the former things are passed away"

(Rev.21:4). When conflict is missing from reality it's hard to believe it will persist as entertainment!—especially when you consider that even in this *present* world, God not only condemns the physical manifestations of the works of the flesh, but also those people who, while not doing them themselves, "have pleasure in them that do them" (Rom.1:29-32).

It could be argued that reading and watching conflicts for enjoyment is having pleasure in those that do them. Though perhaps it's more a matter of *how far* what you read or watch goes in its wallowing in human baseness, and the sort of pleasure you derive from it. For many people it's the *resolution* of conflict which they seek in fiction—the "happy ever after" factor that is missing from their reality. But that end doesn't always justify the means of getting there!

I wouldn't want to set any rules here for believers; they'd probably be ignored anyway. It's for each believer to decide what is acceptable. Not to themselves, that is!—but to God. A peep at the list of "think on these things" items in Philippians 4:8 will usually help decide.

Hatred *(echthra)*

Hatred begins the list in this category of strife. In fact, the category might equally have been headed hatred rather than strife, because there's an element of hatred in all these manifestations of strife. The Greek behind hatred is *echthra*, and Galatians 5:20 is the only place in the New Testament where the word is translated hatred. On every other occasion (five) it is translated enmity. It's helpful to know that *echthra* is a form of *echthros* which means enemy. To have feelings of *echthra* towards another is to consider and treat that person as your foe.

The Septuagint's use of the word is telling, because a number of times it uses the word to refer to bad feelings which are submerged, hidden in the heart, unexpressed. The Proverbs especially use *echthra* this way. It is in the heart, of course, that all hatred resides and festers: it's not in the fist or the mouth or the gun. These things merely express the hatred in the heart. But mostly the hatred stays in the heart, unexpressed. This line from Jeremiah 9:8 RAV describes the situation: "one speaks peaceably to his neighbour with his mouth, but in heart he lies in wait." That is to say, in his heart he's thinking murderous thoughts.

Here lies the particular danger for believers: the problem of concealed hatred. I think it's fair to say that believers feel more strongly than many other people that they have to keep up appearances. It is unacceptable for believers to express hatreds if they have any. And, instead of resolving them through forgiveness (the spiritual fruits of longsuffering and patience), we may be tempted to speak peace to our neighbours while harbouring enmity. There's plenty of scope for play-acting and self-deceit among believers. Part of the self-deceit is to pretend that *hatred* is far too strong a word for what *we* feel towards certain others. *We* have only a mild dislike. And justifiably so, we might think, when you consider what they did, and what they are like. Well, who could blame us? So we avoid them if we can. We wouldn't go out of our way to help them. We wouldn't do them any real harm, of course, but we do communicate our 'mild dislike' of them to other people if we get the chance.

What it all adds up to is that we treat that other person as an enemy. It's enmity, pure and simple. Or how differently would we treat an enemy?

Variance *(eris)*—The Corinthian Games

Variance is a word fast falling into disuse. The newer translations don't use it. The Revised Authorised gives *contentions*, which gives more of a clue to the meaning behind *eris*. Contentions exist where there are contests. And while contests are all very good and healthy in games and sports, they are decidedly *un*healthy in our daily interactions with other people.

Back in the first century, the Apostle Paul had to write to the Corinthian believers about a contest that was going on, not in the local arena, but in the church. News had reached Paul that "there are contentions [*eris*] among you" (1 Cor. 1:11). Factions were forming in the church at Corinth. Some were saying, "I'm a follower of Paul", others "I am of Apollos", others "I am of Peter", others "I am of Christ." Groups of Corinthian believers were lining up behind different leaders, just as they might form rival groups of supporters for the red, blue, green and yellow chariot teams at the local races!

Each group of believers had created its own special "hero". Naturally, this was beginning to fragment the church at Corinth. If Paul couldn't stop it in time, this contest was going to produce *four* churches at Corinth, not one, each preaching essentially the same gospel under a different banner. Worst of all, each group would then start eyeing the others with suspicion and feeling superior to them because it alone had the truth. In time the slight differences would be magnified out of all proportion, and four different versions of Christianity would have been born—*all* wrong! This is what is called being at variance.

Could it happen today? You'd have to be extremely naive to say it couldn't. There has been no noticeable improvement in human nature over the last two thousand years. Whenever believers make the mistake of grouping round a personality instead of a true set of Christian doctrines, there will be contentions

Hero worship is a sad human failing. It's a symptom of our own insecurity if we must attach ourselves to another who appears to have all the answers. It relieves us of the difficult task of having to sort things out for ourselves. In reality the 'hero' is no better qualified to guide our understanding than we are ourselves. But perhaps he speaks well, and thinks faster than we do; perhaps he has a striking appearance and a forceful personality, and a high-flying job. For any number of reasons we may set someone on a pedestal and look to them for the answers to life, the universe and everything. It certainly saves thinking. And it can take the place of searching the Scriptures for ourselves—which will make us all the more easily led.

Though, to be fair, hero worship can sometimes work to our advantage. As when Paul said, "Be ye followers of me, even as I also am of Christ"—a quotation, incidentally, from that same letter to the Corinthians in which he denounced hero worship! Paul told them, in effect, "If you want to follow something, then follow me *in the way I follow Christ*. Don't just follow *me*. See the way I follow Christ and get behind that! That way we shall all be together following the same thing."

Thankfully, in every generation there have been those who set an example of following Christ well worth following. But even with these we should never be so trusting as to lose the ability to think and study for ourselves.

To keep your 'hero worship' in perspective, follow Paul's golden rule: follow the other person's good example of following Christ rather than the person for him- or herself. This effectively demolishes all the wrong reasons for following, and acts as a guard against the sort of contests that went on at Corinth. Let's do our best to keep the Corinthian games out of our places of worship.

Emulations (*zelos*)—"Not according to knowledge"

Emulations is an unlikely word to find in a list of works of the flesh. Why?—because it's the Greek word *zelos*, meaning zeal. How can it be wrong to have zeal? Zeal is enthusiasm, commitment, eagerness, passion, a burning desire to get things done or defend what you have. So how can it be wrong?

Normally it isn't. In his second letter to them, Paul praised the Corinthians for it, *twice* (2 Cor.7:11 & 9:2), and he praised Epaphras for his. Generally speaking it's good to be zealous. Finding it among the works of the flesh tells us there must be another side to it. There is.

When Paul wrote to the Galatian believers he singled out for censure a group who were zealously affecting the church, but in a bad way (Gal.4:17). They were still hung up on the Old Testament Law of Moses. They wanted Christ, but they didn't want to let go of some of the rituals of the Law, like circumcision. They couldn't cope with freedom from the Law they'd known so long. They were like an old, long-stay prisoner who can't cope with life on the outside. God had given them a better New Covenant in Christ, but they hankered for the familiarity of the Old.

This group at Galatia were zealous for the wrong things. Their enthusiasm was infectious, and dangerous, leading the church away from the Truth. So Paul warned: "It is good to be zealously affected always in a **good** thing...." Zeal is not good unless it is zeal over something good. Great enthusiasm, like deep sincerity, does not *make* something right. How easy it is to get carried away over an idea, especially the enthusiastically broadcast ideas of others, and forget to check the validity of what they are so excited about. The Jews of Paul's day, as he said, had "a zeal of God, but not according to knowledge" (Rom 10:2).

However wonderful it may seem, it is nevertheless a work of the flesh to be carried away by anything other than the Truth. Some wonderful new concept of how to worship God, filled with great gusts of emotion, song and dance, and melon-quarter smiles, will be nothing more than a work of the flesh if it ignores God's own pre-requisites for worship: spirit and truth. How good it makes *us* feel is not always the best indicator of how correct it is! Zeal isn't truth, and it doesn't validate anything we care to attach to it. A huge emotional investment, with very little understanding of the Word to back it, will lead to spiritual ruin.

Zeal is also sometimes a sign of spiritual immaturity. All too often we have seen someone begin the new life in Christ with portentous enthusiasm only to fall by the wayside in a few years. It's another form of zeal that is "not according to knowledge". Learners in the Faith can quickly experience spiritual burn-out trying to maintain a constant religious high. They believe this is how they *ought* to feel. They rush around, and burn up a lot of energy—and more energy still trying to get others to rush around as much as they are! It seems so right, so committed, that they don't recognise it as good old-fashioned legalism. They push themselves because they feel they must, and probably blame God when they finally can't cope.

If you ever see yourself going down this road, put the brakes on fast. Such people are described in the parable of the sower as those who, "when they hear, receive the word with joy; and these have no root, which for a while believe, and in time of temptation fall away" (Luke 8:13). Because they live in an unreal world of their own creation, they are not ready for the reality of hard knocks. Their zeal is not sustainable; it's only good when things are going well. Little by little the essential trials of faith begin to produce all the wrong responses. A more realistic (Biblical!) understanding would have told them that life—even in the Truth—can never be lived in a state of perpetual elation. Even an incurable positive thinker like me has to face that!

The joy which is a part of the fruit of the Spirit is a warm glow of certainty at the very heart of your being that comes from your meditation on the Word and tells you that you can survive all the buffeting in the world. It's not a shallow hyped-up excitation of the emotions. As the proverb says: "If thou faint in the day of adversity, thy strength is small" (Prov.24:10).

As a footnote to *zelos*, I should mention that in some versions (e.g. RSV, NIV, NKJV.) *zelos* is translated in Galatians 5:20 as *jealousy*. In fact our English word jealous has its roots in the Latin *zelos* (pronounced *zelus*), which is a distant cousin of the Greek *zelos*.

The meanings of zealous and jealous are very close. If you have zeal over something you may also be jealous over it—want to guard it closely. You can be equally jealous and zealous of your rights and honour, if you have a mind to be. Paul wrote to the Corinthians that he was "jealous over [them] with godly jealousy" (2 Cor.11:2). But he didn't mean that he was *envious* of them (or that God was sometimes envious of anybody!). He meant that he cared a great deal for them. He was concerned and protective for the best of reasons: he loved them.

But jealousy is better known for its darker side. Loving concern can become twisted out of shape by self-interest and insecurity. It becomes deformed and turns into the green-eyed monster. This has nothing to do with "Godly jealousy"; this is fleshly jealousy. And what a cause of strife it can be!

As *zelos* appears in Galatians 5 without a context to define it, the word could have any or all of the connotations given it here. Most likely *all* of them. It's not rare for a word to have a number of meanings. Such a feature adds to the richness of Biblical allusion.

What a shame that we have this tendency to distort good things like zeal and Godly jealousy. It's probably true to say that everything that is wrong with us is a distortion of something that could be right with us if only we applied it correctly.

Wrath (*thumos*)—Slow anger (without the slow)

Remember *makrothumia*? the Greek for longsuffering? In chapter Nine we saw that *makrothumia* is two words joined together, *makro* and *thumeo*, literally slow anger. *Thumos* is the back end of *makrothumia*: it's the anger without the slow.

Thumos is generally anger that is expressed in harmful ways, usually physical and verbal abuse. It's the form of anger that caused a posse of synagogue authorities in Nazareth to throw Jesus out of their synagogue and then proceed to a clifftop to throw him down! (Luke 4:28,29).

It's the kind of anger that made Pharaoh send an army after Moses and the Israelites when they fled Egypt (Heb.11:27). It's the anger that caused Demetrius and his fellow makers of metal gods at the town of Ephesus to lay hands on Gaius and Aristarchus, Paul's travelling companions, and then try to have Paul himself set upon by the mob that gathered (Acts 19:28). On all these occasions, the word *thumos* appears in the text.

In all these cases it's apparent that *thumos* is the sort of anger that surfaces when people feel threatened. It occurs when self-sufficiency is under attack. It would occur only rarely if more people knew how to place their trust in God.

Imagine how different history would have been if Pharaoh had not worried about the sudden dearth of slaves in his country; if he'd not been greatly concerned at the blow to progress on his building projects; if he'd not considered the departure of the Israelites such a blow to his pride. Imagine if Pharaoh had readily agreed to Moses' request to let his people go. We'd probably be reading of the ten *blessings* upon Egypt rather than the ten plagues.

And what if the people of Nazareth had not reacted with predictable scorn to a 'prophet from their own country'? How warmly the notion of being a Nazarene might have passed down the centuries. The name could have become a byword for all those who honoured their successful neighbours.

And what if Demetrius had seen the light and given up casting metal gods for a living in order to worship the true, living God? What a force for good a man of his forthrightness might have been in the early church! What good he could have done! Even if at first his livelihood had suffered, he'd not have been left destitute, as he feared. He'd have wound up a lot better off in more ways than just his pocket.

But alas, they were all small-minded men who believed they had to protect their own interests: Pharaoh his reputation, the Nazarene authorities their 'good' name, and Demetrius and his fellows their livelihoods.

It would be pleasant to think that believers never felt so threatened in the ordinary course of events to resort to verbal or physical abuse. But experience tells us differently. Generally, though, we are inclined to give vent to aggression in more subtle ways. Keeping up appearances again! We may speak sharply, or write the 'stiff' letter, or pass someone over for a good turn we could have done them, because their words or actions were threatening to us, or *appeared* to be. The aggression may not be obvious but it's still aggression. And we are apt to compound the felony by justifying it. "They jolly well deserve it."

What do *we* deserve, I sometimes wonder?

Strife *(eritheia)*—Selfish ambition

The foulness of *eritheia* is selfish ambition. It's the strife provoked by those who want to climb the ladder of success at almost any cost. Even if the ladder is against the wrong wall—which it usually is.

Not that ambition itself isn't a good thing. It's good for us to have goals and aspirations for this life and the next. There are few people more listless, and more joyless to be with than those who have no purpose. They seem to have switched life off at the mains. Ambition gets us fired up, gives us direction.

But there are two things (at least) which can go wrong. One is to be ambitious over **the wrong things.** The other is to have **the wrong motives** behind your ambition. Bring the two together and you really have a problem!

Eritheia is more connected with wrong motives. Often it's the perennial problem of doing the right thing for the wrong reasons. Sometimes we are so devious with *ourselves* that it's difficult to catch ourselves at it! Those familiar words from Jeremiah say it all: "The heart is deceitful above all things, and desperately wicked: who can know it?" We often don't even know it ourselves. Or we don't care to admit to ourselves that we know what's going on in our own heart.

Delight and meditation in the Word is the only way to find out. "For the word of God is living and powerful, and sharper than any two-edged sword, piercing even to the division of soul and spirit [who we *are* and what we *think*?], and of joints and marrow, and is a discerner of the thoughts and intents of the heart" (Heb.4:12 NKJV).

In addition to confessing our sins, it can be helpful now and then to ask for help to know what they are. Follow the lead of the Psalmist in Psalm 139:23,24, when he prayed: "Search me, O God, and know my heart: try me and know my thoughts: and see if there be any wicked way in me, and lead me in the way everlasting." A prayer like that will surely be answered. The answer may come through our attention to the Word: we may come across exactly the information we need. Or events may conspire to tell us what we need to know about ourselves. It may be none too pleasant, perhaps, but instructive all the same.

Almost all human motives are mixed. Even the purest can have a few grains of selfishness in them. A genuine altruist is a rare animal. You may have more hope of finding a dodo. We can't help mixing a little selfishness in whatever we do. But perhaps that's not such a bad thing. Even the disciples of Jesus are on record for asking "What's in it for us?" "Then answered Peter and said unto him [Jesus], Behold, we have forsaken all, and followed thee; what shall we have therefore?" (Matt.19:27). Jesus didn't reproach them for it; he simply told them what they had to look forward to. It's risky to argue a case from silence, I know, but that lack of a rebuke must tell us something!

An element of self-interest lies behind even our religious aspirations. If you doubt that, give yourself some *honest* answers to the question of why you want to be in the Kingdom of God. Honest ones, remember. Are you totally devoid of self-interest? Not even a smidgen? I doubt it. I'm certainly not.

It has been rightly observed that 'God-manifestation, not human salvation' is the purpose of God. Your salvation and mine are not the supreme elements in God's plan. Yet that's how we think of it, I'm sure, most of the time. Ideally, we should view our personal salvation as an opportunity to become the perfect embodiment of God's love, a small reflection of Him, so that at last we will be able to give Him that pleasure in His Creation for which He designed us. I doubt if we generally see salvation in those terms. How many believers could put their hand on their heart and say that's why they were baptised?—to give glory to God? Most of us see salvation in terms of our own escape from the grave.

Why is the Truth never *preached* from the point of view of God-manifestation? Why is the appeal to the unbeliever always made on the basis of 'believe and be baptised for eternal life'? It's not hard to answer. It's done that way because that's the hook that catches the fish. It's apparent that God *expects* a certain amount of self-interest to play a part in our ambition to be in His Kingdom. Is the reason for this, I wonder, because to be totally lacking in self-interest suggests, not so much a high spirituality, but a low self-worth? I believe that in part we are *expected* to want immortality for ourselves, not only so that we can manifest God in ourselves in the Kingdom.

I know we are to 'lose' our life for Christ so that we may 'find' it (Matt.10:39): meaning we surrender our will to him to obtain a better *spiritual* life leading to eternal life—but even that act of surrender is not without a dash of self-interest. Else why surrender in the first place? What's in it for you? This is not cynicism, it's realism.

However, the gradual development of the spiritual nature, as we coax the fruit of the Spirit into existence, will *lessen* the self-interest we have in the fulfilment of God's plan for this world. The production of the fruit will help us turn our attention away from what *we* want for ourselves to what we want to be for God. But only the arrival of the Kingdom will see all traces of self-interest erased from our character.

If God uses our self-interest to attract us to His Kingdom, it can't be all bad. But again the problem is that we misuse a quality which is meant to work in our favour. Instead of aspiring to the Kingdom of God, we aspire to petty things like recognition among our fellows. And that brings strife. We want more recognition than we have, and more things than we have. So we plot and scheme how to get them.

All community situations are spawning grounds for this kind of strife. Religious communities are no exception. Wanting to be a *somebody* is as much a pitfall here as anywhere. If you feel the urge to run your church, then best forget it—or at least hold back and try digging for your motives. We should even beware our motives for being keen Bible students—and especially good platform speakers. *Why* do we want to do it? Is it because we delight and meditate in the Word and we simply want to enjoy communicating our delight and our findings? Or does the idea of appearing spiritually intelligent appeal to our vanity? Do we fancy the sound of our own voice?

Every student, speaker, writer on Bible matters needs regular self-assessments. It's wonderful to have people say, "That was a good talk you gave," or "I did enjoy that article of yours." And it's right that praise should be given where it's due. But if that's the carrot, then you'd be well advised to give it up. Better still, rethink your motives. What point is there in being helpful to others and corrupting yourself in the process?

The best barometer I know (from experience) for determining motive in most things is how well you take criticism. If instead of "That was a splendid talk", you get "Surely you got the wrong end of the stick"—how do you take it? This test rarely fails. If you feel hurt and defensive, it's a sure sign your ego was riding on what you were saying. Bad motives ahoy! If you do it for the 'applause', you're going to have difficulty with the "boos". And "boos" there will always be. You'll be doing the right thing for the wrong reason—and that wrong reason will most likely be *eritheia*: selfish ambition.

Paul wrote to Timothy: "If a man desire the office of a bishop, he desireth a good work" (1 Tim.3:1), and to the Corinthians: "Covet earnestly the best gifts" (1 Cor.12:31). There is a place for ambition. There's nothing wrong, either, in feeling pleased about a little praise. We all need some encouragement now and then. But if we *need* the praise, and we're irritated when it doesn't come, and when criticism comes instead, then beware the seeds of selfish ambition. You may be trying to make a name for yourself. Spiritually it will be spelt MUD.

Seditions (*dichostasia*)—Two places to stand

We came across *'stasis'* when talking about faith in Chapter 12. It means 'a place to stand'. When you add *dicho*, which means *two* (as in dichotomy), you have the word *dichostasia*, and you have **two places to stand**. *Dichostasia* happens when you stand apart in your own place away from where others are standing. Have you ever played the children's party game *islands*, where you put squares of paper on the floor and each stand on one when the music stops? Well, that's a version of *dichostasia*. The grown-up children's version is known as *divisions* or *factions*.

Religious groups are notoriously good at *dichostasia*. They divide and sub-divide at regular intervals like amoebae. Unlike amoebae, religious groups rarely grow into two healthy units like the one from which they divided. They usually become smaller and weaker. Eventually some of them die. Sadly, those concerned are generally too busy promoting good reasons why they should separate to discover better reasons why they should not. But such are the works of the flesh.

The Scriptures don't condemn all divisions. Where there is heresy (the next work of the flesh), or serious and unresolved misconduct, those who insist on upholding Scriptural teaching and values must stand apart from the offenders and those who support them. But we have to be extremely careful about divisions. Those involved will always say it has to be done, and will claim the best of Scriptural motives, with many a supporting chapter and verse thrown in—and yet here is division listed as a work of the flesh! As with strife, we really do need to give close attention to our motives.

A division may have more to do with *psychology* than *theology*. What I mean is: it may have more (or as much) to do with the sort of people we are than what we believe. There are some personality types who *need* a fairly rigid framework within which to live and worship. For them formalism is a must; it's as much a part of the Truth as the Truth itself. Other believers have little need for formality: they see it as obstructing their approach to God. Between these two poles are the rest of us, believers of varying degrees of attachment and non-attachment to formality, according to the type of people we are.

Each group thinks the other ought to be more like them

I don't believe one group is superior to the other, is any more right than another. Which puts me in about the middle, I guess. There are learned theologians who dabble in something they call 'stage theory'. And these 'stage theorists' (who sound more like drama critics than theologians) haggle over how many stages of spirituality there are, and which manifestations of spirituality are higher on the scale. Professor James Fowler wrote a book called *Stages of Faith* in which he gave six levels of spiritual growth. He actually puts formal, institutional spirituality on a level below the non-formal. And he, like many of his ilk, including M. Scott Peck in his book *Further along the Road Less Travelled*, sees spiritual progress as a journey up through the levels from formality to non-formality and beyond.

But from the point of view of those who prefer formality, a move towards non-formality is a step *down* the ladder, not up!

While I do believe changes can occur during the life of a believer (I'm less attached to an organisational framework than I once was), I still hold that *who* we are has a lot to do with our preference or distaste for formality. Neither group is any higher up the spiritual ladder than the other. There can be as much high spirituality among the formal as the non-formal. The fruit of the Spirit is available to all, and is not the exclusive right of those who worship cross-legged on the floor *or* those who prefer to sit in straight rows of chairs.

I hate being negative, but I don't see a solution to the problem of differing psychological make-up among believers. Don't get me wrong; I do know what the answer is. The answer is for both extremes to reach a higher spirituality and connect at that common level. The answer is for both groups, and all the shades in between who get caught in the crossfire, to develop more of the fruit of the Spirit and thereby learn how to exist in harmony.

But the problem of differing psychological make-up causes believers *not* to aspire to a common level of higher spirituality, but to develop reasons for separating. Eventually something doctrinal will emerge upon which both groups can hang their differences and thereby go their own way. This is not entirely unpleasant for those at the far ends of the formal/non-formal scale. Each can be content that the other no longer blights their fellowship. For all those in the middle it's a disaster. Sometimes they are at a loss to know what has happened. Sometimes their very faith is shattered.

What may appear to be a perfectly Scriptural division may in fact have its roots deep in the psyche of the two parties; so it actually begins as a work of the flesh. At what point, I wonder, does it become right?

Believers are asked to "mark them which cause divisions [*dichostasia*] and offences contrary to the doctrine which ye have learned; and avoid them" (Rom.16:17). We must try to isolate propagators of division. Sometimes it can be done. A believer broadcasting dubious ideas can be asked officially to stop causing unrest, and be stood aside from if necessary. But we must remember that when Paul wrote to the Romans about "them which cause divisions", it was a time when *false* brethren were circulating in the churches stirring up trouble. These trouble-makers were no doubt in the pay of the Jewish religious authorities, who at the time were anxious to disrupt and destroy the fledgling Christianity. Anywhere one of these bogus Christians was spotted trying to stir up *dichostasia* he was to be isolated before he could damage the church. We don't have exactly the same problem

today, but through the works of the flesh we still have
dichostasia.

Heresies *(hairesis)*—Choosing your own 'truth'

Heresy is among the works of the flesh because it
involves the vaunting of human choice and opinion above
the Divine. It means moving away from what *is* true to what
we *prefer* to be true. Only by the surrender of the self is
truth rightly perceived. Only when we get our own
preconceived and socially induced notions out of the way
will Truth shine through. Though it has to be conceded that
because our surrender is never absolute, no-one can lay
claim to absolute truth. We each cast our own shadow over
the light of God's perfect revelation. May that thought keep
us humble when we discuss what we believe.

I'm not suggesting that we cannot discern the *essential*
gospel from God's Word: "the things concerning the
kingdom of God, and the name of Jesus Christ" (Acts 8:12).
That would be nonsense. God would not give us a gospel
we could never hope to understand. Nor would Paul have
been able so roundly to condemn anyone who taught any
other gospel (Gal.1:8) if the true version was unfathomable!

There is a core of indisputable gospel truth. Outside that
core, however, can be uncharted waters for many a Bible
student. That's one of the things that make Bible exploration
such an enthralling occupation. But it can also lead us into
the folly of making pronouncements about parts of
Scripture that are way off beam, and yet over which we
become immovable.

I have two somewhat contradictory emotions about
people who are absolutely cast-iron certain about their
interpretation of some of the backwaters of Scripture. On
the one hand I envy them their certainty. On the other hand
that certainty frightens me. I would dearly love to be that
confident about various prophecies and other things, but I
would also *hate* to be so rigid that I closed my mind to
other possibilities—and closed it to something that turned

out to be the truth! I don't believe that an open-minded approach to topics outside first principles is wishy-washy, lacking in conviction, but that it is an approach which makes Bible study all the more stimulating. One should be alive to new possibilities all the while.

Of course, new possibilities should not conflict with the core gospel truth that we spoke of earlier. As somebody wisely said: "Keep your mind open, but don't let your brains fall out."

Differences over matters which fall outside core gospel truth are nowhere near as serious as those that fall within it. The latter are the *true* works of the flesh. These are the *hairesis*. They constitute **a denial through choice** of any of the elements of the core gospel.

Now I'm aware when I use the term 'core gospel' that I'm open to questions like: "What *is* the core gospel? *Who* decides what is essential belief and what isn't?" Well, we do, of course, from our reading of the Word. Again I say, God would not have given us a basic gospel we couldn't grasp. The major truths, or first principles, such as the nature of the Kingdom of God, the resurrection and the return of Christ are self-evident. They form the core. Other truths, like the origin and salvation (?) of angels, are less easily pinned down, and a proper understanding of them is not essential for salvation.

Disagreement about the meaning of a core gospel belief, a belief self-evidently vital for salvation (which if you don't have, you don't have the Truth), must involve heresy on one side or other. *Both* cannot be true, as they are almost certain to be mutually exclusive.

But why would any believer opt for a doctrine that isn't true? Why would someone reading in the Bible that "the dead know not anything" (Ecc.9:5) decide that the Bible teaches the survival of the soul? Probably because they are not reading the Bible, but taking their 'truth' from somewhere or someone else. They may prefer to believe something cosier than extinction at death. I don't specially like the idea myself! They don't notice that the Bible teaches resurrection and judgement *en masse* for believers, and not a swift transition to heaven. And where does the idea of heaven-going come from, anyway? If the meek are going to inherit the *earth*, does that mean meekness will make you a second-class citizen of the future?!

Why would any believer opt for a doctrine that is not true? The answer is *hairesis*. People make their own *choices* about what they believe instead of sorting out for themselves what is true. They mix human and Divine thinking. Generally people prefer a softer religion and a softer God to those presented in the Bible. They want a religion and a God that will leave them alone to do pretty much what they want, and then give them eternal bliss as their reward for doing it! This is the way of heresy. It's not a fruit of the Spirit; it's a work of the flesh. Truly God is good—He has all the aspects of the fruit of the Spirit, but also, "God is not mocked; for whatsoever a man soweth, that shall he also reap. For he that soweth to his flesh shall of the flesh reap corruption; but he that soweth to the Spirit shall of the Spirit reap life everlasting" (Gal.6:7).

Envyings *(phthonos)*—Wanting a less than perfect life

At the trial of Jesus, Pontius Pilate was wrong about many things, but he was absolutely on target about one thing. "He knew that for envy they [the religious authorities] had delivered him [Jesus]" (Matt.27:18).

The Jewish religious leaders of the day *envied* Jesus. More than they feared him or hated him, or pretended to despise him, they *envied* him. More than anything else, it was this deep-seated envy that led them to engineer his crucifixion.

What caused them to envy him so much? *They* had the positions of authority in the land. *They* had the comfortable lifestyle. *They* had all the learning and power. So why envy this 'carpenter's son' from Nazareth? What did he have that they didn't?

To begin with, the common people "were astonished at his doctrine, for he taught them as one that had authority, and not as the scribes" (Mark 1:22). Jesus was a far more informed teacher of God's Word than any of the learned men of his day. But those learned men, instead of taking their cue from the common people and *listening* to what he taught, they resented him. They saw him undermining their influence with the people as teachers of the Law.

Added to this, Jesus went about doing miracles of healing. Great crowds followed him sometimes as he moved about the country. The authorities could perform no miracles. All they could do was try and discredit his. They tried to discredit him as a teacher, too, by asking trick questions in front of the people. Infuriatingly for them, he always had a powerful answer, and their questions only served to amplify their own ignorance before the people.

You would think that, seeing the miracles, hearing him teach, hearing the answers he gave to their questions, and confronting the man himself, they would begin to reason that perhaps this man *was* someone extraordinary after all. Maybe he *was* who he said he was. But the works of the flesh got the better of them. Most of them never got beyond envy to appreciate who Christ truly was. They blinded themselves, didn't want to know. They envied his ability as a teacher and his popularity with the people. And because they couldn't best him as a teacher, they set about destroying his popularity.

They wanted him out of the way. They used all their sway with the people to discredit him. One can detect in the narrative of the New Testament that they were increasingly successful at this. When Jesus asked his disciples, "Whom do men say that I am?" (Mark 8:27), not one of them answered that the people were saying he was the Son of God, the promised Messiah. He was hailed only as a prophet from God. That must have saddened Jesus. The religious authorities were getting to the people, taking advantage of the regard in which *they* were traditionally held. The leaders also had power to excommunicate from the synagogue any who were too zealous for this 'self-styled Messiah', as they no doubt referred to him. Their jealousy, their envy, knew no bounds, leading them ultimately to the excess of the judicial murder of an innocent man. **They could not bear the success of Jesus.**

Why is it that we find it so difficult to rejoice in the success of others? We have an instinct for envy, an inborn desire to pull down the successful. James wrote, "Do ye think that the scripture saith in vain, The spirit that dwelleth in us lusteth to envy?" (Jas.4:5). We naturally envy others. It's a work of the flesh of which we are made.

Incidentally, you won't find the quotation James appears to be making *anywhere* in the Scriptures. There is no verse that actually says, "The spirit that dwelleth in us lusteth to envy." James didn't mean us to understand it as a direct quotation. If I said the Bible says we should read the Word of God to understand the meaning of life, that would be true, but there's no verse which literally says, "we should read the Word of God to understand the meaning of life." However, I could bring together a few verses which *mean* that. And so it is with what James said. The Scriptures don't tell us for nothing that there is within each one of us a natural spirit of envy.

Those to whom James wrote had "bitter envying and strife in [their] hearts" which he condemned as "earthly, sensual, devilish" (Jas.3:14,15). It certainly wasn't heavenly, spiritual and Godly! James told them the wisdom they needed from above was "full of mercy and good fruits" (v17), a comment which The Authorised Version translators are absolutely spot on, in their marginal note, to relate to Gal.5:22: the fruit of the Spirit.

That's exactly what they required. Those to whom James wrote were having a particular problem with envy. It was the problem of hostility between the 'haves' and the 'have nots'. Material differences have been a source of envy that has plagued every generation of believers. An imbalance of riches nearly always produces strife.

But the division between 'haves' and 'have nots' is purely man-made. It has no bearing at all on the way God divides up society. When He sees sheep and goats, He takes no account of the socio-economics of their situation. God is not the least impressed by what anyone has materially. In reality, nobody has *anything*: it's all on loan. We came into the world with nothing and we go out of it with nothing. When you die you will leave behind exactly the same as billionaire Howard Hughes left—everything! You will need no pockets in the last suit you wear.

If God isn't impressed with material status, neither should Godly people be impressed with it. But it isn't easy. We have that old spirit of envy in us. We envy the better house, car, garden, job, income, education... and so on. The list even includes spiritual things like better expounders of the Word, or more courageous and successful preachers, or those with more senior positions at the church. If all this 'spiritual' envying acts as the catalyst for improving ourselves and the quality of our collective service to the Lord, then fine, let's envy some more! But a more likely outcome is resentment, a "Who does he think he is?" mentality. And that *stunts* spiritual growth.

Of course the problem is not always solely the fault of the less well-off. A responsibility rests with the 'haves' not to flaunt their possessions or talents and provoke the resentment of others. That, too, is a great temptation. Do you remember at the swimming baths, as a youngster, that there was no point diving off a high board if no-one was watching!

The very worst aspect of envy is that it can be a criticism of God. Sometimes when you envy you are, in effect, saying, "God, I should have that," when God hasn't seen fit to give it to you. We think we know better about what's good for us. We might even think we could serve God better if only we had more money, more free time, a bigger house... one like the Jones's. It's a wrong outlook. It's the sort of murmuring that God particularly dislikes. If you truly believe that "all things work together for good" for you, and you're generally doing what you can to please God, then whatever situation in life you have right now is perfect. You're right where you should be.

"Perfect!" did I hear somebody shout? *"With my mortgage!"* *"With my redundancy!"* *"With my arthritis!"* *"With my _____."* You fill in the blank. Yes, perfect. If you believe that whatever you have in your life is what you most need from God to help form your character for the Kingdom of God (and it is), then what you have is perfect. A million pound windfall might seem a little more perfect than your current bank balance, but if your lack of funds makes you look to God and a windfall would make you look to the world, which is really better?

Wanting *too much* what you don't have, and what you enviously see other people have, *has* to be a form of criticism of God. We all do it. None of us is one hundred per cent spiritual. And even Jesus, who *was* that spiritual, would have preferred not to go through with the crucifixion. The gospel writers tell us he prayed in the garden of Gethsemane, "O my Father, if it be possible, let this cup pass from me." He didn't *want* to be crucified. Nobody in his right mind would. But when he knew it was God's will, he accepted that it must be endured.

Most people aren't expected to go that far. Most of us couldn't handle it, and no more is ever expected of any of us than we *can* handle. That being so, we arrive at the comforting fact that whatever we have in our lives we can handle—and whatever we don't have, we can handle that, too! Only the prompting of our fleshly nature makes us hanker overmuch after more and better. The spiritual mind directs us differently. To envy is, in fact, to want your life to be less than perfect. What you have now is right. Why spoil it?

This isn't to say that you shouldn't aspire to better things. There are hundreds of thousands of legitimate goals in this life (including the Kingdom of God). But it *is* to say that your wanting should be tempered by an acceptance of what is the Lord's will for you, so if your lack continues you don't become bitter. And your wanting should be without the ill-will of envy towards those who already have what you want. Perhaps, when you accept God's will for your life, and remove all envy, you will thereby remove the blocks to your own prosperity: the lessons will be learned and you can move on.

Footnote to the above

I appreciate that some of you reading this may have *very* serious problems in your life. To you what I've said may seem insensitive and unrealistic. How can your bereavement, you terminal illness (or your child's), your wrecked marriage, or your chronic loneliness or pain, be the will of God that you must accept uncomplainingly? Can God really *want* that for you? And you may be thinking that it's all right for me to offer glib answers when, as far as you know, I don't have your problems.

To these thoughts let me say that I do have problems, and I sometimes have difficulty seeing them as God's will for me, even though on a scale of one to ten they may barely rate a three. But I still believe what I've said about problems being God's will for us. However...

There *are* clearly stated Scriptural principles about God's dealings with us. But there are also differences in the way God allows people to respond to their circumstances. Rom. 8:28 tells us that "all things work together for good to them that love God, to them who are called according to his purpose." 1 Cor.10:13 tells us the God "will not suffer you to be tempted above that ye are able; but will with the temptation also make a way to escape, that ye may be able to bear it." These two verses taken together would seem to constitute a 'theory of everything' for living the Truth. But what do you do when "a way to escape" isn't obvious, or simply isn't there? What if your situation so distresses you that you find it hard to accept it as God's will *and still love God?* Are you wrong to want and pray for your situation to change? Is that a weakness of faith that makes you inferior to other believers and jeopardises your salvation? Absolutely not. We are only human; and God recognises that in His dealings with us. If you can't handle your situation it's not the end of the world. Probably a lot of people couldn't handle it if given it.

There are some cases in Scripture of people changing the will of God for themselves. Hezekiah didn't want his illness to be fatal and God reversed it for him. But Paul didn't want his "thorn in the flesh" and God said he'd have to keep it. Their prayers of 'complaint' were not wrong. Distress is not wrong! We can't all bear up with the same fortitude as Job. The thing to remember about Job is that he was an exceptionally spiritual man, head and shoulders above most people. I couldn't have handled his situation as well as he did. Few people could. But even he didn't suffer in silence.

Having said all that, how should you deal with a situation that you do *not* want, which you feel is not doing you any good, and which you find God does not want to change?—in fact, far from building you up, you feel it's *adversely* affecting your faith. All the kindly words of fellow believers are of little or no avail, well meant as they might be. "You've just got to have faith" only equals "pull yourself together", and isn't any help in these circumstances. You already *know* that! You've told yourself that a dozen times. You only wish you could do it. So where do you go from here? Is it hopeless?

Nothing is ever hopeless. There are solutions. You might like to consider those that follow. The first solution to consider is that you **make a nuisance of yourself.** What I mean is that you *keep knocking* on heaven's door. Okay, I know you've prayed and prayed about the problem, but you have to be *relentless*. I have the parable of the persistent widow in mind (Luke 18:1-8). That parable tells us that God *wants us* to keep knocking. Not because He likes to keep us waiting, but because it brings out our faith. It's often easier to despair than believe. God will answer, "though he bear long with them" (v.7), if we keep asking in the full assurance of faith. Christ's comment at the end of the parable suggests that real faith in the power of God in our lives is not so common *but not unattainable*, and he questions whether he'll find it when he returns: "Nevertheless when the Son of man cometh, shall he find faith on the earth?" (v.8). In addition to your own relentless praying, you should also get as many other believers as you can to pray for you or *with* you about the problem. The Apostle Paul knew the value and power of other people's prayers. In three of his letters he asked his readers to "pray for us", and on one occasion wrote, "for I trust that through your prayers I shall be given to you" (Phm.22). And he offered the same help to others: "making mention of thee always in my prayers" (Phm.4), and "without ceasing I make mention of you always in my prayers" (Rom.1:12).

Another solution is to **praise and give thanks.** It sounds a little radical, and seems like the wrong thing to do in the circumstances, but try it. Actually praise God and thank Him in the midst of your problem. It sounds crazy, I know, and it runs counter to all you feel like doing, but it has the support of scripture. David in the midst of cruel persecution said, "I will praise his word" (Psalm 56:4); and "my praise shall be continually of thee" and as things got worse he said, "I ... will yet praise thee more and more" (Psalm 71:6 & 14). And there in the recommendation from Paul: "In every thing give thanks: for this is the will of God in Christ Jesus concerning you" (1 Thess.5:18). To which we should add his comments in 2 Cor.4, where in the midst of speaking of all his trials and difficulties he says, "that the abundance of grace **through the thanksgiving of many** redound to the glory of God. For which cause we faint not..."(verses 15 & 16). And when you make your requests to God, your prayers and supplications should be "with thanksgiving" (Phil.4:6). To give thanks and praise signifies acceptance of the will of God and helps to chase away any rebellion and anger that might be in the heart. Therefore it helps to open the door of heaven to your cry.

If neither persistence nor thankfulness or anything else seems to be working to change your situation, then that may be because you are an exceptional person. God is saying *no* to you. Which means you are more of a saint than you give yourself credit for. *You* don't believe that you can handle what God has given you, but He does. You have seriously underestimated yourself. Please give due consideration to this, because it's an important point and I don't say it at all lightly. If God says that He "will not suffer you to be tempted above that ye are able; but will with the temptation also make a way to escape, that ye may be able to bear it", and you can see no way of escape after waiting and praying long for it, then the conclusion you must consider is that you *are* able to bear it.

You might also consider that you may be too self-absorbed to see that way of escape. Or your condition could be the illness of clinical depression for which you need treatment, as you would for any other illness. If simply reading the above suggestions depresses you, or you just cannot face the thought of even trying to put them to work for you then you must talk to someone qualified to help, preferably a fellow believer, one with counselling experience, someone who is not going to tell you merely "to have faith". In your case that is inappropriate. Sadly no one can wave a magic wand and put desperate situations right in an instant. How often I've wished it were so! But that's not to say that there is no answer to your problem, or, at least, no way of dealing with it that will satisfy you. *Never* stop believing that it's round the next corner.

Murder *(phonos)*—The culmination of strife

Strife starts in the heart. If it isn't resolved there by forgiveness, by calming it back, it may develop into verbal aggression, which can lead to physical aggression, which can lead to murder. Murder is the climax to which strife can lead. Or rather the depths to which it can sink.

Jesus made the point that strife must be dealt with in the heart before the awful progression can get started (Matt.5:21). The moment strife gets a foothold we are in danger of a capital offence. It's best to catch it early, not give houseroom to any brooding thought that might lead from anger to murder.

Simply put, murder is the deliberate and unlawful killing of another human being. It is any killing which God does not sanction. He is the Great Creator and Sustainer of life. All life emanates from him. Only He can take it away with impunity. We cannot. Those people of ancient Israel who were put to death as punishment under God's Law were not murdered. Neither were all those killed on the battlefield by the armies of Israel under God's direction.

"You shall not murder" (Ex.20:13 NKJV) was the sixth commandment under the Old Law given to Israel. The penalty was death. Under the New and better Covenant brought in by Christ there is no capital punishment. At least no immediate capital punishment. A believer who goes as far as murder is not without hope. He may have time and may be given grace to repent. If he does, the sin will not be laid against him at the judgement seat.

There will be no murderers in the Kingdom of God (Gal.5:21), or anyone who does any of the works of the flesh, come to that. But there will be forgiven murderers, forgiven idolaters, forgiven adulterers, drunkards, etc. To turn from sins—to repent—is to make those sins as if they never existed in the sight of God. His forgiveness is absolute.

There is a verse in James's letter which is usually mentioned when the subject is murder. This is no exception. James 4:2 gives the impression that the believers he wrote to were killing one another! "Ye lust, and have not: ye kill, and desire to have, and cannot obtain...." I somehow think that if they were really killing one another it would have been the subject of the whole letter!

The usual explanation for this reference to killing is to pass it off as hatred in the heart that by extension was murder. But that won't do. I believe the true answer is a simple copyist's error. At some time during the letter's journey through a succession of copyists, one of them wrote the word *phoneuo* (murder) instead of *phthoneo*, meaning envious. It makes far more sense to say, "ye are *envious* and desire to have." Only three verses on from there, James mentions that the "spirit that dwelleth in us lusteth to envy." I can't accept that believers were actually killing one another. But they were committing spiritual suicide with their envy and strife.

The Antidotes to Strife

The two aspects of the fruit of the Spirit which help ward off *all* the aspects of strife are longsuffering and gentleness. Longsuffering, remember, is being slow to anger and exercising forgiveness. Gentleness is the true kindness that comes through understanding others, and making allowance for them. This is briefly how these spiritual qualities react with the flesh.

Hatred: Where genuine kindness is coupled with a forgiving spirit, the weeds of hatred simply cannot flourish. They may spring up now and then, because we're only human, but they soon wither and die. Longsuffering and gentleness are first-class weedkillers.

Variance: The character in which longsuffering and kindness are developing will find increasingly less room for contention. Such a character would prefer to help another rather than compete.

Emulations: As for emulations, the believer who is cultivating kindness will be gracious and make allowance for others and not be dogmatic and domineering. He or she will be aware of others' sensibilities and not be the kind to bulldoze over them with inappropriate zeal.

Wrath: When you have *makrothumeo* you simply don't have *thumos*. With a touch of *makro* you slow down your instinctive fleshly response, and then you dissolve the wrath completely with a liberal helping of forgiveness.

Strife: Selfish ambition is reined-in by kindness. You have no wish to push your own *wants* in front of everyone else's *needs* when you have that sensitive aspect of the fruit.

Seditions: Again it's kindness for this one. The process of making allowance for people and seeking to understand how they tick is fatal to seditious behaviour. With this good quality you're not going to be looking for reasons to separate from others; you'll be looking for reasons to get closer to them. Of course, longsuffering helps also—it helps those who are not seditious themselves but who need the strength to bear with those who are. It stops you losing patience and being confrontational with those who are looking for another place to stand.

Heresies: Even the strife caused by heresies is treatable by kindness and longsuffering. These faculties help prevent a widening of the gap between ourselves and those whose beliefs differ. They prevent us from adding *personal* differences to doctrinal ones. So a channel of communication is left open. Also, if we are trying to understand the other person's thinking, we may discover *why* they believe what they do. It may help to understand the psychology as well as the theology. Differences over the interpretations of parts of Scripture may well be secondary to the real issue of *why* they choose to see the verses that way. A little understanding is a lot more use, sometimes, than a whole lot of argument.

Envyings: Longsuffering helps remove any feelings of resentment we may feel towards those who have more than ourselves materially or spiritually. It also helps us deal with any real or imaginary off-hand treatment we might get from them. Through kindness we take pleasure in the success of others instead of envying them. Or we may be concerned about their success if it appears to be detrimental to their spiritual welfare. And kindness has the good effect of making us honestly sympathetic when successful people fail. When we have envy, we rub our hands together gleefully at the downfall of the better-off. It's called *Schadenfreude*. We English didn't have a word for it so we borrowed one from the Germans. *Schaden* (shame), *Freude* (joy)—together they mean to find joy in the shame of another. It's not a sentiment for believers. So if you have any *Schadenfreude*, kill it with kindness.

Murder: No need to say much here. It ought to be fairly obvious that kindness and longsuffering will keep us from murdering people! But these qualities from the fruit of the Spirit not only keep us from the extreme of murder, they help us overcome all the lesser aspects of strife long before they can ever lead to murder. Longsuffering and kindness strike at the roots, dealing with murder where Christ says it should be dealt with—in the heart.

CHAPTER NINETEEN

EXCESS AND THE ANTIDOTES
(Drunkenness, revellings)

THESE two works of the flesh can be dealt with as a pair. Both drunkenness and revellings are symptoms of the abandonment of spirituality and of a retreat from reality.

Many people these days contrarily believe that spirituality is an escape from reality. They see it as a refuge for those who can't cope with life, a crutch to lean on for the emotionally weak. The fact that it draws the weak has more to do with the pitying eye of the Father than the nature of spirituality itself. I also believe that it takes an extremely *strong* person, sometimes, to realise that they need the crutch of spirituality. And many people don't have the strength it takes to break free from their nature, or from the constraints of society to become a committed believer. It takes courage, as well as belief, to stand out among friends and family and colleagues as a practising Christian. They'll all, no doubt, tell you to "Get back to reality".

The truth of the matter is that *only* spirituality teaches us what is real. Everything about this world seems so permanent: the systems, institutions, customs, the social and political evolution, they seem as if they will always be. The Bible opens our minds to the reality of the fragility and impermanence of what we see. God is in control. He is calling out a people for Himself from every generation who will populate a kingdom that will replace all the seemingly permanent kingdoms on this earth: "...it shall break in pieces and consume all these kingdoms, and it shall stand forever" (Dan.2:44).

The world as we know it will be swept aside ("as a scroll when it is rolled up," in the words of Revelation 6:14 NKJV), and "the meek shall inherit" an entirely revised planet earth, as promised. There's no way they could inherit the world as it is—or would want to!

This is reality. It is understood and appreciated only through spirituality. Drunkenness is used in Scripture as a metaphor for being so confused and drugged by the 'reality' of the present world that we cannot see the truth. The Word keeps us sober. It keeps us from being intoxicated by all the mind-numbing stuff of the world. It keeps the door to reality open.

But that's enough about metaphorical drunkenness. What about *actual* drunkenness? Being drunk affects people differently. It can make us happy or sad, brave or fearful, sleepy or overactive, quiet or brash and foul-mouthed, offensively or embarrassingly truthful, or the biggest brag-gart under the sun. It can also make us physically sick. And if drunkenness becomes a way of life it may rob us of family, friends, home, job, health, wealth, happiness and life. There's not a lot going for it, really, is there?

Like many of the works of the flesh, drunkenness is the misuse of something meant for our good. Alcoholic drinks are good and pleasurable in themselves, making "glad the heart of man" (Ps.104:15). The benefits of 'little and often' are occasionally attested to by the medical profession. I don't know about you, but it seems that every time I hear or read an interview with a person who's over one hundred years old, I hear them say they take a glass of sherry, or red wine, most days!

Drink itself isn't harmful. It's the excess of it that does the harm. In the right *modest* measure it gives a pleasant conviviality and does the system good. In the wrong measure it can destroy the personality and the body. And if it ever becomes an addiction, then even 'little and often' ceases to be a good idea; total abstinence is reckoned to be the best solution. Wine can indeed "make glad the heart of man" but we are also warned that "Wine is a mocker, strong drink is raging: and whosoever is deceived thereby is not wise" (Prov. 20:1). And let's not forget that any amount can be lethal if taken at an inappropriate time, such as when driving or doing anything potentially dangerous that requires proper attention.

I've met people who have told me that they were teetotal because the Bible forbids the drinking of alcohol. The Bible does no such thing. It warns against drinking too much of it, not against drinking any at all. If we are going to argue that a warning not to drink too much means a complete ban on drinking, then by the same token the Bible's warnings about the misuse of the tongue should prohibit talking. Silence was never *that* golden.

Excess is the problem, not drinking. Drunkenness takes away our proper awareness of what we're doing. A modest amount of alcohol merely relaxes us, but if we drink too much we reach the point where most, if not all, of our inhibitions vanish. Okay, so some people could do with losing a few inhibitions? Some do need to loosen up and lighten up a bit? Some of the checks on our personality are needless? But with drunkenness we lose those checks on our personality that *need* to be in place. And once in that state we are going to begin manifesting other works of the flesh. The gate is wide open. Drunkenness drops our guard. That's the worst of it. That's why it's linked with revellings.

Revelling entails brawling and sexual abandon. Peter lumps revelling together with lasciviousness, lusts, excess of wine, and banqueting. And by banqueting I don't think he had in mind a formal lunch at the Guildhall. Peter follows through with an exhortation to be "sober, and watch unto prayer" (1 Pet.4:7). Drunkenness and revellings are to be a thing of the past, if ever, for believers. There's no way you can be watching and ready for Christ's coming if you drink too much. But these things are obvious and don't need hammering home by me.

The Antidotes to Excess

The antidotes to excess are peace (not surprisingly) and meekness. Excessive drinking and the revelry commonly associated with it are often born of the need to escape real life. Someone who can find no peace will often turn to drink to dull the pain of existence. But when the peace of God rules in the heart, because we know that all our circumstances are in God's hands, we don't need a bottle, we need a Bible. But it takes the inner strength known as meekness to realise that and put it into practice.

Troubled people seek an escape from reality. They can't handle all the pressures and disappointments of life. With Biblical peace and meekness we know that all we have to do is trust God, let Him take the strain. The solution is to believe that He is in control, and *act* as if we believe it. Take all your problems to God—**and don't forget to leave them there.**

CHAPTER TWENTY

CONCLUSION
(Critical M.A.S.)

THE fruit of the Spirit "represents the whole, balanced, spiritual personality." If you don't recognize that last phrase, let me remind you that it appeared way back in the Preface. In that Preface I expressed the opinion that the fruit of the Spirit might well encompass everything that Christ will be looking for in you and me at his return. The development of the fruit is one of the prime purposes of life on this planet. It is by our characters, by what we have done with ourselves, and, thankfully, by the grace of God also, that we will be judged at the gate to the Kingdom.

These notions about the fruit remain with me still. I hope that by now, assuming that you've come the long way and aren't just peeking at this last chapter, you will have some sympathy with them. I hope you now realize why the subject of the fruit of the Spirit impressed me as being so important.

The fruit is coaxed into existence by the reading of the Word with an attitude of delight and meditation. This is what the picture of the spiritual man as a fruitful tree by a river shows us. Psalm One gives that picture. And the attitude of delight is not a matter of temperament or inclination; it's a matter of choice. Left to ourselves, how we feel at any given moment, we may not read and delight in the Word. We have to make the choice to do it.

It must also be our decision to meditate on the Word, having read it. Whether we meditate on the Word or not doesn't depend on the amount of time we think we have available. It takes no more time to meditate than to live. For

God's Word to be "our study all the day" (as it is for the spiritual man of Psalm One), our thoughts are to return to the Word constantly throughout the day. We hear the 'voice' of the Word as part of our inner dialogue as we go about our business. "When thou sleepest, it shall keep thee; and when thou awakest, it shall talk with thee" (Prov.6:22).

Gradually, by assimilating the mind of God, the fruit of the Spirit grows in the heart. It's a form of God-manifestation. "God-manifestation, not human salvation," is the purpose of God, to re-quote J. Thomas. Slowly we take in the mind of God and begin to manifest Him in our lives. God is love, and by becoming repositories of that love and channels for it, we begin even now the business of God-manifestation that will culminate for us in the Kingdom when we become, by His grace, perfect embodiments and reflections of the character of God.

We have to emphasize that it is **by His grace** that we are saved. For while it's true that there are things that we must do, we will NEVER bridge the gap that lies between us and perfection. It's a Grand Canyon of a gap. God's grace bridges it in response to our feeble endeavours. The righteousness we could never attain for ourselves is imputed to us by God because of our faith in Him. He finds our faith in Him extremely pleasing. So much so that He's prepared to overlook a lot of other things because of it.

When it comes to trying to bridge the gap ourselves, we are all like the man of the parable (Matt.18:24) who was forgiven a debt of staggering proportions (though not like him, I trust, in not forgiving those who owe us trifling amounts). Simple arithmetic brings home how huge the man's debt was to his master. He owed 10,000 talents. A talent is about 6,000 denarii (the penny of the New Testament, and incidentally the 'd' in the old £.s.d. [pounds, shillings and pence], if you can remember back that far). A

New Testament penny was a day's wages for a labourer. If we conservatively estimate a day's wages today at around £40 for a labourer, multiply that by 6,000 to get the value of a talent at £240,000, then multiply that by 10,000, we reach the astronomical figure of £2,400,000,000! (two thousand, four hundred million pounds).

The parable man hadn't a hope of repaying that amount. And yet he asks time to scrape together the money! Where did he think he was going to get it, I wonder? Work a few extra shifts? He was being totally unrealistic to think he could pay. And so are we if we imagine that by cranking up our spirituality a few extra notches we can gain God's approval. It doesn't work like that. If we think like that, we have totally misjudged the situation—totally misjudged how much we owe.

This reminds me of the story of an enthusiastic young plumber who, shortly after finishing his apprenticeship, was taken to see Niagara Falls. He stood silently watching all those billions of gallons of water plunging over the edge for some moments, then said, "I think I can fix this."

So what is the point of this book if no matter what we achieve spiritually it will never be enough?—if it will always be a drop in the ocean (or the Niagara River). Why bother to improve, to develop more of the fruit of the Spirit, if God is going to bridge the gap with His grace anyway? Why? Because God's grace meets us only part way. Grace doesn't make the whole journey. We have to be moving forwards, towards Him, for Him to be moving towards us. "Draw near to God and He will draw near to you" (Jas.4:8).

We are to be like the prodigal son whose father came out to meet him while he was still a long way off. **The Father saw that His son was travelling towards Him.**

It's not that the more spiritual we become, the less we need God's grace (we may reduce our multi-million pound debt by a pound or two!). In fact, the more spiritual we become, the more we realise how much we *need* God's grace, and the more we realise **that we have it!**

But if we don't make any moves to better ourselves, which is the reason God gave us His Word, and if we think we can leave it all to God, then our attitude is akin to saying, "Shall we continue in sin, that grace may abound" (Rom.6:1). We're saying, "I won't improve myself spiritually because God will make up what I lack with His grace. So let it abound!" That attitude doesn't maintain the status quo; it causes a backward slide. I recently heard living the Truth likened to riding a bicycle: if you stop moving forwards, you fall over.

Maximum Achievable Spirituality

We will never reach perfection in this life. But we must each have what I call a Maximum Achievable Spirituality (**M.A.S.**). It will differ for each of us. It is the maximum, given who we are, and the circumstances in which we find ourselves, that it is possible for us to attain. That for us is our own personal perfection. That's the goal for each of us. It's a long way short of true perfection, but it's as far as we're going to get until the Kingdom comes.

Normally a major pitfall with having such a goal as **M.A.S**. is that it would tend to make us legalistic. We would start setting ourselves tasks like so much Bible reading per week, so much prayer time, so many tasks done for other people, never missing a meeting. But that doesn't happen when we approach our spirituality from the right direction. It doesn't happen when we approach it from the direction of *who we are*, instead of what we do.

Making the decision, the choice, to delight and meditate in the Word is all we need do. "One thing is needful." Continue in that one thing and the fruit of the Spirit is bound to develop. The works will then take care of themselves. You won't need a check-list. You'll do all you need to do and hardly be aware you're doing it. And at the same time you'll be dealing fairly effectively with the works of the flesh. You'll be doing what comes naturally. Or rather you won't. You'll be doing what comes *spiritually*—only it will seem natural to you!

So if you feel as if you're not making any spiritual headway, make a commitment now to delight and meditate in the Word. Then see how your garden grows. Don't put it off. Don't be one of those people who always intends to be a better person. Sometimes when I've given a talk on the fruit of the Spirit I've put a slide of a favourite 'Peanuts' cartoon on the screen to conclude. Charlie Brown's sister says to him: "I've decided to try to be a better person... But not now, of course... Maybe a few days from now."

A few days from now isn't the best time. If you're always planning to be a better person, you never will be.

Never aim low, or be half-hearted about following the spiritual path. There's no enjoyment in that. Real enjoyment in most things in life comes only with commitment, with really throwing yourself into something. Live with passion! And remember you are allowed to enjoy being a Christian— joy is a part of the fruit.

May God bless you in achieving your Maximum Achievable Spirituality.